PRAISE FOR
THE LOGISTICS AND SUPPLY CHAIN INNOVATION HANDBOOK

'During this period of acute innovation and disruption, understanding the logistics and supply chain market landscape is more crucial than ever for investors. Manners-Bell and Lyon provide insight into how to spot the type of companies and innovations that have the best chance of succeeding, and some of the pitfalls which new businesses must avoid.'
Alexsander M Stewart, former Managing Director and Head of Global Transportation and Logistics Investment Banking, Stifel

'The authors intelligently and expertly provide a comprehensive look at the new disruptive technologies and business models that are reshaping the rapidly changing global logistics and ecommerce landscape. The book also identifies both the emerging and established supply chain players innovating this change, providing the reader with an insightful analysis. A must-read.'
John Hextall, CEO and board member, De Well Group

'Companies such as Amazon, Uber and Alibaba have revolutionized parts of the economy. But how will the physical–digital interplay shape the future? How to move beyond innovation to become real game changers? This book provides the knowledge and tools to drive change in the Fourth Industrial Revolution. It will be essential for those who wish to transform their business, build or invest in next-generation technology and shake up the supply chain and logistics industry.'
Wolfgang Lehmacher, former Director, Head of Supply Chain and Transport Industries, World Economic Forum

'This is the best logistics and supply chain book I've ever read, with excellent current insight. There is also a bit of scepticism just under the surface, which lends additional credibility to an already honest, forthright assessment. It

provides common sense, logic and insight, all focused by the innovative disruption that has guided Manners-Bell and Lyon during their rich and extensive global logistics journey.'
Michael J Stolarczyk, author of *Logical Logistics: A common sense primer for your supply chain*, and Vice President, Veristor Systems

'Wow... I hadn't realized the extent of the innovations taking place that could make an impact on this area and the progress that has been made in the last five years. This is a very interesting book with practical insight and examples.'
Graham Sweet, Visiting Fellow, Cranfield School of Management, and former Manager of Supply Chain Strategy, Xerox, London

The Logistics and Supply Chain Innovation Handbook

Disruptive technologies and new business models

John Manners-Bell
Ken Lyon

KoganPage

> **Publisher's note**
>
> Every possible effort has been made to ensure that the information contained in this book is accurate at the time of going to press, and the publishers and authors cannot accept responsibility for any errors or omissions, however caused. No responsibility for loss or damage occasioned to any person acting, or refraining from action, as a result of the material in this publication can be accepted by the editor, the publisher or the authors.

First published in Great Britain and the United States in 2019 by Kogan Page Limited

2nd Floor, 45 Gee Street	122 W 27th St, 10th Floor	4737/23 Ansari Road
London	New York, NY 10001	Daryaganj
EC1V 3RS	USA	New Delhi 110002
United Kingdom		India

www.koganpage.com

ISBNs

HARDBACK	978 1 78966 008 1
PAPERBACK	978 0 7494 8633 4
E-ISBN	978 0 7494 8634 1

British Library Cataloguing-in-Publication Data

A CIP record for this book is available from the British Library.

Library of Congress Cataloging-in-Publication Data

Names: Manners-Bell, John, author. | Lyon, Ken, author.
Title: The logistics and supply chain innovation handbook : disruptive
    technologies and new business models / John Manners-Bell and Ken Lyon.
Description: 1st Edition. | New York : Kogan Page Ltd, [2019] | Includes
    bibliographical references and index.
Identifiers: LCCN 2019007914 (print) | LCCN 2019010426 (ebook) | ISBN
    9780749486341 (Ebook) | ISBN 9781789660081 (hardback) | ISBN 9780749486334
    (pbk.) | ISBN 9780749486341 (eISBN)
Subjects: LCSH: Business logistics–Technological innovations. | Delivery of
    goods–Management. | Electronic commerce.
Classification: LCC HD38.5 (ebook) | LCC HD38.5 .M3638 2019 (print) | DDC
    658.7–dc23
LC record available at https://lccn.loc.gov/2019007914

Typeset by Integra Software Services, Pondicherry
Print production managed by Jellyfish
Printed and bound by CPI Group (UK) Ltd, Croydon CR0 4YY

CONTENTS

Online resources to accompany this book are available at:

www.koganpage.com/LSCIH

ABOUT THIS BOOK

The Fourth Industrial Revolution – a term used for a collection of new technologies and business models – is transforming the societies and economies in which we live. Consumer habits are changing fast, and supply chains are having to adapt to meet the challenges created by this dynamic new environment. Traditional logistics operating models are also under threat – incumbent freight operators across the entire transport and warehousing spectrum have been forced to assess and develop strategies to effectively compete with innovative new start-ups.

The Logistics and Supply Chain Innovation Handbook provides a comprehensive overview of all the major new technologies and business models currently under development. From blockchain to on-demand delivery systems, it offers a straightforward and easy-to-understand assessment of these innovations and their impact on the industry as well as on society as a whole.

Topics covered include:

- the process of disruption and why the supply chain and logistics industry is so vulnerable;
- sharing economy and crowd-sourcing/crowd-shipping;
- on-demand delivery;
- the Internet of Things, artificial intelligence and control towers;
- autonomous vehicles;
- automation in the warehouse;
- electric vehicles and alternative fuels;
- the phenomenon of Amazon and Alibaba;
- blockchain technologies.

This book is intended to provide:

- insight into all the major trends transforming the supply chain and logistics industry using case studies and interviews conducted with key actors;
- help for managers seeking to protect their companies from disruption and how they can ensure the sustainability of their businesses;

- a guide to spotting many of the pitfalls involved in starting up or investing in a new 'disruptor';

- an understanding of how the industry will develop and how all companies in the supply chain must adapt to this new environment to survive;

- a practical understanding of how disruptive technology will transform supply chain dynamics;

- a vision of how supply chains will develop in the coming years and what a future logistics operation will look like;

- insight into why some innovations may never be adopted and why many start-up companies fail.

PREFACE AND ACKNOWLEDGEMENTS

The supply chain and logistics industry has already undergone somewhat of a transformation since we both started out on our careers. Early memories of telex machines in the corner of offices with spools of tickertape, subsequently made redundant by faxes and then email; dispatching drivers with paper manifests, maps and 'telephone money' to call in after they had made their delivery; stock management without a barcode anywhere to be seen. Sometimes it seems incredible that anything worked at all without a computer or a smartphone.

Of course, things did work (most of the time), just not as efficiently as today. Just-in-case manufacturing predominated, just-in-case parts weren't available or were defective (which they often were). Lost shipments, mislaid stock, poor routing, late deliveries, inadequate paperwork and clearance queries were endemic. The result was longer transits, unpredictable production schedules, higher levels of inventory, higher fuel, labour and administration costs as well as a significant impact to the economy.

Over the decades, processes have become much more efficient. Technologies now provide levels of visibility in the supply chain that were unimaginable just a few years ago. JIT has created the need for frequent, reliable transport and e-commerce has placed even more pressure on the sector.

However, in many respects, the industry is still very recognizable to the one we joined. But for how much longer? A new generation of technological developments and innovative new business models mean that disruption is inevitable. Digitization, 3D printing, blockchain, e-commerce, autonomous vehicles, alternative fuels (and many others) are resulting in systemic supply- and demand-side changes.

The pace of transformation is accelerating, and tracking these changes has become an increasingly important – and difficult – job. Therefore, we would like to acknowledge the assistance of the UK research team at Transport Intelligence in helping with the development of material for this book: Nick Bailey, David Buckby, Violeta Keckarovska, Alex Leroy and Andy Ralls.

John Manners-Bell and Ken Lyon

The Fourth Industrial Revolution and the anatomy of innovation

THIS CHAPTER WILL FAMILIARIZE THE READER WITH:

- what is meant by the term 'Fourth Industrial Revolution';
- how emerging technologies are impacting supply chains;
- different types of innovation and how digital and physical technological innovations can overlap to meet business needs;
- how different innovations apply at different points of the supply chain;
- descriptions of organizational innovations such as 'horizontal collaboration';
- the 'physical internet' and proposals to converge a range of organizational and technological innovations.

Introduction

The 'Fourth Industrial Revolution' (4IR) is the term used to describe the transformation of economies through a combination of technological, societal and business-related disruptive forces. It has led to the development of the 'sharing economy' (such as Airbnb and Uber) as well as a change in attitudes towards asset ownership.

Nowhere will the effects of 4IR have more impact than in the development of the transport, logistics and supply chain industry. However, it is far from evident whether the outcome for the industry will be positive or negative – much will depend on choices being made in the coming years.

The impact of 4IR on employment is a case in point. A number of the most significant innovations being considered could eliminate many millions of jobs as supply chain functions become automated by driverless vehicles, robots in the warehouse or 3D printing (WEF, 2016). Unless education and training are put in place that will equip future employees with skill sets that enable them to adapt to the changing economic environment, a large proportion of society could find itself excluded from the benefits.

In fact, the whole future of the supply chain industry has been called into doubt. 3D printing could seriously diminish volumes of components moving through upstream supply chains (especially throughout Asia) as manufacturing becomes consolidated in local plants. This would mean that the ubiquitous subcontractor/assembly model becomes redundant, and the logistics services required to link production nodes are eliminated (Manners-Bell and Lyon, 2015). Instead these will be replaced with lower cost bulk shipments of 'printer' materials originating in large chemical plants based close to where the raw materials are extracted (eg in the Middle East) (see Chapter 7 – 3D printing).

The pace of industrial change (although not the likelihood of change itself) will be impacted by the inertia created by governments and vested interests. For example, regulation often finds it difficult to keep pace with technological change, and this can lead to a vacuum of governance and the lack of a legal framework. This could equally apply to the development of autonomous vehicles, employment in the 'gig' economy or drones.

Although there is always the risk of over-hyping the impact of new technologies, it seems inevitable that there will be significant changes in the very near future. Supply chain and logistics companies need to prepare for this new environment by building flexible and agile structures that allow them to respond quickly to shifting dynamics – whatever they may be.

Themes of 4IR

The World Economic Forum (WEF) has identified five themes related to 4IR:

1 Information services

'Digitally enabled information services will put data at the heart of logistics businesses through initiatives such as logistics control towers and analytics as a service. These will reduce operating costs while improving operational efficiency' (WEF, 2017). The WEF estimates that this presents a US $810 billion opportunity for the industry as analytics can optimize routes, improve utilization and reduce maintenance. It would leverage 'Big Data' generated by the Internet of Things, for example.

The proliferation of internet-connected devices that interact without human intervention is creating new possibilities in data gathering, predictive analytics and IT automation. For example, in conjunction with developments in autonomous vehicles, cities can share data on traffic conditions to optimize routing and create efficiencies.

Creating optimized distribution networks will have an impact on inventory holdings (lower than might have been required with sub-optimal transport). Centralization of inventory will remain possible, without the need for more localized holdings of stock.

The WEF also identifies 'Analytics as a Service' as an important component of information services. It estimates that it would bring benefits such as:

- savings in fuel costs for road freight companies of 5 per cent;
- reduction of repair costs by 30 per cent through predictive maintenance;
- improvements in the utilization of logistics by 5 per cent.

The WEF (2017) suggests that savings totalling US $520 billion could be saved by road freight companies and US $30 billion and US $50 billion by air and sea freight companies, respectively. Likewise, there would be savings of more then 4 billion metric tons of carbon emissions.

2 Logistics services

'Digitally enabled logistics services will grow trade by creating digitally enhanced cross-border platforms' (WEF, 2017). Businesses, particularly small and medium-sized enterprises (SMEs), have struggled with the logistical challenges related to the cross-border shipments of small parcel goods. SMEs are demanding a more simplified process, and technology-powered intermediary platforms are filling that gap.

Digital logistics services, such as road freight platform, will also help satisfy growing customer demand for faster deliveries and promote the concept of city logistics, which will allow firms to operate efficiently in 'megacities'.

The simplification of trade processes could benefit trade platforms by US $120 billion and logistics companies by US $50 billion in additional profits, according to WEF (2017).

CASE STUDY 1.1   eBay's Global Shipping Program

Global eRetail platform eBay has recognized this and has developed a Global Shipping Program to make retailers' products available to millions of buyers in more than 50 countries. The Global Shipping Platform enables fully landed costs to be displayed to international customers. It also provides businesses with the ability to ship any products bound for an international customer to a domestic shipping centre. Customs filing, international packaging and import payments are handled by an intermediary, and the item is then sent to the international buyer with complete end-to-end tracking. The Global Shipping Program is free to join for users of eBay Marketplaces.

The primary driver for the success of the Global Shipping Program is the difficulty associated with international shipping of goods, particularly for small businesses. SMEs are demanding a more simplified process, and technology-powered intermediary platforms are filling that gap. Moreover, SMEs are unlikely to have cross-border operations and therefore they need end-to-end tracking in order to monitor the status of their international shipments.

According to eBay, the Global Shipping Program has been shown to increase sales by 15%. The process is also much easier than for typical international transactions because the domestic small business is merely engaging in a domestic shipment of the good and the intermediary handles the challenges of cross-border logistics. The Global Shipping Program also increases transparency for the buyer by providing fully landed costs up front and providing end-to-end tracking. Finally, the Global Shipping Program provides business cost savings due to the aggregation of outbound parcel shipments by many SMEs.

Key to success has been:

- innovative software that can calculate fully landed costs upfront;
- eBay's global Marketplace platform with over 150 million users worldwide;
- the creation of national logistics hubs where outbound international shipments can be aggregated.

3 Delivery capabilities

'New delivery options such as autonomous trucks and drones mean more efficient ways to deliver shipments' (WEF, 2017). There can be no more disruptive technology to the global road freight industry than 'autonomous vehicles'. Whereas the headlines have mostly focused on cars, many of the world's largest manufacturers of trucks, including Daimler and well-backed innovators such as Tesla, Wrightspeed and Nikola, have already invested billions in the technology.

However, at this stage, removing drivers from trucks is still a very long way off. The technology faces huge challenges, not only from labour organizations but also safety and regulatory bodies and even the wider population.

In summary, vehicle manufacturers believe that the benefits will be:

- reduced fuel consumption and emissions – the computer will drive the vehicle more fuel efficiently;
- 'perfect' route planning;
- diagnostic services, ensuring fewer breakdowns;
- emergency braking, ensuring fewer accidents;
- less congestion;
- zero accidents caused by human error.

See Chapter 12 for a more detailed discussion of the subject.

Technological and regulatory barriers will constrain the development of these innovations, although over the next 10 years the WEF still believes that they will contribute US $50 billion in economic value add.

The WEF also includes 3D printing within this category. It effectively delivers product without the need for transportation, apart from the printer materials. For this reason, operating profits of logistics providers may fall by US $1 billion by 2025 (WEF, 2017).

4 Circular economy and sustainability

'A circular economy will foster a more sustainable product life cycle, helping to lessen the industry's environmental footprint by reducing carbon dioxide (CO_2) emissions, air pollution and waste material' (WEF, 2017). The WEF estimates that digital initiatives could reduce emissions from logistics by 10 to 12 per cent by 2025.

A structural change from petrol and diesel fuel powered vehicles is also underway, prompted not least by government bans on conventionally powered trucks in urban areas. Health concerns are growing over the impact of particulates as well as over carbon emissions. This will mean that operators will require fleets of alternative fuel vehicles (including electric) as well as traditional diesel, until the operational effectiveness gap between the two narrows (see Chapter 13 for more details on alternative fuels).

5 Shared economy

'Shared warehouse and shared transport capabilities are expected to increase asset utilization in the near future' (WEF, 2017). Crowd-shipping is a major opportunity – and threat – to the industry, and the WEF believes that traditional trucking companies could lose US $310 billion of profits to companies using crowd-sourced platforms.

Using 'smartphone' technology, crowd-shipping apps are better able to match demand with supply (either road freight operators or individuals). In an urban context, moving parcels by bus or train could reduce congestion on roads. Drivers could use 'Uber-like' platforms to utilize spare capacity in their own cars, making money and reducing the volumes of vans on the road.

Traditional operators may benefit from higher load factors. However, the platforms could also attract more car owners to undertake parcel deliveries – actually exacerbating traffic congestion rather than improving it (see Chapter 11).

Total benefits of the 4IR to the logistics and supply chain sector

The WEF, in conjunction with consultancy Accenture, estimates that there could be up to US $1.5 trillion of value at stake for logistics providers by 2023 and an additional US $2.4 trillion of societal benefits. (See Table 1.1 for benefits of logistics innovations in 2023.)

Table 1.1 Benefits of logistics innovations in 2023

	New business value	Logistics cost reduction	Emission and congestion
Data analytics	600	–	–
Control towers	210	–	–
Trade facilitation	170	600	–55
Crowd-sourcing	310	800	180
Autonomous transport	–	50	–
Shared warehousing	–	500	70
Total	1,290	1,950	195

SOURCE WEF (2017)

The anatomy of innovation

'Innovation' has been a much used – and many would say over-used – term in the past 20 years. Logistics companies have often been accused by their customers of lacking innovation, while they in turn have levelled accusations that manufacturers and retailers have been more focused on cost cutting than creativity. In fact, the truth is that, with few exceptions, most logistics companies and their customers have been happy with the status quo. That is, until the latest breed of e-commerce disruptors and digital service providers transformed consumer expectations.

There are many types of innovation. Logistics innovation itself has been defined as, 'creating logistics value out of new products or services, new processes, new transaction types, new relationships or new business models' (Verweij and Cruijssen, 2006). They divide innovations into five separate categories, as shown in Table 1.2.

In many cases, these innovations are inevitably inter-related. Amazon's success, it could be argued, has been brought about by innovation in all these categories. It has developed new products, relentlessly innovated the way in which these services have been delivered and implemented new ways of selling as well as initiating new relationships with customers and suppliers. This has led to the transformation not only of its business but of an entire sector.

The new technologies highlighted in this book play an important role in all these categories. It is important to note that the development of technology is not an end in itself. It is only worthwhile if it delivers demonstrable

Table 1.2 Categorization of innovation types

Innovation	Explanation
Product and service	Research and development of new products and services
Process	Changes in the way these products/services are performed or produced
Transactional	New ways of selling
Relationship	Development of new relationships with customers or suppliers
Business model	Transformation of operational model

SOURCE Based on Cruijssen (2006)

benefits to a business, either by releasing value or cutting costs. It is against this metric that the hype surrounding 3D printing, drones or blockchain must be judged.

Digital and physical technological innovation

Figure 1.1 illustrates the relationship between business needs and technological innovation. Without a business need there is little requirement for a new technology. This may sound self-evident, but of course it is often very difficult for developers to truly understand if there is a market for their new application or product. There is also the risk that developers will create a new application, for instance, just because they can and not because there is a need for it. The other point to make is that some business needs may not be easily identified by the customer. For instance, the inertia of being a big corporate can militate against adopting new ways of doing things.

However, given that a need has been identified, the technological innovation to meet that need generally falls into either a 'physical' or 'digital' innovation type. As Figure 1.1 shows, physical innovations can include alternative propulsion systems, drones, 3D printing and robots. Digital innovations involve the

Figure 1.1   The relationship between technological innovation and business needs

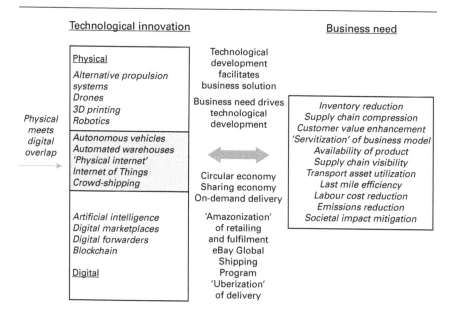

flow of data and the enhanced decision-making that this facilitates. For instance, artificial intelligence, digital marketplaces and blockchain.

Of course, sometimes the physical and digital worlds overlap. Autonomous vehicles can start making decisions without human interaction as AI interprets vast streams of data provided by a combination of sensors, GPS, cameras and radar. Automated warehouse technology can synchronize many hundreds of robots as they efficiently pick orders. The Internet of Things can use sensor technology to allow decisions to be made on the maintenance of vehicles or the reordering of parts. Likewise, people, smartphones and digital marketplaces combine to enable crowd-shipping.

At the nexus point of these innovations and business needs lies 4IR and its sub-themes, for example, the 'circular economy', 'sharing economy' or 'on-demand'.

Some companies have become inextricably linked with the innovations they have been responsible for. Amazon, for instance, has transformed the retail sector and created a new model for shared fulfilment within its facilities. eBay's Global Shipping Program seeks to do the same in cross-border e-commerce and, of course, Uber has become synonymous with the transformation of sectors through its exploitation of smartphone technology and digital platforms. As Figure 1.1 indicates, *business needs* drive technological development, but *technological development* facilitates business solutions.

Figure 1.2 shows the impact that disruption and innovation are having on the various parts of the supply chain. The Internet of Things will have a supply chain-wide impact on the movement and storage of goods from manufacturer to end-user and back again. Others, such as 'crowd-shipping', will impact on a specific leg of the delivery. Wearable technology, augmented reality glasses and 'cobots' will be found in the warehouse.

Figure 1.2 is helpful in showing that some innovations are wide ranging, whereas others are very specific in their impact.

Organizational innovation

Many of the innovations occurring within the supply chain and logistics industry are organizational, that is, they relate to relationships, operational processes or business models. Although they may involve an element of technological innovation or indeed are facilitated by new technologies, they generate value predominantly through changes in the way things are done or in the relationships between customers and suppliers.

Figure 1.2   The positioning of technological innovations in the supply chain

Upstream supply chain	Downstream distribution			End-of-life/ spare parts
Product design/production/ sourcing	Warehousing	Transport	Last mile delivery	
Internet of Things				
Blockchain				
Artifical intelligence				
Payment methods (crypto-payment)				
E-commerce				
Cloud-based data visibility systems				
3D printing	Robotics and automation	Increased vehicle utilization (telematics)		3D printing
Circular economy design	Wearable technology	Mileage reduction (route optimization)		Circular economy design
Temperature controlled packaging innovations and sensors				
Cross-border consolidation	In-warehouse camera-based code readers/scanning	Systematic freight dimensioning	Crowd-shipping	
Product miniturization	Pick by light/ pick by voice	Drive safe/in-cab training system	Lockers and alternative delivery locations	
Smart packaging design	Augmented reality warehouse picking	Asset tracking	Drones	Increased returns velocity
		Freight platforms	'Uberization' of delivery systems	
Mass customization of design	Green warehousing	Alternative fuels		
		Autonomous vehicles		
Near-shoring/ re-shoring	Intralogistics	Predictive maintenance	Alternative addressing systems	Ease of returns
			Click and collect	

'Horizontal collaboration', as outlined in Case Study 1.2, is one such innovation, as is the 'physical internet' concept. Both rely heavily on technological developments, but their success will rely predominantly on a transformation in business culture and a more 'open' approach to sharing volumes, customers, assets and networks.

CASE STUDY 1.2   Horizontal collaboration

An important organizational innovation that seeks to address inefficiencies in the warehouse and road freight transport market is 'horizontal collaboration'. The term refers to cooperative supply chain and logistics relationships between manufacturers (Horvath, 2001).

By collaborating, these partners are effectively merging their shipment volumes and distribution networks to achieve a range of efficiencies. Another term for this is 'insyncing' (as opposed to 'outsourcing') (Cruijssen, 2006). One of the most compelling benefits of horizontal collaboration is that it has been shown to bring fast and measurable benefits and is relatively cheap – an important factor in today's market environment.

Within the warehouse environment, combining inventories can increase distribution centre utilization. It has been used to good effect when, for example, a supply chain re-engineering project has resulted in the reduction of stock held at centralized facilities. This then leaves an underutilized warehouse that usually has to be disposed of, incurring property and employee costs. By inviting another manufacturer to share the premises, these costs are avoided and efficiencies are increased.

On the transportation side, there are also benefits. By co-loading shipments there are synergies to be gained, especially where the product is being distributed to similar retail outlets in the consumer goods sector, automotive dealerships or high-tech service parts drop-off points.

One particular project between two collaborating consumer goods manufacturing companies found that 80 per cent of delivery locations were the same. A research project for a Dutch university believed that a saving of 31 per cent in transportation costs could be achieved (Cruijssen *et al*, 2007a).

However, collaboration not only benefits warehousing and transportation operations. It can also enhance customer service by providing a critical mass that allows increased frequency of deliveries. Shippers do not have to weigh up the benefits of increasing the number of consignments to customers against the cost of dispatching half-empty vehicles. Co-loading with a partner ensures that vehicle breakeven points are met.

The last major benefit in terms of bottom line profitability is the leverage that shippers can gain in terms of negotiating freight rates. Consolidating shipment volumes can ensure small- and medium-sized manufacturers can compete in the market on the same basis as larger rivals.

Horizontal collaboration can also deliver important environmental benefits through:

- reducing congestion by better utilizing the vehicles deployed;
- enabling modal shift by creating unit loads through consolidation of shipments;
- encouraging sustainable distribution networks and partnerships;
- reducing waste;
- facilitating and consolidating returns.

Collaboration does not work for all companies. Beyond the obvious corporate cultural barriers that may preclude working with other competitors, there is a range of pre-conditions that need to be met. In many cases, collaboration will work best if the products and distribution profiles of the collaborating companies are similar. Even if the products themselves do not need to be identical, it certainly helps if handling characteristics, lifecycles, inventory velocity and seasonality, as well as environmental control and security needs, are compatible. In addition, similar patterns of spatial distribution will certainly drive cost savings (Manners-Bell, 2010).

Impediments to collaboration

Of course, there are reasons why collaboration can be difficult to achieve in practice. For example, it can be difficult to find suitable partners with whom to work. To aid the process, cross-industry forums have developed that foster discussions between manufacturers, consultancies and logistics providers.

However, another problem is finding a partner that can facilitate collaboration and act as an independent facilitator. The role, which can be undertaken by a third-party logistics provider or consultancy, may involve promoting the concept, identifying partners, quantifying the benefits, managing data (for confidentiality as well as operational reasons) and operations themselves. If competing companies are collaborating, there may well be anti-trust issues involved. In fact, this also makes the role of the third party even more important to act as a 'Chinese wall', as it might be termed.

For any partnership to be long lasting, the allocation of the cost savings as well as any costs involved in establishing the venture need to be seen to be fair. This will involve an openness that again may challenge many companies.

Although collaboration is considered to be a 'cheap' supply chain initiative, there may be investment needed, depending on the complexity of the relationship. For example, information and communication technology investments may be required to enable data-sharing (Cruijssen *et al*, 2007b).

Finally, if a company sees its supply chain as a competitive advantage, then it may be best not to collaborate with a competitor. Collaboration will bring benefits, but it also nullifies advantages. Therefore, while providing cost savings, it may well additionally improve a competitor's speed to market, customer service and inventory levels. In this case it may be better to collaborate with a complementary product manufacturer instead.

The convergence of innovations: the 'physical internet'

Some academics believe that maximum value will accrue to the supply chain and logistics industry, as well as the wider economy, only if a completely new system can be designed to leverage the benefits of the new technologies and organizational structures (and cultures) being developed.

A discussion paper written for the International Transport Forum (Tavasszy, 2018) describes the 'physical internet' (PI) as 'the only comprehensive vision [in which] these innovations could converge into a single logistics system'. The concept was developed in the United States, the brainchild of Professor Benoit Montreuil, in the mid-2000s and was supported in Europe by ALICE (Alliance for Logistics Innovation through Collaboration in Europe), a European-funded research organization.

The concept is certainly bold as it calls for the reimagining of the entire logistics industry on a system level. In the keynote speech at the 2017 Physical Internet conference, Professor Montreuil described the PI as a 'hyperconnected global logistics system enabling seamless open asset sharing and flow consolidation through standardized encapsulation, modularization, protocols and interfaces' (Montreuil, 2018b).

The basic ambition of the PI is to make logistics networks as efficient as those in the digital world. But for that to occur there needs to be root-and-branch transformation of the existing systems that have been in place, in many cases, for centuries (Montreuil, 2018a).

Montreuil believes that the industry will evolve from one that could be described as fragmented or atomized, to integrated, to collaborative, to finally one that is 'hyperconnected'.

Transport and delivery

Perhaps the biggest change will be to the existing distribution structures. The proponents of the PI see private networks, hubs and transportation fleets as inherently inefficient. To achieve a step change in efficiency, logistics companies will need to open their networks to competitors, allowing interoperability across transport assets, information technology platforms and warehousing.

Logistics hubs would become public in much the way that ports deal with containers from a multitude of shipping lines, freight forwarders or other cargo owners. They would be cross-docked rather than stored, leading to a compression of the supply chain. Long-distance journeys would be eliminated, as each consignment would be dropped at a regional cross-dock hub and then collected promptly by another driver. Driver overnight rest periods would no longer be an issue, cutting overall transit time significantly.

By sharing logistics assets, it has been estimated that there could be up to a third in cost savings. In addition to this, greenhouse gas emissions would be reduced by 60 per cent.

Although relevant on a regional basis, the need for better utilization of transport is even more pressing in an urban context as congestion levels and emissions rise. This is a key area in which it is hoped that the PI would have an impact.

Packaging

Within the PI, all goods would be stored and moved in standardized modular containers. These, according to Montreuil, would be a cross between 'a lego block and a Russian doll' (2018b). That is, smaller containers could be consolidated into larger ones efficiently with a minimum of wasted space.

These modular containers would be 'smart', re-usable, recyclable and secure. As in the shipping industry, these standard containers would allow faster flows through warehouses and transport hubs as well as providing better visibility and traceability, to item level. The PI doesn't deal as such with freight but only the containers in which the freight is stored, in much the same way that modern ports only deal with containers.

Supporters of the concept believe that it is a development of the sharing economy, as exemplified by innovators such as Flexe (see Chapter 10). Amazon, by opening up its distribution centres to third-party retailers through its Fulfilled by Amazon programme has already gone some way to creating a hyperconnected logistics network.

However, the key challenges that must be overcome before the PI can become a reality will be to prove to shippers and logistics companies:

- that it makes financial sense to share networks and assets;
- that containerization of all products leads to more efficient use of space, not less;
- the technology exists, or will exist, that facilitates the data sharing;
- operationally, the processes work.

In addition to this, there is the cultural barrier of giving up elements of competitive advantage. Would DHL be happy to ship UPS or FedEx packages and vice versa? This may be the biggest stumbling block to adoption. Those promoting the idea certainly don't believe the PI to be imminent, setting 2050 as the year in which they hope it will become a reality.

Summary

The 'Fourth Industrial Revolution' as a concept brings together a range of digital, physical and organizational innovations. Significant forces for industry transformation exist within the supply chain and logistics sector due to high levels of structural and sometimes operational inefficiency. Sometimes these innovations will create value at a specific point within the supply chain, such as in the warehouse, while other innovations are far more wide-reaching, such as the Internet of Things and blockchain. The success of an innovation can be measured in different ways:

1 It may generate new business opportunities, creating new markets or customer value.

2 It may deliver operational efficiencies, cutting costs while enhancing service.

3 It may reduce environmental impact, for example by reducing greenhouse gas emissions.

For managers to develop a compelling and comprehensive vision for their businesses in a transforming market environment, it is critical for them to understand the interrelationship between the physical and digital world as well as the opportunity for organizational innovation. Most value will be created where these innovations converge and, as such, the 'physical internet' is the most ambitious initiative.

Bibliography

Cruijssen, F (2006) *Horizontal Cooperation in Transport and Logistics*, University of Tilburg, Netherlands

Cruijssen, F, Braysy, O, Dullaert, W, Fleuren, H and Salomon, M (2007a) Joint route planning under varying market conditions, *International Journal of Physical Distribution & Logistics Management*, 37, pp 287–304

Cruijssen, F, Cools, M and Dullaert, W (2007b) Horizontal cooperation in logistics: opportunities and impediments, *Transportation Research Part E: Logistics and Transportation Review*, 43, pp 129–142

Horvath, L (2001) Collaboration: the key to value creation in supply chain management, *Supply Chain Management: An International Journal*, 6 (5), pp 205–207

Manners-Bell, J (2010) *How Collaboration Can Improve Your Bottom Line and Benefit the Environment*, Transport Intelligence Ltd, Bath

Manners-Bell, J and Lyon, K (2015) *The Implications of 3D Printing for the Global Logistics Industry*, Transport Intelligence Ltd, Bath

Montreuil, B [accessed 10 May 2018a] Towards a Physical Internet: Meeting the Global Logistics Sustainability Grand Challenge, *Logistics Research* [Online] https://doi.org/10.1007/s12159-011-0045-x

Montreuil, B [accessed 11 May 2018b] *Sustainability and Competitiveness: Is the Physical Internet a Solution?* Graz, Austria [Online] www.pi.events/IPIC2017/sites/default/files/IPIC2017-Plenary%20keynote_Montreuil.pdf

Tavasszy, L (2018) *Innovation and Technology in Multi-Modal Supply Chains*, Delft University of Technology, the Netherlands

Verweij, C. and F. Cruijssen (2006) *Verbeterpotentie van Europese logistieke netwerken*, Transumo, Netherlands

WEF (2016) *The Future of Jobs*, World Economic Forum/Accenture, Geneva

WEF (2017) *Impact of the Fourth Industrial Revolution on Supply Chains*, World Economic Forum/Accenture, Geneva

Breaking the paradigm 02

The rise of the disruptors

THIS CHAPTER WILL FAMILIARIZE THE READER WITH:

- how innovation can lead to disruption of industries and companies;
- the type of supply chain waste that innovations seek to address;
- drivers of waste and innovations in the logistics industry;
- the difficulties in identifying a business need for a start-up innovator;
- how disruption can release value by addressing 'waste' in a supply chain;
- the key attributes of a successful innovator.

How to be a successful innovator: addressing supply chain inefficiency

It is exceptionally difficult to judge which of the many thousands of new start-up companies in the supply chain and logistics space will be successful or not. There are many key qualities that an innovator must exhibit. However, fundamental to success, it is essential for an innovator to tackle an industry problem that, if fixed, will release value fully or partly to the innovator.

In some cases, as will be discussed, an innovation can lead to an efficiency saving, for example, completing a task more quickly or by using fewer resources. In others, it can lead to a completely new way of doing things, disrupting existing systems and the companies that operate within them. In the term used by Braithwaite and Christopher (2015), 'breaking the paradigm'.

This chapter examines the different types of 'innovation' and the inefficiencies they seek to address. It will also show how difficult it is for innovators (and potential investors) to be sure that the new product or service has a market due to the difficulties of measuring 'waste' in the supply chain and logistics industry. A long list of innovators – Shyp being among the more recent – have found this to their cost.

Types of supply chain waste

One of the key targets of many innovators is to address supply chain inefficiency or 'waste'. In a lean supply chain context, waste is defined as anything that doesn't add value to the customer or, in other words, is 'useless' as opposed to 'necessary' consumption or expenditure. The Japanese word 'muda' is often used to refer to this waste. Although the aim of this chapter is not to discuss the best approach to eliminating wasteful processes *per se*, it is always critical for innovators to understand and quantify the extent of the problem that their product, new business model, service or technology seeks to address.

These 'wastes' can be categorized into the following:

- **Over-production:** Making too much of a product or, for retailers, over-stocking a product, occurs when forecasts overstate expected demand. The flow of information from customer to manufacturer is a key supply chain issue.

- **Time/inventory related:** How can the supply chain be compressed? Releasing capital tied up in inventory has long been the main goal of many manufacturers' and retailers' supply chain strategies. Reducing time-in-transit is a key issue in terms of logistics.

- **Productivity:** How can organizations become more productive? In the warehouse, this may be achieved by increasing the efficiency of the work force by the use of technologies related to put away or picking (such as augmented reality glasses) or replacing workers with automation.

- **Imperfect market knowledge:** In terms of transportation, waste is created when shippers with cargos are unable to access enough suppliers to make a competitive market. This may mean that they are charged more than is necessary or indeed they do not use the fastest or most appropriate transport available to them. The corollary also exists, that transport providers miss the opportunity to utilize all available space on their vehicles.

- **Space mismanagement:** This could relate to sub-optimal loading of vehicles, containers or other unitized devices. Alternatively, it could relate to poor space utilization in warehouses.

- **Inappropriate processing:** Unnecessary work, such as phoning numerous shipping lines or forwarders to get a quote, or the rekeying of data into trade and customs' documentation. Not only is this time consuming but risks errors. Digital innovations such as cloud computing or blockchain could address this.

- **Market regulation:** A high degree of regulation exists in the transport markets, some quantitative but most qualitative. That is to say, numbers of operators are not directly restricted in the way they were, say, 50 years ago, but most governments around the world impose minimum standards on the industry. This may hold back innovations (think autonomous vehicles or drones) if safety concerns are overstated. Regulations on cabotage are another example of how the European road freight sector is forced to operate sub-optimally at the expense of better capacity utilization.

- **Transport:** The movement of goods is regarded as a 'necessary' waste. Companies, after all, have to get their goods to market. However, there are efficient and inefficient ways of managing this part of the supply chain process, some more wasteful than others. Containerization, hub-and-spoke networks and direct-to-consumer models are all attempts at balancing the cost of transport with the time taken in transit. 3D printing may eliminate some transport needs completely.

An element of the 'wastes' identified above can be addressed by planning and efficient management. It needs no innovation. However, there are times when innovations drive efficiencies by providing new tools for managers. There are also times when innovations can lead to the complete system transformation of operating and business models, although innovating to create efficiency does not in itself necessarily lead to disruption. Figure 2.1 illustrates that while the first two steps are often closely linked, the third, disruption, should be regarded as distinct.

It is often very difficult for senior management to provide the necessary internal backing to ideas that will disrupt their existing business model. For this reason, disruptors often come from outside the company or, indeed, from outside the industry. They have no vested interest in retaining the status quo.

Addressing inefficiency

Table 2.1 examines five different logistics segments: air cargo, warehousing, road freight, freight forwarding and shipping. For each segment a number of 'waste drivers' have been identified (there will be countless more). Against

Figure 2.1   Process efficiency and disruption

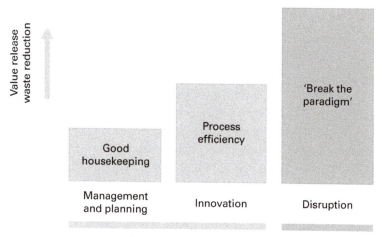

Innovation steps for waste reduction

each of these an innovation has been identified that seeks to address the inefficiency, and the last column shows the result: either a release of value or a reduction in waste (and sometimes both).

Quantifying waste

It is one thing to identify inefficient aspects of the logistics industry; it is another to quantify the level of waste and hence assess the potential market for an innovator. The road freight/trucking sector is a good example.

In theory it should be possible to put a figure on one aspect of waste in road freight transportation, that is, underutilization of capacity. Many statistical bodies have published figures on this metric, not least because unnecessary road transportation is regarded as having a deleterious effect on the environment in terms of emissions. A widely quoted figure, from the European Commission, for the proportion of vehicles running empty is 26 per cent (European Commission, 2018). However, this only tells part of the story as it doesn't take into account partial loading, which arguably is more important in judging how well vehicles are being utilized. The only statistical measure relating to 'average lading' is published by the UK government, which puts it at 60 per cent (McKinnon, 2015). Consequently (at first look), it may be concluded that an operator has 40 per cent of any one if its vehicles' payloads available for additional loads at any one time.

Table 2.1 Drivers of waste and innovations in the logistics industry

Sector	Waste driver	Innovation	Value release/waste reduction
Air cargo	Rekeying of data Paper documentation	Digitization Cloud computing Data standardization	Visibility and instant access to data Performance improvement Reduction of processing costs Reduction of waiting times
Warehousing	Peaks and troughs of demand Labour shortage Errors in put-away/picking Workplace accidents	Automation Co-packing robots Augmented reality glasses Drones	Fewer warehouse workers Better productivity~100% picking accuracy Fewer training costs Fewer accidents
Road freight	Capacity underutilization Traffic congestion Sub-optimal routing Waiting times Route and delivery bans Vehicle inefficiency Sub-optimal driver behaviour	Digitized marketplaces Open data Dynamic routing systems Electric/hydrogen vehicles Autonomous vehicles Platooning Internet of Things sensor technology	Fuller trucks Better productivity Fewer vehicle emissions More productive urban deliveries Lower fuel costs Effective driving re-training Lower maintenance costs and breakdowns
Freight forwarding	Customs delays Quotation delays Document re-keying and errors Lack of trade finance	Single window customs procedure Electronic tariffs Rate quotes on demand Digitization of paperwork International Transport Management Systems Blockchain	Faster clearance Fewer agencies to slow down transit Less corruption Better and faster rates Better visibility Better access to finance for SMEs
Shipping	Overloaded/misdeclared containers Drayage delays in port Inefficient networks Stowage management	Digital database of tare weights 'Uberization' of drayage Algorithm powered network design Stowage planning and container management software	Lower risk of overloading Faster transit of containers through ports Better fuel consumption Better asset utilization

Therefore, it would seem that an innovation that was able to match trucking companies with loads more effectively would:

- reduce the number of trucks required to move the same amount of freight;
- improve operators' profitability by more regularly exceeding breakeven load factors;
- improve overall industry efficiency;
- reduce freight costs for shippers;
- reduce emissions per tonne moved.

This logic has led to the development of numerous freight exchanges. However, the reality is much more complex, a fact that explains why digital road freight marketplaces have not been as successful as might be imagined, despite providing much more visibility of loads.

Figure 2.2 illustrates this and shows that there are a host of reasons why the truck may not be fully loaded in terms of weight. For example, in the consumer goods sector volumetric 'maxing out' is a particular issue. Low density packages may mean that a truck is fully loaded long before the weight limit on the vehicle is reached. Consequently the 'real' addressable market that electronic road freight platforms seek to penetrate is much, much smaller. The percentages used in Figure 2.2 are purely hypothetical as it is impossible to identify which waste is 'necessary' and which is not. However, they are illustrative of the problem faced by digital exchanges that are chasing a market that may not be as big as they had hoped.

Figure 2.2   Addressable waste in the road freight sector

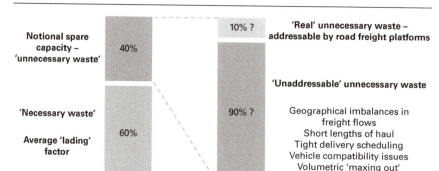

The 4Ds of disruption

Much has been written about disruptive technologies and their impact upon societies and economies. One such book, *Bold*, by authors Diamandis and Kotler (2016), looks at the various stages of what could be called the disruptive process. Although not all of the stages apply to the disruption of business models related to physical processes such as the movement of goods, their argument still holds good in parts and is a useful framework for analysis.

The first stage of the disruptive process involves the 'digitization' of aspects of an industry sector. Although it is easier to imagine the effect that this would have, say, on a sector such as photography (the well-documented bankruptcy of Kodak, for example), digitization has also had a big impact on parts of the transport and logistics industry. The most obvious impact has been the migration of letters to email, reducing the number of documents being sent through postal operators and express parcels carriers.

Relevant as this may be, it is not the most important aspect of the digital revolution in terms of the logistics industry. More transformative has been the digitization of documents carrying the 'metadata' accompanying goods throughout their storage or movement. While once this would have involved a paper trail – a delivery note or airway bill for instance – there is no reason why this data cannot be digitized, and it most frequently is.

This means that this data can be accessed more efficiently and used in ways that could never have been anticipated even a few years ago. This not only has implications for logistics operations but can provide far greater levels of supply chain visibility. Despite the ability of most companies to capture vast amounts of data, many are still unable to work out what to do with it all. Even if they have the capability to mine this 'Big Data' resource effectively, most will use it as a way of making their existing operational processes more efficient. However, more excitingly, for some smarter operators, it is an opportunity to replace out-moded and inefficient business models.

This leads on to the second stage, that of 'disruption'. In the road freight industry one of the major problems has been the inefficiency of the market (as discussed earlier). Part of the problem is that the sector is split into silos of unitized transport capacity, ie private fleets of vehicles. The allocation of these resources is only as good as the access of each individual company to demand (loads). Obviously, the capacity has to be of the right quality, have the right attributes (eg temperature controlled/bulk, etc), be in the right place at the right time and, of course, available at the right price. However, these are largely secondary considerations. If the transport manager doesn't have access to the market information in the first place, these considerations are irrelevant.

The inefficiency is entrenched as each company sees its ability to access loads as a key competitive advantage. This is compounded by many shippers being unwilling to share contracted assets with companies, competitors or not.

It is this environment of understandable vested interests, inefficiency and the poor utilization of data that suggests the transport industry is ripe for 'disruption'.

The development of platforms that can match supply and demand by providing a closer-to-perfect market than presently exists could deliver huge value, which presently lies latent. It remains to be seen whether this will happen by incumbents being provided with additional loads, or by a more far-reaching move, such as disintermediating the industry to allow shippers to strike deals directly with owner-drivers. It could indeed be through the consumerization of the industry: by allowing private individuals to earn additional revenues by dropping parcels on their way to work, perhaps using public transport. Whichever form it takes, given the conditions that exist, a major shift is inevitable.

The third (and for transport companies most worrying) stage of the disruptive process is 'demonetization'. In the Kodak example, this is the stage at which consumers stopped buying its film products in favour of new digital cameras. Could something similar happen to transport companies? Could the giants of the industry – UPS, FedEx and DHL – go the same way as Kodak? It seems highly improbable as, unlike the camera industry that went through an additional stage of 'dematerialization', products still need to be moved to market. That is, of course, unless 3D printing removes the need for transport completely.

However, there are still considerable risks for medium and large transport companies. If disruptive technology providers are able to allow shippers (the cargo owners) to access the vast pool of owner-drivers that exists in every country in the world, they would be able to benefit from vastly lower cost bases. Owner-drivers do not have legacy IT systems or pensions to fund, brands to support, or massive head office overheads and so on. These of course are all being funded indirectly by customers through higher-than-needed rates. Some of the largest shippers (eg Unilever) have already started the process of disintermediating their logistics operations by dealing directly with 'local heroes', rather than through regional or global logistics service providers. New disruptive technologies would give them even better visibility of the market and the opportunity to leverage its potential.

The final of Diamandis and Kotler's 'Ds' is 'democratization'. It could be argued that the logistics industry is already highly democratized as there are few barriers to market entry and exit. All that is required is a relatively small sum of money with which to buy or lease a truck. Contrast this with establishing a factory to manufacture camera film, which needed vast investment in production facilities and brand marketing. However, disruption could lower the barriers in the transport sector even further, increasing the size of the relevant supply side market from a few thousand transport entities in each national market, to millions of individuals. Using either the capacity in their own vehicles or indeed public transport, it is foreseeable that parts of the industry (especially mail and parcels) could be transformed (see Chapter 11).

So, is this the beginning of the end for the global 'mega-logistics' companies, their business model eroded by an upsurge in micro-enterprises and individuals? Not necessarily. Although it is highly probable that some companies will fall victim to a changing market, due to either being unwilling or unable to adapt to the new environment, others will seek to harness the new technologies and change the market to their own advantage. At the same time, not every new start-up will be successful. Many, if not most, will fall by the wayside.

Consequently, the largest players in the logistics industry should not feel threatened by every new 'disruptor'. The smartest players in the industry are often, although not always, the largest companies who have been able to invest in new technologies. They are staffed by high quality and creative IT professionals. However, at the same time, the size and inertia that many large companies exhibit mean that they are at risk from these new start-ups, regardless of how many internal innovation or research and development departments are created.

Releasing value through disruption

Looking for sector-based inefficiencies can ignore the greater potential for releasing value by dismantling and rebuilding existing systems. Referring to the example of containerization in the shipping industry in Chapter 3, waste existed in every aspect of the shipping supply chain. This was caused by factors such as regulation of routes and rates, lack of investment in automation, long waiting times, theft and corruption, and multiple calls with small ships. Containerization was so successful as a disruptor as it not so much reduced waste in existing processes, but it led to a strategic transformation of the entire maritime supply chain. To illustrate further, containerization did not result in the ports of New York and London becoming incrementally more efficient, in fact the opposite. It led to the design and development of an entirely new network of mega ports and, further, to the globalization of the world's economy.

Innovation can spur three different types of disruption at different levels. These are:

- process;
- operating model;
- sector;
- company.

The warehousing sector is a good example, as illustrated in Figure 2.3 and explained in the following text.

First, inefficiencies can be addressed by **good management and planning**. This could involve better training of the workforce, flexible use of labour across multiple contracts, investment in warehouse management systems and optimization of inventory placement.

As already discussed earlier in the chapter, **process innovation** is next, addressing inefficiencies through new technologies. Augmented Reality Glasses are an example of this. Not only do they guide the worker to the right picking location, saving time and increasing pick rate, but they also check what they are picking, reducing errors. This means that a process becomes more efficient, but that process is essentially unchanged.

Figure 2.3   The innovation and disruption process in the warehouse

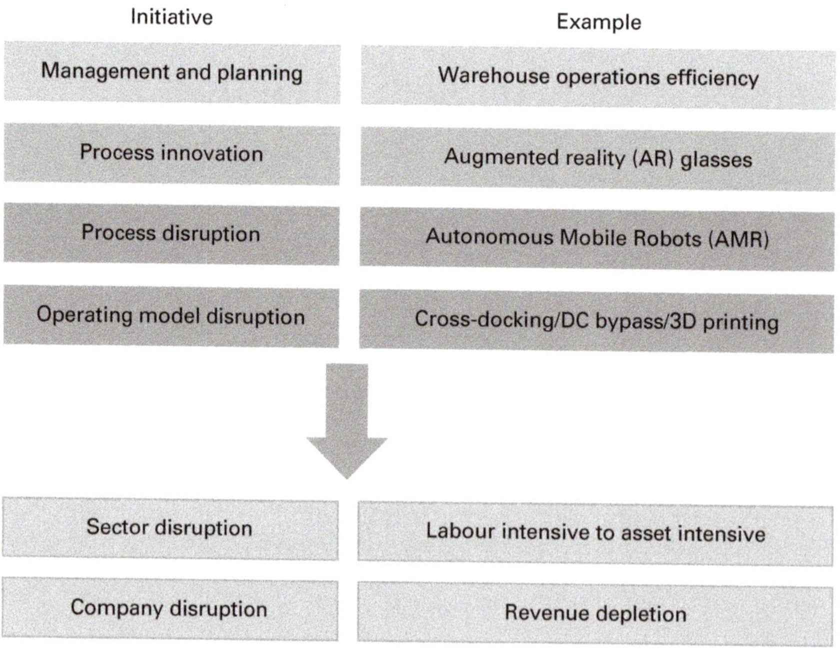

Initiative	Example
Management and planning	Warehouse operations efficiency
Process innovation	Augmented reality (AR) glasses
Process disruption	Autonomous Mobile Robots (AMR)
Operating model disruption	Cross-docking/DC bypass/3D printing
Sector disruption	Labour intensive to asset intensive
Company disruption	Revenue depletion

This contrasts with an innovation such as the use of Autonomous Mobile Robots (AMRs), such as those used by Amazon or Alibaba. These bring the pick face to the picker, resulting in **process disruption**. Where once workers would have walked several kilometres along the aisles, they are now entirely redundant from the process.

A step further is **operating model disruption**. Examples of this are cross-docking (goods are not stored in a warehouse; the shipments are unpacked, combined with other shipments and then immediately dispatched) or Distribution Centre (DC) bypass, where shipments miss out the warehouse completely and are delivered directly from a port, say, to the customer's premises. Ultimately, a technology such as 3D printing could eliminate the need to store goods completely. Instead, for sectors such as service parts, components could be 'printed' by an engineer as and when required, doing away with tiers of global, national, regional and local holdings of inventory.

Changing customer requirements such as these have a subsequent effect on the logistics industry, both in terms of the **sector** dynamics and at a **company** level. Automation in the warehouse will mean that the sector will transform from one that is highly labour dependent to one that is focused on assets (that is, the robots). This will mean a significant change in management skills and financial structure. Logistics companies must prepare themselves for a considerable loss of revenue as costs in the warehouse tumble.

Table 2.2 shows some of the most important operating model disruptions of the last 70 years.

Table 2.2 Logistics operating model disruptions

Logistics sector/activity	Disruptive business model
Breakbulk shipping	Containerization
Road freight	Express parcels network (hub and spoke)
	Pallet networks
Freight forwarding/air cargo	International express ('integrators')
Warehousing and distribution	E-commerce logistics
	Direct delivery/cross-dock
	Robotics
Supply chain technologies	Blockchain
	Cloud computing
Express parcels	E-commerce B2C last mile delivery
Freight forwarding	Digital freight platforms

Another example of disruption is in the road freight sector. Transport management systems have long made existing road operations much more efficient in terms of routing and loading of vehicles. However, of more strategic importance was the advent of hub-and-spoke networks that developed in the 1980s in the freight and express sectors. These were highly disruptive in that they enabled the fast delivery of shipments while reducing costs and increasing capacity utilization. They led to the rise of a new wave of road freight and trucking companies.

So, in summary, innovation within existing operations can be used to optimize processes. This has an important but limited role in the development of the supply chain and logistics industry. Optimization would never have brought about the systemic transformation of the shipping industry, nor the creation of the international express sector or pallet networks. These disruptive phenomena were brought about by companies and individuals willing to break the existing paradigm.

Innovators vs disruptors: which is which?

It is useful to differentiate between process innovators and disruptors. Some companies, as has been discussed, have developed products to make the logistics process easier, thereby benefiting all supply chain partners without altering industry sector structures or having a negative impact on the market incumbents. For example, tech company Freightos has created a digital freight rate platform that will significantly decrease the time it takes to get quotes. This will benefit shippers and also freight forwarders, who can integrate the product within their own offering. The proposition offers a way of addressing 'unnecessary waste' without radically altering the freight forwarding landscape.

Flexport, in contrast, has entered the market using new technologies that have allowed it to offer a compelling proposition to global shippers and capture market share from the incumbents. It has gone head-to-head with the world's largest forwarders, which has resulted in what was referred to above as 'revenue depletion' at a company level.

Of course, Amazon has been the most successful disruptor of all. Its new way of business has had a massive impact on the retail sector, cloud computing, fulfilment and last mile delivery. It is yet to be seen what the consequences will be for air cargo, freight forwarding and other key logistics sectors.

Table 2.3 lists just a few companies categorized in this way.

Table 2.3   Example process innovators and market disruptors

Process innovators		Market disruptors	
Freightos	Digital freight platform	Flexport	Digital freight forwarder
Fleet	Digital freight platform	Amazon	E-commerce logistics
IContainers	Digital freight platform	Rethink Robotics	Collaborative robots
Cargobase	Digital freight platform	Starship Technologies	Self-driving robots
Elementum	Supply chain operating network	FreightHub	Digital freight forwarder
Atheer	Augmented reality for warehouse	Convoy	On-demand trucking service
Ubimax	Augmented reality for warehouse	Drive	Driverless technology
Project44	API developer	Deliv	On-demand
SeeGrid	Forklift automation	Uber Freight	On-demand
E2Open	Cloud-based supply chain management	Fast Radius	3D printing

SOURCE www.ti-insight.com

Disintermediation in the air freight forwarding sector

A key element of disruption can be 'disintermediation'. As Professors Braithwaite and Christopher say in their book *Business Operations Models* (2015), 'The design of disruptive business operations models is generally about disintermediating existing inefficient channels and forming new and responsive relationships with customers'. For many years, the role of the air freight forwarder has been questioned. The argument is that if travel agents can be largely eliminated from the air travel market, why shouldn't freight forwarders be bypassed by shippers working directly with air cargo carriers? In the 1990s, the airline KLM attempted to build direct relationships with shippers such as global high-tech manufacturer Philips but was prevented from doing so by the power of its large forwarder customers – it had too much to lose if competitor airlines were not willing to change their business models too. However, times and technologies have moved on, so do forwarders have a future now?

The answer is that they do. For the most part, the travel agent fulfilled the simple task of finding the best price for the passenger, a function that multiple platforms can perform very effectively (if the passenger doesn't want to book directly with a low-cost airline). The passengers then ensure that they themselves conform with documentation requirements (passports/ID cards) and security requirements before making sure that they arrive at the right terminal at the right time and catch the right airplane.

This contrasts with the complexity of a freight movement. Finding a competitive price is just one part of the process, albeit one that will be increasingly automated. As well as identifying the best route, the forwarder will also ensure that each international shipment must conform with a whole host of regulatory requirements from phytosanitary to certificate of origins, air cargo security, duty and tariff declaration obligations, letters of credit, insurance and risk as well as being responsible for all the documentation. In addition, the forwarder will arrange collection and liaise with an agent in the destination country to fulfil the final delivery.

In summary, it is likely that many processes in the movement of international goods will become more efficient. The benefits will be:

- Rates will fall as shippers are able to access more market information through new rate platforms.
- Rates will be accessible more quickly (instantly) to shippers; seconds compared with days.
- Blockchain will mean fewer delays in air cargo handling operations at airports.
- This technology will also mean smart contracts become the norm, automatically releasing payment when goods are received.

However, it seems unlikely that there will be any root-and-branch transformation of the industry, at least for a large proportion of volumes. The complexity of the process is such that there will be the requirement for a freight forwarder for many years to come. In fact, beyond this, forwarders are well placed to understand their customers' value chains and help them restructure to release value.

How to spot a successful innovator

Banks, venture capitalists, private equity, hedge and investment funds spend a large proportion of their time – and of course money – trying to identify which innovative new company will succeed and which will fail.

Although this is difficult, indicators to success do exist:

1 The start-up is tackling a problem within an industry (such as inefficiency), which, if fixed, will release value (partly, at least, to the start-up).

2 The existing market incumbents are failing to address this problem.

3 The market is large enough to support the business model.

4 There is potential for scalability of the product or solution.

5 Regulatory issues have been addressed.

6 The solution can be counter-intuitive, leverage technologies present in other sectors or bundle existing technologies in unique ways.

7 Its product is differentiated sufficiently from other start-ups.

8 The innovator has a committed and determined founder and a strong management team.

9 It has customers on board testing the concept (even if not paying).

10 It has sufficient funding – critical to provide scale to compete with incumbents and other start-ups.

11 The solution works in the real world (especially when involving the movement of physical goods).

12 It has effective PR and marketing.

To some degree it is possible to quantify some of these indicators. For example, it should be possible to size the market opportunity as well as identifying which needs of customers are being addressed by incumbents and which are being ignored. In other words, a diligent investor should be able to assess the prospects of a start-up by using a quantifiable set of metrics. However, it is very easy to misinterpret data and market opportunity, as we will see below in Case Study 2.1.

In addition to this, many of the points above are not quantifiable, albeit very important. For example, however good a product, the company is not guaranteed success unless it has strong and visionary management as well as

Table 2.4 Weighted scorecard for start-up

Success indicator	Score (0–10)	Weighting (adds up to 100%)	Weighted score (score × weighting percentage)
1 Size of inefficiency or problem addressed (large = 10)			
2 Strength of incumbent competition			
3 Addressable market size			
4 Scalability of solution/ product			
5 Regulatory compliance			
6 Level of innovation and uniqueness			
7 Product differentiation			
8 Strength of management team			
9 Existing customers			
10 Sufficient funding			
11 Real-world testing			
12 Strength of PR and marketing team			
Total		100%	

excellent communications. Although every investor will look for different attributes, a weighted scorecard approach could be employed using the template in Table 2.4.

Why do even 'good' start-ups fail?

Even if this systematic approach to analyse the prospect for a start-up is employed, many still fail. This is because it transpires they are either offering a solution nobody wants or is willing to pay for, or they misunderstand the fundamental behaviours that created the problem in the first place. This was certainly the situation in Case Study 2.1.

CASE STUDY 2.1   Palleter

Palleter, established by ex-Skype founder, Märt Kelder, aimed to transform the European freight market by creating a road freight platform that it claimed would better match supply and demand. The company was very successful in raising investment due to a compelling case:

- Management believed that its solution would address the 'inefficiency' in the European road freight industry. They relied on Eurostat figures to make this case.
- It developed what was regarded as very smart technology, linking fleet GPS telemetry providers and shippers' freight offers.
- The integration process between carrier and system was fast ('less than three minutes').
- The model would replace ad hoc communication mechanisms.
- The shipper/carrier transaction would take place on the platform.

However, in 2017, Palleter closed down and returned money to investors, a year and a half after it was established. Why? Despite the 'neat' solution addressing a major industry problem at a macro level, operational and technological problems were not addressed. Kelder provided the following reasons for the failure:

Technology

- Companies were unwilling to spend money and time on data extraction from their existing systems.
- IT departments were focused on keeping existing systems running, not on new initiatives.
- No potential customers were willing to gamble on replacing legacy systems with new operations platforms.
- The complexity of data sharing between supply partners was underestimated.

Operations

- Much of the vaunted spare capacity on trucks was, in reality, not accessible.
- Companies were unwilling to re-route trucks even short distances due to time constraints from existing customers.

- The platform required the cooperation of existing road freight operators and a cultural shift.
- The rates quoted on the system were often higher than other traditional operators using hub-and-spoke systems.

Even though a problem had been identified, Palleter's solution only overcame some of the challenges. Its solution did not factor in its true cost to users or opposition to change at grass roots level.

Start-up value ratio: what it means for innovators

In order to understand what went wrong for Palleter in more detail, it is possible to employ a variation of the Value Ratio as laid out by Braithwaite and Christopher in their book, *Business Operations Models* (2015). This seeks to answer the question: did the solution offer compelling value for both suppliers and shippers?

$$\text{Start-up Value} = \text{Perceived benefits} / \text{Total cost}$$

In Palleter's case:

Perceived benefits = Value of increased loads for suppliers, lower rates for shippers

Total cost = charge for using service (negligible, in Palleter's estimation)

However, Palleter's mistake was to underestimate the tangible and intangible costs for suppliers (and hence shippers). Total cost should have included:

- costs to make changes to suppliers' and shippers' technology systems as well as management time;
- intangible costs such as changing operating practices (and unwillingness to adopt new operating models);
- time taken to re-route trucks.

The result was:

- not enough carriers to create competitive market;
- not enough shippers to provide attractive enough volumes;
- higher prices on Palleter than on the open market;
- incumbents were actually more price competitive for less efficient transport.

Summary

There are many types of innovation. Some, as we have seen, result in process efficiencies; others release much greater levels of value by disrupting entire business models or the market status quo. Small start-ups do not have a monopoly on innovation – many of the large incumbents have been very successful at leveraging their resources – technological and intellectual – to continually meet the developing needs of the market and their customers. However, smaller companies can be better able to take risks and can be more agile in the development of new products and services. Often led by people from outside the industry, they can offer new perspectives and thinking. Despite this, as the recent demise of on-demand delivery company Shyp demonstrates, not all innovators and disruptors will be successful, however well backed. Innovating is an inherently risky business, especially when it so difficult to identify the size of the market opportunity.

Bibliography

Braithwaite, A and Christopher, M (2015) *Business Operations Models: Becoming a disruptive competitor*, Kogan Page, London

Diamandis, P and Kotler, S (2016) *Bold: How to go big, create wealth and impact the world*, Simon and Schuster, New York

European Commission [accessed 21 February 2018] *Road Freight Transport by Journey Characteristics* [Online] http://ec.europa.eu/eurostat/statistics-explained/index.php/Road_freight_transport_by_journey_characteristics

McKinnon, A (2015) *Performance Measurement in Freight Transport: Its contribution to the design, implementation and monitoring of public policy*, Kuehne Logistics University, Hamburg

Lessons from the past

03

What present day disruptors can learn from the containerization of the shipping industry

**THIS CHAPTER WILL FAMILIARIZE
THE READER WITH:**

- the high levels of inefficiency in the shipping industry that led to disruption;
- the challenges faced by the pioneers of shipping containerization;
- technological, social, legislative and political barriers placed in the way of industry reform;
- opposition from market incumbents;
- the economic benefits that resulted from containerization and the consequent rise of globalization;
- lessons for modern day innovators.

Introduction

In terms of innovation in the supply chain and logistics industry, the introduction of the shipping container is perhaps unrivalled as regards its impact upon the industry and the global economy. The reduction in transport costs that it brought about enabled retailers and manufacturers to access low cost products and labour forces in previously remote parts of the world, leading to a revolution in the way that supply chains operated.

The adoption of the new technology was not, as many would expect, quick and without challenge. Companies had experimented with unitizing freight for several decades, but it was not until the 1950s that containerization started to take root (Levinson, 2016).

The way in which the introduction of shipping containers transformed the industry has many lessons to the disruptors of today, and it is therefore useful to analyse this period of systemic change.

The economic case for containerization

Before containerization, one of the greatest sources of time and cost lay in the inefficient handling processes of loading and unloading ships. Typically, this could include:

- unloading of rail freight wagon/truck at the port;
- handling and storage on dock;
- potentially use of a 'lighter' (barge) to move freight to the dock;
- the carriage of goods onto the ship (by manual labour);
- stowage on board.

When the ship docked the reverse process was undertaken. Loading and unloading ships took a long time, was labour intensive and the work was often dangerous. In addition to this, most ports had a problem both with corruption and cargo crime. This was endemic across the world.

Governments, shippers, ports, rail companies, trucking lines and shipping lines were not blind to the inefficiencies and the costs involved. Many studies had been undertaken over the years that identified the waste. However, as will be shown, the 'silo mentality' (as it would be called now) was a powerful factor against change. With the exception of shippers, the industry benefited from many of the barriers to change that were in place. This was reinforced by resistance to reform from labour organizations fearing (rightly) that automation would reduce employment in the sector.

Shippers, it might be said, were the victims of these cosy relationships that existed across the logistics sector. However, the high levels of fragmentation that existed in the demand-side prevented any customer pressure for reform. In any case, it was unclear that the containerization of shipments would produce savings. Early indications were that unitizing freight without systemic changes to the truck and rail industry, without specialized loading equipment and, of course, without the specialist container vessels on which to stow the boxes, would be costlier than the existing 'breakbulk' process.

Getting every sector to buy in to the case for reform was the real challenge, and even then, it took many years for the economic value to be released.

In retrospect, it is clear that containerization was the first materialization of 'total supply chain management'. Before this, each logistics sector acted independently without much regard for the opportunities to connect to other modes. Each sector believed its role was to operate its assets in the most efficient way – not to create efficiency in the supply chain as a whole. The early pioneers of containerization started to change this mind set.

So why did it take so long for a new system to be developed? Looking at the barriers to the adoption of the new technologies and processes involved in containerization provides an indication to present day would-be disruptors.

Social and political barriers

At the time, national and local politicians were some of the most influential opponents to change in the transport industry. They had an interest in retaining the status quo, largely due to the large labour forces employed in the sector, however inefficiently.

Labour organizations (which had a large influence over the politicians) saw as their role the protection of the jobs and employment rights of their members. In many ports they also benefited from taking kickbacks from shipping lines, and they had a monopoly on handling. Even politicians favourable to free markets were frightened of the power of the unions – and rightly so. In the UK a boycott of the new container terminal at Tilbury by unions led to London losing its position as one of the leading ports in the world. Instead, non-unionized Felixstowe was able to grow from a backwater to one of the world's largest terminals within a matter of years.

The resistance to the new, less labour-dependent operating model brought about by containerization has echoes in the antipathy shown to automation and robots that are starting to be deployed in warehouses. Politicians in North America, Europe and Asia are already talking about a tax on robots to slow down the onset of automation. This has echoes of the campaigns (ultimately futile) fought by labour organizations in the 1960s and 1970s to protect dockworkers' jobs and the income guarantees negotiated by many unions such as the 'Economic Stabilization Program' in the United States in the late 1970s.

Legislative barriers

In the post-war era in large parts of the world, the shipping and transport markets were heavily regulated. This was no more the case than in the United States where the Interstate Commerce Commission (ICC) controlled most aspects of the freight market. Rates were set (generally on a per commodity basis) and routes allocated to trucking companies by the ICC who saw as its role the maintenance of stability across the US transport market. Huge barriers were placed in the way of companies that wanted to innovate either with new routes or even to start hauling commodities for which they had no permit. This created massive inefficiency.

The ICC was used not only by the government to maintain stability (or stymie innovation depending on your view point) but also by various parts of the industry to prevent competition. For instance, rail companies could challenge trucking companies over the rates they were charging. Likewise, shipping lines might challenge rail companies over the routes and services they were providing if they thought it would impact on their profitability.

The regulatory climate is perhaps less proscriptive in the present era than it was in the mid-20th century. This, however, has not stopped regulators from taking aim at disruptors such as Uber (licence revoked in London) and Airbnb (banned in various cities in Europe and Asia). As far as the logistics sector is concerned, tax authorities look to be clamping down on employment practices in the 'gig economy', which could limit the operations of many on-demand, last mile delivery companies. With many cities also implementing 'diesel bans' to create clean air zones, the additional traffic caused by on-demand couriers could come under scrutiny. Implementation of drones has also been held back while regulators assess safety, security and privacy issues.

Regulators very unwillingly gave up their control of logistics markets when it finally became evident that even the largest incumbent players could not operate within the sclerotic systems that had been created. The signs are that there is a renewed appetite for re-regulation of many parts of the industry, which may well constrain the development of new generation innovators.

Technological barriers

The technological challenges (albeit in the 'hardware' rather than software) involved in the development of containerization should not be underestimated. There was a long period of trial and error before successful designs were adopted of the container boxes, the ships, the trucks and the inter-modal rail wagons as well as the cranes and handling equipment capable of moving and stowing the containers. For instance:

- The boxes had to be sturdy enough to be stacked, but not too heavy to make the tare weight uneconomic.

- There had to be a quick way to pick up and load the containers by crane.

- The system had to be standardized so that the boxes could be moved by any truck or by any rail company.

- The system used to stow the boxes on board ships had to be robust enough so that the containers would not shift during the voyage.

At the outset many companies tried different systems. For example, was it best to deploy shipboard or dock-based cranes? What was the best size for the containers, maximizing economic value of weight and volume? How many containers could be stacked on a ship without it becoming unsafe? It is easy to look back at this period and think that containerization was inevitable, but this was certainly not the thinking at the time.

Likewise, there have been many false starts for other innovations. E-commerce spawned the dot-com bubble of the early 2000s; RFID tags have been around for many decades, although it is only recently that low-cost sensor technology has taken off; excitement over delivery by drones is subsiding; how will 3D printing develop? Picking the technology that will win out today is just as difficult as it was for the pioneers of containerization 60 years ago.

Resistance from market incumbents

The majority of the incumbent shipping lines of the time were hostile to the prospect of innovation in the form of containerization. The shipping industry had always been focused on moving ships rather than the cargo, and there was what might be termed cultural indifference to improving supply chain efficiency. This was perhaps why one of the major innovators in the disruption of the sector, Malcom McLean, came from outside of the sector – trucking rather than shipping. The existing shipping lines had a vested interest in avoiding change, despite acceptance that processes were highly inefficient.

One of the reasons for this was that, from their perspective, there was little economic case for change. Although ships would spend long times in port, this was only partly problematic. Unlike today when it is important for shipping lines to maximize utilization – ships should be generating ROI by steaming at sea and not tied up in harbour – post-war, merchant ships were very numerous and cheap, sold off by navies. Shipping pre-containerization was not asset intensive. Stevedoring was likewise asset-light, using temporary labour rather than investing in materials handling equipment and new technologies.

In terms of the present market incumbents there is also resistance to change, albeit for different reasons. Many large logistics companies have invested heavily in technology systems over the past 30 years, and these systems are in place today. Even though there is no doubt that at some levels all companies have committed to embracing the opportunities that innovation can bring, making changes to these legacy systems is easier said than done. This has sown the seeds for disruptors such as freight forwarder Flexport to enter the market. With the benefits of working off a blank sheet of paper, the company has been able to develop systems from scratch rather than add on components to 1980s architecture. A large proportion of its employees come from outside of the freight forwarding sector, providing an alternative perspective on many of the challenges faced.

Unpacking the economic benefits

Although there was a good economic case for unitizing shipping volumes in the 1950s due to the reduction in handling costs and time, the benefits were certainly not clear cut. Many shippers exported or imported small consignments not large enough to fill a container (these days this is called less-than-containerloads or LCL). Therefore, there was a large amount of consolidation to be undertaken, which, of course, involved extra handling. Whereas these days the container market is dominated by large importers, such as Walmart, filling many thousands of full containers, this was not the case in the 1950s when the market was far more fragmented. What to do with the empty containers was (and still is) also a problem. Trade imbalances around the world have led to a pile up of containers in major import markets (ie North America and Europe), and their restitution is only possible due to the overall economic value created elsewhere in the system.

There was also the view (at least at the outset) that containerization would be unnecessary for international shipping, as the time spent loading and unloading was a much smaller proportion of the overall travel time. When a journey might take four to five weeks, a few days extra in port was less critical than in a short sea shipping operation.

However, this was a very limited view of the potential of containerization. Very quickly it was evident that shipping volumes could (and would) consolidate around a few, very large terminals serving large containerships. Feeder services would move containers to these hubs from smaller ports where they would be transhipped. The huge levels of efficiency and the economies of scale that this new system created meant that rates fell significantly, leading to industry transformation.

Today's innovators are trying to address inefficiencies in other transport sectors. In theory, a technological solution that better matches capacity with demand should release economic potential, and for precisely this reason, many freight forwarding, warehousing and road freight platforms have developed over the years. Unlike containerization, however, there has been no revolution. Why is this?

There are many reasons, but perhaps the most important is that while shippers can benefit from lower freight rates using such platforms, the asset providing operators don't do so well. The 'reverse auction' nature of such platforms can lead to a race to the bottom in terms of rates. While rate reductions also occurred in the shipping industry, of course, the leading shipping lines were able to consolidate, build bigger ships to provide lower costs, maximizing economies of scale, and call at fewer, larger, faster ports to improve asset utilization. The potential for other sectors is very much more limited in these respects. For example, delivery frequencies and just-in-time or on-demand delivery have driven the need for smaller, less-efficient commercial vehicles, not larger ones.

Summary

Containerization was not a solution to a shipping problem. Rather it addressed inefficiencies within the entire supply chain. The fact that it impacted on so many parties – shippers, shipping lines, rail operators, truckers, port authorities, stevedores, labour organizations, governments to name but a few – created major barriers to its wholesale adoption. Eventually these barriers were overcome by the sheer weight of the economic case and the power of free markets.

The lesson for today's innovators is that it is not enough to design a solution that addresses the symptoms of a problem – a deep understanding of the underlying issues and the needs of all the stakeholders concerned is required. Just because something becomes technologically possible, doesn't mean that it will be successful. Social, political, cultural and regulatory factors have to be taken into account as well as the basic economic case. There have to be benefits for all (or at least most) stakeholders, not just a few.

Bibliography

Levinson, M (2016) *The Box: How the shipping container made the world smaller and the world economy bigger,* Princeton University Press, USA

Sector Case Study　　04

Disruption in the express parcels market

**THIS CHAPTER WILL FAMILIARIZE
THE READER WITH:**

- how the express parcels market is being disrupted by new market entrants;
- the key innovations that are being implemented by carriers, large and small;
- the potential for Uber to compete effectively against the major parcels carriers;
- how some technology innovators allow small carriers to compete with larger rivals;
- the response of the major express companies in terms of process innovation.

An evolving sector

The express parcels industry has undergone a major transformation over the past 20 years due, not least, to the impact of e-retailing. In the early 2000s, when the internet shopping revolution was in its infancy, it was far from certain that many of the major express players, such as UPS, FedEx or DHL, would embrace home delivery. This was largely due to the high costs of undelivered parcels caused by not-at-home end-recipients and the lower density of deliveries to rural locations.

Higher margin B2B services, especially in the buoyant economic years in the run up to the recession of 2008, drove innovation in the industry, with huge corporate budgets resulting in initiatives such as electronic proof-of-delivery notes, providing greater levels of visibility in the supply chain. B2C home delivery companies, often off-shoots of traditional home shopping retailers, were seen as belonging to a separate sector.

Today, it is hard to convey the extent of the change in management sentiment and operational and technological focus. B2C has become a critical part of the major players' strategic thinking and revenues. No doubt the external demands being placed on express parcels carriers to meet the needs of e-retail customers will continue to drive changes in the industry for many years to come.

Key themes in the development of the express parcels market

1990s onwards – express companies invest in supply chain visibility technology

1995 onwards – build out regional and global operations networks

Mid-2000s onwards – development of B2C capabilities

2015 onwards – adapt operational models to take advantage of new technologies and defend against market disruptors

---

However, across mature markets it is becoming increasingly evident that the sector cannot continue in its current form with huge inefficiencies brought about by failed deliveries and the costs of B2C deliveries unaccounted for.

Sources of market disruption

It might be considered that the major express parcels companies, especially the 'Big 3' UPS, FedEx and DHL, have built operations and businesses that are so strong as to make them immune to disruption. It is a fact that the global networks they have developed, their brands, their technology and the depth of their finances would seem to make them impregnable. However, this hypothesis is only partly true. There are four types of new market entrant that could compete effectively against the market incumbents (whether the 'Big 3' or national/regional players):

- a small number of market entrants that have the resources and the innovative operating models to challenge the 'Big 3', not least in terms of brand, for significant parts of their business (eg Amazon and Alibaba); see Chapter 17 for more information on these companies;

- market entrants that can compete effectively at a micro-level, eg execution of last mile delivery;

- innovators that can provide platforms that allow shippers to disintermediate larger parcels networks and connect direct to small- and medium-sized carriers;

- innovators that can provide low-cost technology to SME carriers allowing them to compete with large companies.

Case Studies 4.1 and 4.2 look at two such market entrants, one challenging parcel delivery systems and the other looking at a cloud software company that is disrupting first and last mile deliveries.

CASE STUDY 4.1 Alternative delivery systems
Uber's threat to the parcels sector

The 'sharing economy' has become a disruptive force challenging government regulations and disrupting industries such as transportation, delivery, hotels and more. The logistics and supply chain sector will need to evolve to meet these challenges.

A number of start-up delivery companies have emerged such as Deliv, Postmates and TaskRabbit, which all address the same day/local delivery sector. However, most attention is focused on the plans of personal mobility app, Uber.

Founded in 2009, Uber offers transportation and taxi services in the United States and over 50 countries around the world. Uber has developed from its roots as an app-based taxi network that uses technology to direct and connect vast taxi capacity with would-be travellers more efficiently. The app, which allows customers to see the location of nearby taxis and offers a choice of driver based on proximity, price and a review system, has proved to be hugely popular.

Its success in the transport sector has caught the attention of express parcel companies, which are beginning to see significant potential for an app such as Uber. The prospective adoption of such innovative technology has wide-reaching implications for the express sector and could render once viable business models obsolete.

Uber has already begun to apply its technology to the express sector, running a trial of Uber Cargo in Hong Kong. The service works in much the same fashion as the Uber taxi app: customers select a vehicle from the app and direct it to pick up a consignment. The customer then loads the goods and tracks their journey in real time through to their arrival and delivery. Prices for the trial are based on the distance and time of the trip, with no extra charge applied for weight and volume.

Similar services to this have already been created in Asia Pacific by companies such as Lalamove and GoGoVan, both of which are operating in multiple cities in China and South East Asia. With the introduction of Uber's brand, and the critical mass it has the potential to bring, the express sector in Asia Pacific could be about to witness a revolutionary change and lead markets in Europe and the Americas to follow suit.

New technology platforms have the potential to dramatically increase efficiency with higher load factors, shorter trips between pick-ups and fewer missed deliveries. These applications will therefore move to the forefront of delivery companies' strategic agendas.

However, some delivery companies may look upon the application of Uber's technology with caution, especially those whose business models are currently predicated upon the use of sub-contractors and attempts to squeeze as much value out of them as possible. Uber technology has the potential to empower smaller sub-contractors with the technology they need to secure business independently of the large delivery firms.

CASE STUDY 4.2   Urbantz
Facilitating market disruption

Urbantz is a small Belgium-based first and last mile delivery cloud software developer that has raised approximately €750,000 in funding. Its proposition is to save its customers (small courier companies) time by increasing delivery efficiency of parcels rounds.

Its software allows for the automatic ordering of delivery schedules and informing drivers via real-time end-to-end tracking. According to the company, it can improve efficiency 'by up to 50%' – from 140 deliveries per day to 210 (at peak) (company website).

Another advantage is management says that negligible training is required to use the product, meaning that new drivers can easily be brought in at short notice to deal with peaks of demand.

The company is also believed to be developing dynamic delivery options involving the geofencing of end-recipients. This means that the delivery can be re-routed to find the end-recipient if they are not at the original delivery address.

The product that Urbantz (and many other small developers like them) provides allows small- and medium-sized courier companies to compete with much larger companies with 'corporate quality' transport management systems capabilities. This ultimately can be disruptive, as these companies will often be more flexible and cheaper than larger rivals.

Incumbents: fighting back

Although it would be easy to characterize the businesses of major express players as being vulnerable to new disruptors, or on a 'burning platform' as some like to term it, this may not be quite the case. It is perhaps more accurate to say that some of their present operating models and the technologies they deploy are on the 'burning platform' rather than companies themselves. Although vast in size, companies such as UPS, FedEx and DHL have shown themselves in the past to be flexible enough to adapt to changing economic and technological environments.

Many of the innovators that are transforming the industry at present are providing services that can be used by the incumbents rather than actually threatening them. The rate platform Freightos is a good example. It has received large amounts of funding that has allowed it to develop a product that will make freight forwarders' operations more efficient. Likewise, the many road freight marketplaces that have sprung up can be used by freight operators, large or small, to improve vehicle utilization. They offer no real threat to the market leaders and are not designed to.

Therefore, although there is little doubt that the conditions exist for the express parcels industry to be disrupted by new technologies and business models, this is not to say that the giant corporations that dominate parts of the industry face an existential threat. In fact, these companies have been at the forefront of innovation over the years, and there is no reason to believe that they cannot take advantage of the latest technologies to exploit new markets.

All the leading express companies have substantial internal resources that are focused on developing new technologies and solutions. DHL's Innovation Centre, for example, was responsible for developing its 'SmartSensor' for the pharmaceutical sector, monitoring temperature, humidity, shock and light data in packages. The company has also been a pioneer in crowd-shipping trials in Stockholm with its MyWays app.

Case Study 4.3 looks at UPS and how it is investing in innovation.

CASE STUDY 4.3 UPS
Investing in innovation

UPS has its own Strategic Enterprise Fund, which exists to provide it with insight into emerging business models, technologies and markets (Figure 4.1). UPS identifies new investment opportunities, which it hopes will be repaid several times over in terms of financial and knowledge gains through its contacts within the venture capital community and internal referrals.

Figure 4.1 UPS Strategic Enterprise Fund strategy

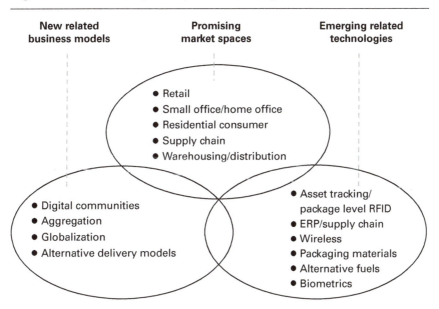

| New related business models | Promising market spaces | Emerging related technologies |

- Retail
- Small office/home office
- Residential consumer
- Supply chain
- Warehousing/distribution

- Digital communities
- Aggregation
- Globalization
- Alternative delivery models

- Asset tracking/ package level RFID
- ERP/supply chain
- Wireless
- Packaging materials
- Alternative fuels
- Biometrics

One of its best known investments was in Shutl, the London-based courier platform provider that offers the rapid fulfilment and delivery of online shopping orders within a 90-minute time window. After joining other investors, including GeoPost, UPS finally sold out its share when eBay acquired the whole company in 2013.

On a far bigger scale was UPS's US $28 million investment in Deliv in February 2016, one of the best-known on-demand delivery networks. Working specifically within the US e-retail and multichannel sector, Deliv provides the platform with same-day crowd-shipping delivery solutions. Among its customers it names Best Buy, Walgreens, Macy's and Office Depot.

UPS, of course, is well known for its express and parcels services through an extensive, asset-intensive global network. However, management has recognized that crowd-shipping is both a threat to its established business as well as being an opportunity.

The investment also gave UPS a seat on the Deliv board, which critically allows the company to understand its operations. Beyond this, UPS has also rolled out Deliv services to its small- and medium-sized customers through its UPS Store network. This has proved particularly popular for print on-demand customers looking for the rush delivery of orders.

As Deliv says in its own promotion, 'For the first time in history, the fastest and most flexible same-day delivery is now also the cheapest shipping option'. This is an interesting point, as traditionally same day services have been charged at a premium and have only appealed to a very niche market. Now, however, there is the potential that they will become a significant mainstream delivery provider.

Summary

It might be considered that the express parcels sector would be vulnerable to disruption given the advent of so many new technologies applicable to this vertically integrated business model. Indeed, the impact of e-retail giants such as Amazon is already being felt, as in key markets it has disintermediated the major carriers in favour of working with local providers. In addition to this, smaller parcels companies will also benefit as software-as-a-service developers (such as Urbantz) provide them with the tools to compete more effectively.

However, it would be easy to overstate the threat to the major integrators. Many of the new innovations in the industry are being harnessed by the incumbents to release value and, as has been discussed, UPS, FedEx and DHL have invested heavily in making sure that they remain at the cutting edge of the market.

The Internet of Things, 'Big Data' and artificial intelligence

05

THIS CHAPTER WILL FAMILIARIZE THE READER WITH:

- what is meant by the term 'Internet of Things';
- the application of the technology in supply chains and how it will impact on consumers, retailers and manufacturers;
- the benefits of the new technology to the logistics industry and how it will be applied;
- the role of artificial intelligence (AI) in analysing the vast levels of data being generated in part by the Internet of Things;
- AI's importance to the successful integration of the digital and physical world;
- how AI will impact upon the logistics and supply chain industry;
- AI's role in the development of logistics innovations.

'Internet of Things' in the supply chain

The 'Internet of Things' (IoT) is a term used to encompass the use of sensors, technology and networking to allow buildings, infrastructures, devices and additional 'things' to share information without requiring human-to-human or human-to-computer interaction. It can create richer data and deeper intelligence for all parties in a supply network.

According to research company IDC, the IoT and the technology surrounding it is expected to be a US $1.1 trillion market in 2021, growing at 14.4% per year between 2017 and 2021 (IDC, 2018). IDC further suggests that the installed number of 'things' connected will be 212bn by the end of 2020, including 30.1bn connected autonomous things:

> The internet has changed the way we consume information and talk with each other, but now it can do more. By connecting intelligent machines to each other and ultimately to people, and by combining software and big data analytics, we can push the boundaries of physical and material sciences to change the way the world works. (Jeff Immelt, former CEO of GE)

With the lower cost of production, sensors will become more economical for use in a range of supply chain applications. They provide visibility down to item level, a level of granularity that has thus far come at a significant cost. These visibility gains will result in substantial financial benefits as supply chains become far better at locating and securing inventory.

The connected consumer

Domestic automation, enabled by the IoT, includes a wide range of functions and appliances in the home, many of which are not supply chain related (controlling heating and lighting for instance). However other appliances can be integrated into the supply chain, such as the refrigerator. Using sensors and video cameras (monitoring the contents of the fridge), the appliance can be a portal for ordering and re-ordering perishable goods. Software can learn to recognize items, such as milk or tomatoes, and track buying behaviour. Eventually, smart packaging should even be able to identify when products are out of date.

The same principle applies to other household appliances. For example, washing machines and dishwashers can automatically re-order detergent, perhaps in conjunction with a virtual assistant.

Sensors can also be attached to appliances in order to perform predictive maintenance. This may enable them to perform self-diagnostics, alerting the service company to the fault and which parts are required.

According to a Worldpay report, 44 per cent of consumers used connected home devices and virtual assistants such as 'Alexa'. Of those interviewed for the company, 46 per cent said that they were happy for the devices to place orders automatically without human intervention (Worldpay, 2018). Other connected innovations will also change buyer behaviour. 3D bodyscanners, for example, will encourage more consumers to buy clothes at home without going to the store to try them on.

Although the advent of the connected home is inevitable and to be welcomed, there is also the need to improve cyber security. Either manufacturers will need to ensure their products are harder to subvert, or users will need to reinforce their domestic infrastructure. This topic is often ignored by both media and manufacturers but will become a significant issue over the next few years.

Supply chain inventory management

Digital shelving

Using sensors on products to identify when stock is running low in store (so-called 'digital shelving') will enable re-ordering automatically. Stock levels on the shelves and in the stockroom and distribution centres as well as other stores can be linked and viewed, theoretically, on a real-time basis. This may allow returns to be re-routed to stores where there is demand rather than being routed to a central warehouse.

Container and product tracking

There are many different levels of sophistication of sensors used in the tracking of containers. Some log data for download at a later point, while others can use GPS technology to provide real-time tracking, alert when the door has been opened or environmental parameters have been exceeded (temperature, for example). While sensors have been around for many years, integrating them within a cohesive management system and gaining visibility of the consignments within the container will be the ultimate goal. Eventually this will provide 'from floor to store and beyond' item-level tracking capabilities.

Inventory optimization

A study by Harvard Business School found that 8 per cent of all retail items are out of stock at any given time (Corsten and Gruen, 2018). With IoT systems in place, the likelihood of stock-outs can be reduced by as much as 80 per cent according to Zebra Technologies, as the improved visibility generated by the technology allows retailers to locate and replenish their stock far more rapidly (Zebra, 2018). Automatic re-ordering when the weight or height of items reaches a certain level would replace stochastic, rule-based methods. Item-level visibility also allows buffer stock to be reduced, delivering cost savings on both over- and under-stocking. McKinsey Global Institute (2015) suggests that inventory optimization could deliver savings in inventory carrying costs of 10 per cent a year.

The same concept also applies in other sectors. McKinsey estimates that gains are even bigger than in the retail environment, with the potential value gain ranging from 20 to 50 per cent reduction in manufacturing/hospital inventory costs. One example is the use of sensors and cameras to monitor stock levels in supply boxes. When they have reduced to a certain point, an order to replenish the bins is made. Consequently, the IoT allows decisions to be made on real data rather than on forecasts.

Inventory shrinkage

Furthermore, visibility at the item level allows retailers to keep much tighter control over shrinkage, which cost an estimated US \$46.8bn in the United States in 2017, according to the US National Retail Federation (NRF, 2018). A notable success in this area is the French sporting goods retailer Decathlon, which reported that the deployment of sensors across its 951 stores had the impact of reducing shrinkage by 9 per cent in 2014 (Swedberg, 2018).

Application in the logistics industry

Fleet and asset tracking is one such capability that IoT can provide, and many logistics operators have already installed new tracking technology across their fleets of vans, trucks, trailers and intermodal containers. Tracking technology can deliver continuous, real-time information regarding the location and load status of each trailer and container, often using solar or cellular power. This allows companies to pinpoint the exact location of empty containers and trailers, making the planning and dispatch process more efficient, while reducing drivers' wasted time and empty miles.

The increased level of sensor use and vehicle telematics allows logistics managers to gather data daily on mechanical performance of vehicles and behavioural patterns of drivers. This includes: vehicle speed, direction, braking, performance of engine and mechanical components. This can be used to improve driver behaviour, reducing wear on vehicle and fuel consumption (thereby reducing CO_2 emissions). This results in the improved maintenance of vehicles, less downtime and fewer breakdowns.

Sensors are not just being introduced to the road freight industry. Aircraft engine manufacturers have been capturing engine performance data in flight for years. This data is constantly being transmitted to the manufacturers so that any variation from expected norms generates an alert. This information is then used to trigger specific inspections at the next point the aircraft lands, along with the appropriate recommendations for resolving the issue such as having a replacement part available at the airport, which is then installed before the plane is allowed to continue.

This regime is well established and has resulted in enormous gains in reliability, a reduction in flight delays due to engine problems and improved engine efficiency in terms of jet fuel use. The engine manufacturers (eg Rolls Royce, GE, Pratt & Whitney) now have massive amounts of data that is constantly analysed for improvements and greater insight into how the next generation of engines can be made more efficient and effective. Every flight that takes place continues to add to these data stores and is only part of the data that is now being captured from the numerous systems on board aircraft.

Other benefits of IoT include:

- monitoring the status of assets, parcels and people in real time;
- measuring how assets are performing (and what they will do next);
- reducing fuel costs by optimization of fleet routes;
- automating business processes to eliminate manual interventions;
- optimizing how people, systems and assets work together, and coordinate their activities;
- applying analytics to identify wider improvement opportunities and best practices;
- monitoring inventory to reduce stock-outs.

CASE STUDY 5.1   Using IoT for yard management

DHL Supply Chain, together with Huawei Technologies, has launched a Narrowband Internet of Things (NB-IoT) application at an automotive site in Liuzhou, China. Leveraging existing infrastructure and limited investments, the implemented IoT solution is designed to facilitate and streamline yard management for inbound-to-manufacturing logistics, leading to improvements in inbound processing time at the site. The proof of concept ran until the end of 2018, with 100 DHL drivers at a section with 30 docks.

DHL and Huawei are integrating NB-IoT chipsets for their solution, which use common cellular telecommunications bands with the benefits of a more simple and cost-effective implementation. Vehicle detectors are embedded within these chipsets, which do not require any infrastructure investments. Within each terminal, DHL Supply Chain is now able to automatically collect clear dock availability in real time, which in return provides visibility to the dispatcher and drivers. When a truck arrives, its driver checks in via an app on his or her mobile, receiving a queue number and an estimated waiting time. The yard management system then automatically screens the docks for their availability, providing each driver with real-time status updates visible via the app. As soon as a dock is free, the driver is notified to proceed accordingly. This way inbound trucks can be prioritized to the site's needs, and shipments are unloaded at the most appropriate dock.

The innovation is halving the waiting time for drivers from an average waiting time of 40 minutes, significantly reducing the risks of manufacturing delays as materials arrive in time and resources are optimized appropriately.

DHL's proof of concept is expected to be enhanced with additional features such as automatic number plate recognition and geofencing.

The future: printable electronics

Although much attention has focused on the use of sensor technologies such as RFID, considerable potential also exists in conventional printing systems.

Inkjet systems are built for mass production, employing rollers to transfer ink onto the surface being printed, whether that be paper or plastic. If this technology could be effectively applied to the production of integrated circuits and antennae, then it could completely transform the market for sensors and unlock greater potential for the IoT.

Currently, most 'passive' sensors (the most commonly used) cost a minimum of 5 cents per tag, which is far too expensive for widespread use in consumer-packaged goods, for example. The reason it is difficult to produce tags at scale for a lower price is that the traditional manufacturing technique used to make integrated circuits and conductive antennae, the basic components used in passive RFID tags, is copper-etching, a process that requires several phases and wastes as much as 70 per cent of the material. While etching is considered an efficient process overall, it places a floor on the minimum cost of production.

As such, the application of inkjet printing systems to the production of microchips is something that has been talked about for some time, with silver or copper ink used as a conductor. Unfortunately, many circuits produced using the latter have suffered poor performance, while those using the former have been uneconomic.

Nonetheless, there are potential ways around this problem. Researchers have explored the use of graphene particles as a component of conductive inks in place of silver nano particles, with promising results. In October 2015, a team led by Dr Tawfique Hasan of the Cambridge Graphene Centre (CGC), in collaboration with local company Novalia, announced the successful development of a commercially viable system that prints at a rate exceeding 100 metres of material a minute. Moreover, the cost of the graphene ink used is around £40 per kg, compared to a cost of at least £1,000 per kg in the case of silver-based inks.

It is important to note that printable tags are still held back by a lack of economies of scale. Nonetheless, with the success of existing solutions, and with the expected cost reductions to the manufacturing process, this technology could become a lot more practical in the near future.

'Big Data' and artificial intelligence (AI)

The ubiquitous nature of low-cost sensors has led to the rise of 'Big Data'. The trillions of data points that are now being generated mean that the availability of information is no longer a problem. However, the challenge remains being able to use such high levels of data to make informed decisions.

Control towers are a step towards utilizing this data (see Chapter 6), but on their own they are insufficient. The potential of 'Big Data' can only be exploited by removing human involvement from the decision-making process. Humans are just no longer capable of analysing the overwhelming levels of data that are being generated. This is where AI becomes critical.

Figure 5.1   The cyber-physical relationship in the supply chain

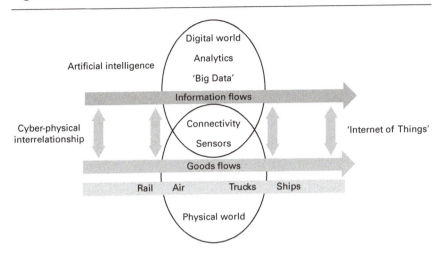

Figure 5.1 shows the relationship that exists between the physical world and the digital world. Sensors in transport assets and actual products are able to communicate data about their status, location, condition and environment at every stage of the supply chain. The 'Big Data' generated then requires real-time analysis if it is to be of any use, allowing decisions to be made that will create supply chain value. This could be:

- exception management, resulting in re-routing or change of delivery time;
- intervention, such as precautionary maintenance on a truck or ship;
- deciding on the most efficient position for put-away in a warehouse.

All of this occurs without human interaction, working to a set of algorithms or rules that hard wires efficiency into the supply chain.

What is AI?

AI is a broad concept, traditionally conceived as a definition for a self-aware machine with an ability to think and act as an autonomous agent. AI within the current commercial context is now broadly accepted as a term to convey a machine capable of performing tasks that would formerly require human intelligence, such as visual perception, speech recognition, decision-making and language translation. For a machine to be artificially intelligent, it may be informed by human reasoning, but it does not necessarily need to function in the same way.

A fundamental component of AI is machine learning, a term that refers to the ability of a computer to identify patterns in streams of inputs and learn by association. For example, through this process, a computer can 'learn' to distinguish a dog from a cat by filtering through a data bank of thousands of categorized images and respond to human corrections to build an association between the data.

In order to leverage the benefits of AI, it is first necessary for the computer in question to have access to vast amounts of data, which is where 'Big Data' becomes relevant. Moreover, in understanding the analogy of 'Big Data' as the 'fuel' for an AI 'engine', it is also important to recognize the significance of the IoT as a means of extracting useful data to be analysed. As these technologies progress and mature, they will be increasingly embedded within a mutually supportive ecosystem that operates and improves physical and virtual networks, such as supply chains.

Supply chain and logistics applications of AI

Delivery flexibility

One area of logistics that will be increasingly influenced by AI is the operation of last mile delivery systems. Delivery flexibility is a vital enabler for e-retailers aiming to keep up with changing consumer demands, which also vary between countries and regions. For example, customers in the UK are keen on instore 'click and collect', while German consumers prefer to use parcel lockers, but neither preferences are static.

Overall, customers are becoming more demanding. In a 2016 survey by MetaPack, 46 per cent of survey respondents said that if there were an option available that allowed them to change their delivery preferences after placing an online order, they would use it (Metapack, 2018). However, any company offering a flexible range of delivery options faces an increasingly difficult task in coordinating last mile flows, and this is where the application of AI can dramatically improve delivery services.

Besides optimizing the distribution of shipments, AI can also submit alternatives by crunching customer data; for example, proposing that a customer pick up their consignment from a designated access point, based on geo-location data showing that it will be located on their route home as they commute from work. By analysing consumer behaviours and location data provided by mobile devices, it is likely that AI will enable companies to become increasingly capable of customizing delivery options for individual customers.

Connected consumers

The key to unlocking such advanced functionality is data. Notably, while the success of Amazon's Dash Button (released in 2015) in driving sales is reportedly negligible, it has been an invaluable source of information on consumer behaviours.

At present, one of the main weaknesses of machine learning systems is that the data inputs they receive are restricted. Google knows what you are searching for, Facebook knows who your friends are and Apple knows what music you listen to, but none of them can combine this information to gain a more complete understanding of you as an individual.

The companies winning this race are those that have realized the potential of home-based assistants for acquiring and interpreting data. Amazon's Echo is the most prominent of these systems, which, by leveraging integrations with other smart devices, can produce helpful suggestions and enact orders. For example, by connecting to the data embedded in a user's smart fridge, such an assistant could suggest that a customer would be out of milk tomorrow morning; but if they were to submit an order they could receive a delivery in time to eat cereal for breakfast.

Autonomous vehicles

Arguably the most visible manifestation of AI within the e-commerce supply chain is autonomous vehicles, chiefly in the form of drones. As the last mile delivery of products constitutes the only visible segment of the supply chain for individual consumers, drones have captured the popular imagination and account for a sizeable proportion of the news coverage relating to AI (CNBC, 2018). This notwithstanding, the development of autonomous delivery drones is significant from a commercial perspective.

Warehouse automation

Warehouse automation is another area that has already been significantly impacted by AI. The distribution of products in an Amazon warehouse, for example, is not predetermined by category but uses an organic shelving system where products are arranged by the company's Warehouse Management System, which uses algorithms to optimize placement based on picking routes.

The company's 2012 acquisition of Kiva systems allowed it to optimize fulfilment further, by deploying robots to streamline the picking process; bringing the shelves of goods to the human picker, rather than vice versa. This has speeded up picking operations and has enhanced the use of AI within the company's facilities.

This is only one model for the application of AI within a warehouse setting, however. Rather than a top-down system that controls the movements of all robots within the picking area, other companies have exploited machine learning to 'train' autonomous guided vehicles (AGVs) to operate in a mixed warehouse setting, alongside humans.

US start-up Seegrid has embedded this capability within several materials handling systems, which learn by association. Each AGV is set up with multiple cameras before being 'walked through' a designated warehouse route by a human operator. The company's proprietary software allows each of the vehicles to recognize a specific route based on the visual data, with each route 'memory' available to all AGVs operating within the system. The system is flexible, relies on relatively cheap hardware and, unlike Amazon's robots, does not need to read specific instructions from floor markings. Seegrid AGVs have been adopted by the United States Postal Service, and Amazon themselves, among others.

Summary

The IoT has the potential to provide unparalleled levels of data related to just about every aspect of the supply chain. From consumer behaviour and needs to the location of products in the warehouse; from wear and tear on vehicle engine components to the tracking of shipments across continents. Nevertheless, generating these huge quantities of data is pointless if the data resource is not analysed in a timely fashion and the resulting intelligence not acted upon. This is where AI will play a critical role.

Fears over the unintended consequences of AI experimentation are likely to become a recurring topic of debate over the coming years in the media and for politicians. However, despite concerns, AI is set to significantly increase the efficiency of major organizations. Within supply chains, a more effective allocation of assets in response to demand peaks and troughs will reduce costs. In addition, the prospects for using AI in a creative manner will allow organizations to solve problems in different ways. For supply chains, AI applications have already allowed control towers to introduce predictive and prescriptive functions to navigate unforeseen events. As AI applications become more advanced, this will eventually create a self-correcting supply chain that is adaptable and responsive to changing circumstances. Combined with strategic analysis, this could result in an evolving system that is able to recreate itself to support different requirements.

It is also likely that AI will cause a significant upheaval in employment, as many jobs become automated. Automation has significantly reduced manufacturing employment over time, but the potential for this to also impact service jobs is a significant change.

Bibliography

CNBC [accessed 10 April 2018] Amazon Wins Patent for a Flying Warehouse That Will Deploy Drones to Deliver Parcels in Minutes, *CNBC* [Online] www.cnbc.com/2016/12/29/amazon-flying-warehouse-deploy-delivery-drones-patent.html

Corsten, D and Gruen, T [accessed 10 April 2018] Stock-Outs Cause Walkouts, *Harvard Business Review* [Online] https://hbr.org/2004/05/stock-outs-cause-walkouts

Daimler [accessed 8 April 2018] The Mercedes-Benz Vision Van. Intelligent Delivery Vehicle of the Future [Online] www.daimler.com/innovation/case/electric/mercedes-benz-vision-van-2.html

IDC [accessed 15 April 2018] IDC Forecasts Worldwide Spending on the Internet of Things to Reach $772 Billion in 2018 [Online] www.idc.com/getdoc.jsp?containerId=prUS43295217

Kolodny, L [accessed 10 April 2018] Postmates and DoorDash are Testing Delivery by Robot with Starship Technologies, *Techcrunch* [Online] https://techcrunch.com/2017/01/18/postmates-and-doordash-are-testing-delivery-by-robot-with-starship-technologies/

McKinsey Global Institute (2015) *The Internet of Things: Mapping the value beyond the hype*, McKinsey & Company, New York

Metapack [accessed 15 May 2018] MetaPack Study Shines a Light on the Short-Fall Between Consumers' eCommerce Delivery Expectations and Reality [Online] www.metapack.com/press-release/2016-consumer-research-ecommerce-delivery-expectations-vs-reality/

NRF [accessed 15 May 2018] NRF/University of Florida Survey Says Retail 'Shrink' Decreased to $46.8 Billion in 2017 [Online] https://nrf.com/media-center/press-releases/nrfuniversity-florida-survey-says-retail-shrink-decreased-468-billion

Swedberg, C [accessed 15 May 2018] Decathlon Sees Sales Rise and Shrinkage Drop, Aided by RFID, *RFID Journal* [Online] www.rfidjournal.com/articles/view?13815/3

Worldpay [accessed 15 May 2018] The Connected Retailer [Online] www.worldpay.com/global/insight/articles/2017-11/internet-of-things-the-connected-retailer

Zebra [accessed 10 April 2018] Item-Level RFID Tagging and the Intelligent Apparel Supply Chain, *Zebra Technologies* [Online] www.zebra.com/content/dam/zebra_new_ia/en-us/solutions-verticals/product/RFID/GENERAL/White%20Papers/WP_Item-Level_Supply_Chain_0413.pdf

Control towers and supply chain visibility

06

THIS CHAPTER WILL FAMILIARIZE THE READER WITH:

- the difficulty in achieving visibility of shipments in the supply chain due to the large number of parties involved;
- the trend towards building so-called 'control towers' to monitor and manage supply chain activity;
- the role of 'control towers' in analysing the data generated in part by the IoT;
- how control towers can direct and drive product flows through the client's supply chain effectively at the most efficient cost;
- the opportunities for logistics providers to develop their roles in monitoring, directing and driving product flows;
- new opportunities to build scalable solutions through cloud computing.

Introduction

One of the consequences of a 'Big Data' world, created by innovations such as the IoT, is the challenge faced by supply chain managers in analysing the mass of information generated and making timely, fact-based decisions.

As has been the case for many years, running logistics operations at any scale requires the support of information systems. The difference between then and now, is that sophisticated technology is generally available to almost anyone, at very low cost.

The application of technology in supply chain management operations has always been focused around specific areas of functionality. This usually means transportation, warehouse, inventory and order management. Complementary systems for planning and forecasting, materials and requirements planning (MRP) and obviously accounting, were also designed as separate functional programs. Support services for integration and collaboration have also been created to underpin these functional silos, helping to provide mechanisms for message exchange and file transfers both within and outside the organization. Now, however, barriers between these functional silos are being challenged and new platforms are required.

This highlights the reality that existing IT structures are not the best foundation for addressing future needs. The following section will describe what is required to support the operations of logistics service providers (LSPs) over the next few years.

The role of the LSP

As a prelude, it is perhaps appropriate to point out that the business models for funding technology acquisition and support are changing so fundamentally that many large LSPs will have to exploit new operating models. At the same time, they are managing a very complex transition away from legacy solutions and supporting contracts costing millions, much of which may never be recovered.

Information systems and services underpin all logistics operations (Figure 6.1). For decades only the biggest players have been able to invest in large, scalable solutions supporting individual operational functions. But the seismic shift resulting from the evolution of cloud services and mobile computing is challenging every aspect of the industry.

Major investments have been made in systems that manage and control the internal operations of large enterprises. These systems, usually described as Enterprise Resource Planning (ERP) suites, codify and structure information flows through the organization. They have done an excellent job inside organizations that have clear, established processes that seldom change. This is assuming that they have been able to endure the costs and time required for implementation. Unfortunately, they are not proving to be well suited to the needs of nimble and agile LSPs who are subject to a constant stream of changing requirements. This is unsurprising given the origins of ERP solutions in the world of finance and accounting.

Figure 6.1 Sharing information in the supply chain

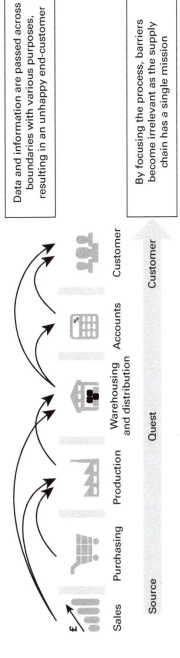

Data and information are passed across boundaries with various purposes, resulting in an unhappy end-customer

By focusing the process, barriers become irrelevant as the supply chain has a single mission

Sales Purchasing Production Warehousing Accounts Customer
                                and distribution

Source   Quest   Customer

Figure 6.2 Control tower management

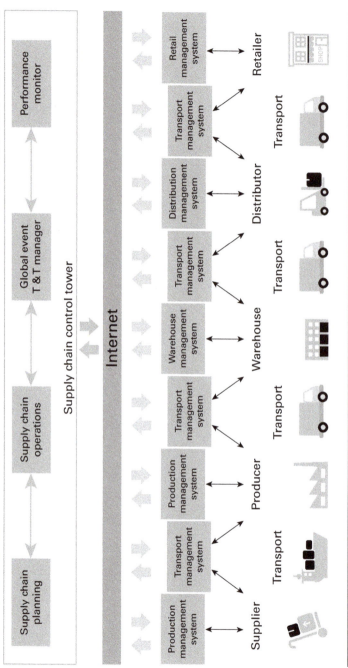

LSPs today are having to operate in a much more networked and collaborative world. It is necessary to integrate with a variety of different systems and services across the operating spectrum. At the same time, streams of data from a range of devices and sensors need to be captured and processed in support of the ever present demand for visibility.

Many LSPs are exploring the adoption of an operations 'control tower' to monitor and manage supply chain activity on a global basis (Figure 6.2). In essence, this is really another description for the provision of complete supply chain visibility.

True supply chain visibility has been an elusive goal for many years, the closest approximation being found in the track and trace systems operated by the global integrators. These systems provide excellent visibility, all the time the orders and shipments remain in the custody of the integrator. However, the moment they are transferred into the domain of another operator or partner, information flows pause or disappear completely. Even now, a shipment involving movement on more than one carrier will require the manager to check multiple systems and collate the results on behalf of the client.

This has triggered a number of mergers and acquisitions (M&As) between various logistics system vendors. The migration of several functional applications onto hosted platforms, accessible via the internet has exacerbated this trend. This is commonly referred to as moving to 'the cloud', but not every application described in this way has been designed for this environment or can appropriately exploit the advantages of cloud infrastructure.

The architects of these M&A efforts are attempting to provide a single solution platform that can support all of the operational needs of an LSP. While they hope this will be a tempting solution for larger companies, it is more likely that they will be exploited by smaller LSPs or start-ups. This is probably down to political motives rather than operational logic. If the CIO of a large logistics service provider has a significant budget at their disposal every year, they are unlikely to explore solutions that conflict with that construct. This is not universal, as there are some enlightened technology executives who understand that the constant demand for modifications and changes to existing systems are unlikely to reduce any time soon.

Cloud-based services

The introduction of cloud services also heralds the new subscription-based business models that are creating huge challenges to traditional application vendors. They are having to migrate existing solutions into the cloud, invariably requiring a fundamental rewrite of the software at huge cost, while supporting existing customer service contracts. At the same time, customers are moving away from expensive licensing and support agreements in favour of more flexible, lower-cost alternatives.

It can be seen in many organizations that business units are implementing numerous low-cost applications from external cloud vendors, as they are unable to wait until the internal IT function can start servicing their requests. This has resulted in a 'Tower of Babel' inside many large companies, with numerous point solutions attempting to exchange data between themselves. This also poses a potential security and data management challenge, as much of the critical client and operational data ends up on various mobile devices operating outside of the organization.

Established LSPs, with extensive legacy investments in ERP and other internal server-based applications, are having to identify how they can migrate critical operating data onto cloud service platforms. Smaller LSPs and new market entrants can commence operations almost immediately, selecting from a variety of applications as requirements demand.

It is this realignment of cost for technology services from an inhouse focused capital expense, to a more flexible subscription-based operating expense cost model that is so disruptive. It means that small LSPs can exploit these new platforms and provide solutions to customers very quickly. They can do so without having to make the massive investments that incumbent players have made and so enjoy a considerable cost advantage. Another benefit is that the inherent flexibility of new solutions means that they can implement and adapt to whatever the client needs, often within days and sometimes within hours.

The new platforms are immensely scalable, highly secure (even 'large' companies cannot match the size of the security teams available to Google, Microsoft or Amazon) and are all subject to reduced cost, while capability is increased thanks to 'Moore's Law'.[1]

Enabling supply chain visibility

One major advantage of this new approach is the increasing availability of the technological components to enable total, global supply chain visibility. This is beguilingly simple to express but notoriously hard to achieve. True supply chain visibility extends from procurement, through to final delivery of the finished product and sometimes beyond, if the service and support cycles are included. This is somewhat easier to achieve if all of these activities take place within the same organization, but in today's outsourced and networked world, where many functions are shared with partners, it is extremely difficult.

The sophisticated track and trace systems of the global integrators probably come closest to achieving visibility. However, they only work when orders and shipments remain within the integrator's operational network. This way they can guarantee the data and status updates are captured in a timely manner and can be authenticated. They have invested billions of dollars in extensive networks, scanners and sensors, ensuring the identification and location of almost everything passing through their chain of custody. This is great if the operating model and related cost are acceptable, but for many companies this is not workable. So, what should they do? Fortunately, the relentless innovation in technology since the late 2000s has made available all of the necessary components needed to do this, at an affordable cost.

The most efficient logistics operators are now becoming experts in managing process flow. This is because it is very difficult to restrict efficiency improvements to just one functional discipline. In the past, improvements to a particular functional silo usually involved pushing inefficiencies and problems across into the two adjacent functional silos, which did nothing to improve the process flow across the organization. As the barriers between the silos have fallen away, being able to control the flow of orders and shipments relies on instant and accurate data. This is where a supply chain visibility system, of which track and trace is just one component, is essential.

The visibility platform should act as a link between various operational systems running across the supply chain. It should provide context and reference resolution between all of the various data sources. The more data sources, the greater the clarity of what is happening. Precision of available inventory status, volumes and location is essential, and with this information it is possible to derive all kinds of efficiencies.

At the same time, accurate information about the contents of the shipment provides options to the supply chain management team. These come into play when there are inevitable delays or disruptions within the supply chain. As an order is moved through the supply chain, it changes as it is consolidated with other shipments, or is handed to other carriers. This usually results in the original references and identities being subsumed into a plethora of additional references, most of which only make sense to their parent data management systems.

It is this fact that makes it very hard to identify a specific order as it moves across the supply chain. Any unique shipment references only apply if the managing logistics service provider has identified and linked other references assigned to the order.

A great analogy for this problem is a set of Russian dolls. Each doll may (or may not) nest inside another doll. The viewer only sees the outermost doll but has no knowledge of how many other dolls it may contain without opening them all. A good visibility system has a flexible and robust design that is able to deal with this problem. The original order may be placed in a package, which is put in a box with other packages, added to a pallet, which in turn is put into a container or airfreight unit load device, each with its own unique reference ID. A client hoping to track the original order will expect that any visibility system they access is able to resolve this puzzle.

LSPs who have great visibility can direct and drive the product flows through the client's supply chain effectively and usually at the most efficient cost. Depending on the nature of the visibility platform, new parties and data sources can be easily accommodated. The ability to extend access to the visibility platform to the edges of any supply chain is critical in being able to develop a 'single version of the truth'.

Mobile devices and RFID-enabled sensors (radio frequency identification) are all capable of collaborating and cooperating with visibility platforms. As these platforms exploit emerging cloud technologies to extend their scope and scale, they become the principal operating base for all supply chain activities. Case Study 6.1 looks at supply chain visibility for a global engineering company manufacturing very high precision components.

CASE STUDY 6.1 Supply chain visibility for an engineering company

A global engineering company manufacturing very high precision components was challenged to improve the availability of materials in the production process. Raw materials and semi-finished components originated from a handful of partner companies. Each partner received demand forecasts from the engineering company, and these forecasts spanned a very long time horizon. As the dateline moved closer to call off and supply, the partners were expected to match their delivery schedules to the demand plan. Unfortunately, the source of the demand plan was a large ERP system that only understood the world of its owner: the engineering company.

This meant that the published demand plans carried parts references that did not match those of the suppliers, so considerable manual efforts were needed to comprehend the demand plan. More to the point, when the suppliers responded to the plan with their own schedules, there was often a reference mismatch in the other direction. As a result, the variability between demand and supply was difficult to comprehend and was addressed by the operations team consistently over-ordering to compensate.

An experiment using a visibility system was tried to see if it was possible to resolve this. The visibility solution understood the referencing conventions of all the parties and contained inventory levels and status across the supply chain. It was a unique application that was accessible across the internet and not under the control of any of the involved parties. Each company had their own access and could manage their own data, and the system maintained the links between the various references and stock keeping unit data.

One important point to note is that there was no master item database, as this would have been impossible to create and maintain, given the number of different parties involved.

In operation, the ERP system generated the demand plans as usual, but a copy of the plans was ingested into the visibility system and could be viewed by the partners in a form that made sense to their operational constraints. This meant that every party was looking at the same information, rather than trying to guess its interpretation.

The partner companies could then respond by putting their inventory availability and delivery schedules into the system, and again it translated the information back into a form that the ERP system was able to process. In addition, an event management capability within the visibility system was able to generate alerts if there were any deviations or unexpected problems with scheduled deliveries into the manufacturing process. These alerts automatically generated graphs that highlighted the deviations and why they were happening, and they were then automatically emailed to the logistics managers.

Although it was a pilot project, it demonstrated that considerable savings could result if the system was implemented across the entire production process. It also demonstrated the power of collaboration, provided the correct systems and visibility tools to augment it.

However, the most surprising fact about this example is not the results, but that it took place some 15 years ago, using technologies that are now commonplace, but that back then were deemed too experimental for full-scale deployment.

Summary

Although supply chain visibility has been talked about for many decades, it is still difficult to achieve. This is not due to a lack of data, which is being generated in enormous quantities by various applications, not least the 'Internet of Things'. Rather it is the quality of this data that is the key issue as well as the capabilities to interpret and act upon it. Control towers are an important innovation in this respect. Eventually, powered by AI, supply chain and logistics management decisions will be made seamlessly to deliver customer service, while minimizing inventory. They will also provide LSPs with an important new product and lead to their reinvention as valued supply chain coordinators.

Note

1 Moore's Law is the observation that the number of transistors on a chip will double every two years, while at the same time, prices will continue to fall.

3D printing

07

A review of its implications for the supply chain and logistics industry

THIS CHAPTER WILL FAMILIARIZE THE READER WITH:

- what is meant by 3D printing and the technologies involved in additive manufacturing;
- the benefits it has over traditional manufacturing techniques;
- the challenges to adoption faced by the technology;
- the potential for the technology to disrupt supply chains;
- how the technology is being applied in industry sectors such as automotive and aerospace;
- investment by logistics companies in the technology.

Introduction

3D printing is a major technological innovation with significant implications for the logistics and supply chain industry. Additive manufacturing, as it is otherwise known, is a key element of the Fourth Industrial Revolution. This chapter examines the development of the technology, the reality and the fantasy.

What is 3D printing?

3D printing was originally developed as an automated method of producing prototypes. Although there are several competing technologies, most work on the basis of building up layers of material (sometimes plastic, ceramics or metal powders) using a computer aided design. Hence, it is referred to as an 'additive' process; each layer is 'printed' until a 3D product is created.

The logic for using 3D printing for prototypes is compelling. Traditional 'subtractive' manufacturing techniques (where materials are removed) can take longer to set up and are more expensive for short runs. Mechanical parts, shoes, fashion items and accessories and other consumer goods, can all be printed for review by the designer or engineers, and revisions printed equally as easily. Whereas mass production is viable due to economies of scale, it is uneconomical for 'one-offs' and prototypes.

The end 3D printed product also has other benefits. Products can be lighter but just as strong. There is also less wastage. In comparison traditional subtractive manufacturing is highly inefficient in the use of materials.

For many industry sectors, the use of 3D printing is already widespread, although confined to certain specialist parts of the manufacturing process. It has many benefits over traditional reductive production techniques, these being:

- faster iteration of prototypes;
- lower lead times;
- elimination of tools and moulds;
- reduction of component weight without compromising on strength ('light weighting');
- reduction in number of parts required;
- reduction of material loss;
- replacement of parts quickly and easily;
- optimizing computer aided designs;
- customization of parts;
- postponed manufacturing opportunities;
- reduction in supply chain risk through less outsourcing;
- elimination of 'bull whip' inventory effect and safety stocks of intermediate goods.

According to a report by consultancy Deloitte (2018), 3D printing will be most widely adopted in automotive 'design-rapid' prototype printing, aerospace and defence parts printing. The authors predict that the market will grow from US $13bn in 2016 to US $36bn in 2021.

The way in which each product is individually manufactured means that it is ideal for 'mass customization' techniques. Consumers will, in theory, be able to have a much greater say in the final format of the product they are buying and have it manufactured to their precise specifications.

As yet, traditional manufacturing holds sway in sectors where mass production is still required but, as we will see, this is likely to change as printer technology becomes cheaper and printers get faster.

The range of materials used in the 'printers' is also developing. These now include:

- plastic;
- nylon;
- graphite;
- ceramic;
- glass-filled polyamide;
- epoxy resins;
- silver;
- titanium;
- steel;
- wax;
- polycarbonates.

There are many types of technologies involved, perhaps the most popular being Selective Laser Melting (SLM) and Direct Metal Laser Sintering (DMLS). These techniques both use a laser to melt metal powder particles together, building up a part layer-by-layer, but the latter can use powder composed of several materials to form an alloy.

Challenges to adoption

Although the technology has been around for some time, progress towards adoption has been slower than first thought. Nobody expected the industry to be transformed overnight, but progress has been inhibited by the following factors:

- inherent inertia of big manufacturers;
- complacency around the need to change;

- fear of failure;
- regulatory burdens;
- lack of available talent;
- unwillingness to take risks;
- time taken to print parts;
- cost per piece;
- lack of standardization of raw materials;
- quality assurance, reliability and liability;
- risk of counterfeiting;
- concerns over intellectual property.

Only when these issues and worries have been addressed will the technology become more widely adopted. Many of the above are related to corporate or operational concerns. However, there is also a logistics-related challenge linked to the international movements of goods, that being the role of customs. Presently, customs authorities collect tariffs and duties on imported goods, as well as playing an important role in preventing the shipment of counterfeit or substandard goods.

First, from a tax revenue generating perspective, if products are produced locally by 3D printer there is a strong possibility that tariffs and duties will decline in line with a drop in international shipping volumes, thus creating a shortfall for national exchequers. Will duties need to be levied on a download of a design if that design is originated overseas? This seems unlikely as in a cloud computing world, digital libraries could be located anywhere.

Second, how will authorities react to the risk that businesses (and individuals) will be able to produce goods that may be lower than regulated standards (electrical fitments, for example, made from inadequate materials) with no traceability?

At present, the low volume of parts produced by 3D printing and the oversight of the major manufacturers producing these goods has ensured that these issues have not made it onto the political agenda. The democratization of the technology will ensure that this will not remain the case for long.

Why will 3D printing disrupt supply chains?

In a White Paper on the subject (Manners-Bell and Lyon, 2015), it was asserted that 3D printing had the potential to become the biggest single disruptive phenomenon to impact global industry since assembly lines were introduced in the United States in the early 20th century. The authors went on to say:

> New technologies which are currently being developed could revolutionize production techniques, resulting in a significant proportion of manufacturing becoming automated and removing reliance on large and costly work forces. This in turn could lead to a reversal of the trend of globalization which has characterized industry and consumption over the last few decades, itself predicated on the trade off between transportation and labour costs.

This assertion still holds true, although the adoption of the technology has been slower than originally thought. Many people focus on the higher cost per piece as a reason for the slow take-up, although lower prices for 3D printers and the materials they use will address this issue. Likewise, the speed of 3D printing will also increase as technology develops.

However, it is likely that these challenges will be overcome not least due to the enormous value that will be released within the supply chain. One estimate suggests that inventory and waiting comprises 92 per cent of assembly time in the automotive industry and that transport output related to these parts amounts to 45.3 billion ton-miles in the United States alone (Dohnalek, 2018). These 'hidden' costs are rarely taken into account when comparing traditional manufacturing techniques with 3D printing. Presently, in lean supply chain terms, transport is seen as a 'necessary waste' – this may well change to 'unnecessary waste' in the coming years.

3D printing will mean that the intermediate goods in the supply chain will be replaced by the raw materials needed to make the printing materials. Multiple tiers of inventories held upstream and downstream will be eliminated as will be the need to move them from location to location, often on a global basis. Instead, much simpler supply chains involving the bulk storage and movement of printer materials will develop.

An example of this is the material 'graphite'. Currently used for 3D printing in the electronics sector due to its superior conductive capabilities, the mineral is predominantly sourced from a mine in Tanzania where very pure forms can be extracted. The Australian mining company involved has partnered with a specialist 3D printing company to develop a variant 'graphene'. The relevance of this is that tiers of suppliers presently involved in traditional supply chains will be removed as mineral resource companies can supply materials direct to processing companies that supply the printer materials to be used in the production of components or final product. The implications of this to the supply chain are highlighted next.

A supply chain transformation

To illustrate the supply chain changes that could occur, it is useful to examine a number of scenarios starting with an analysis of present structures.

In the simplified supply chain in Figure 7.1, it can be seen that, upstream, a complex lattice work of interconnected 'tiered' suppliers exists. Although the diagram just shows two tiers of suppliers, many supply chains consist of more than five tiers. They will supply each other as well as the final assembly operations undertaken by an original equipment manufacturer (OEM) or by

Figure 7.1 Existing global supply chain networks

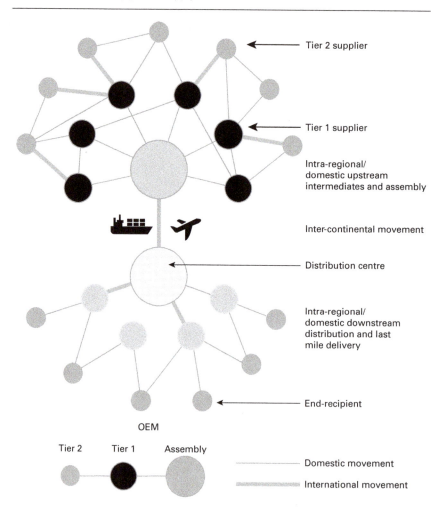

its contract manufacturing company. This results in intensive transport requirements on an intra-regional basis, typically across Asia, supported by air cargo, shipping, road freight and freight forwarding resources. The final products are then shipped to ports in North America or Europe, moved inland and then stored and distributed possibly to more localized warehouses before last mile delivery to the end-recipient.

In what could be considered as Stage 1 of the evolution towards the adoption of 3D printing throughout industry, many of the existing suppliers of semi-fabricated goods become redundant as a result of the introduction of 3D printing plants. The final assembly plant also adopts this technology, doing away with the need for a proportion of its labour requirements. The goods are then shipped to ports in the developed world and stored at distribution centres in a 'vanilla' state, ie in a format that will allow further customization for local markets. 3D printers at the distribution centre will undertake this customization. These goods are then shipped through logistics networks to the end-recipient via more localized distribution locations. These locations also double up as 3D printer plants for spare parts, using their proximity to the customer and service engineers to meet tight service level agreements (Figure 7.2).

In the next stage, global manufacturers are able to exploit the technology to produce goods without the need for large labour forces. Hence, China and Asia lose their competitive advantage as a manufacturing location and production is 're-shored'. Raw materials are shipped direct from the regions of extraction, typically Africa, Latin America, parts of Asia and Australia to 3D printing plants in North America and Europe (Figure 7.3).

There are obviously many variations of these scenarios, but one that provides an alternative structure is highlighted in Figure 7.4.

In this example, the customer requests a 3D print shop or facility to download a design from a database (either generic or customized), which is then manufactured. The final product can then be dispatched to the end-recipient or collected. The system is very simple in comparison with the previous models that describe the impact of 3D printing on enterprise-wide structures.

Adoption by industry sectors

Automotive

Presently, 3D printing is used for concept modelling and prototyping as well as the printing of some production parts and low-volume replacement parts.

Figure 7.2 Hybrid industrial 3D supply chain networks

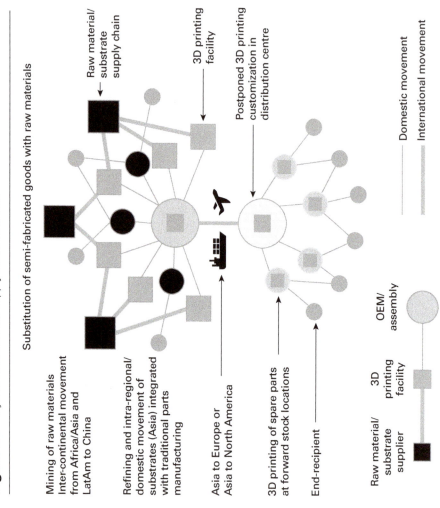

Substitution of semi-fabricated goods with raw materials

Raw material/ substrate supply chain

3D printing facility

Postponed 3D printing customization in distribution centre

Mining of raw materials
Inter-continental movement from Africa/Asia and LatAm to China

Refining and intra-regional/ domestic movement of substrates (Asia) integrated with traditional parts manufacturing

Asia to Europe or Asia to North America

3D printing of spare parts at forward stock locations

End-recipient

Raw material/ substrate supplier

3D printing facility

OEM/ assembly

Domestic movement

International movement

Figure 7.3 Re-shored 3D supply chain networks

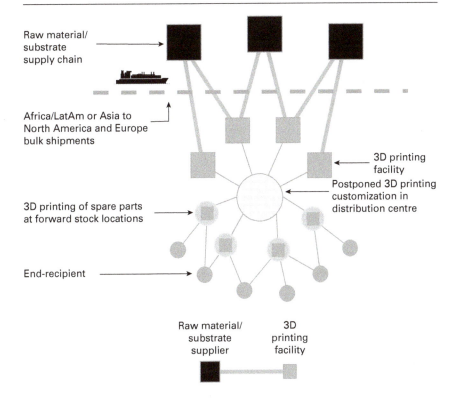

Raw material/
substrate
supply chain

Africa/LatAm or Asia to
North America and Europe
bulk shipments

3D printing of spare parts
at forward stock locations

End-recipient

3D printing
facility

Postponed 3D printing
customization in
distribution centre

Raw material/
substrate
supplier

3D
printing
facility

Figure 7.4 3D print shop model

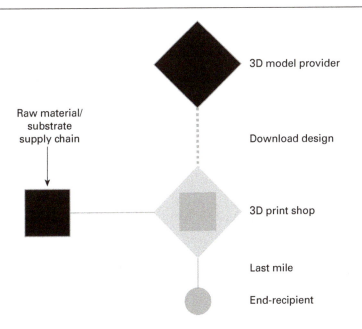

3D model provider

Raw material/
substrate
supply chain

Download design

3D print shop

Last mile

End-recipient

In the future, the technique will be extended to much longer runs, creating lighter components using innovative materials and completely new designs that do not try to replicate existing parts, but fully optimize the potential that 3D printers offer. This includes computer aided honeycomb and lattice designs that would be impossible to produce with traditional techniques, but which offer a combination of weight and strength.

Engines

Very large 3D printers have now been developed that can be used for printing whole engine blocks. Developed by German company Roush Industries, it is aimed at companies looking to design engines rather than for large-scale production. However, management believes that soon the technology will be fast enough for the production of engines to be considered feasible. Quality and size issues are no longer inhibitors. Of course, if electric vehicles replace existing internal combustion engine-powered vehicles, the need for printing engine blocks will become redundant.

Spare parts production

As mentioned earlier, many automotive manufacturers are testing the concept of 3D printing spare parts. It has become popular for 'vintage' cars where parts are very slow moving and consequently costly to store (and source). This involves manufacturers developing digital libraries of parts that can then be printed off on demand. 3D printers are still located at central locations so that quality can be assured, although in the future it is conceivable that printers based in garages or dealerships would be able to provide the parts, eliminating the need for transportation completely.

Manufacturers actively involved in testing the technology for parts include:

- Renault;
- Audi;
- Rolls Royce;
- Caterpillar;
- Porsche (classic cars);
- Daimler Trucks North America (pilot project).

Tyres

Tyre manufacturers such as Michelin are in the process of planning a new generation of tyres leveraging the potential of 3D printing to manufacture products from complex, biomimetic designs and using recycled materials. According to the company, the future tyre will be airless, recyclable, puncture-proof and strong. It will also be possible to 3D print a retread for the tyre.

Aerospace

3D printing offers enormous potential for the production of components primarily due to their lightweight nature, essential when the weight of aircraft is so critical in the aerospace industry. The sector can claim leadership in the application, with Boeing using 3D printed parts since 2003 originally in the air defence sector. The US Department of Defense has been interested due to the potential to print parts quickly and 'in theatre'. Today, Boeing has 50,000 3D printed parts flying in a variety of aircraft. The company is now in the process of introducing titanium parts for the 787 Dreamliner, although this will require approval by the FAA, the US regulator.

GE's initiative is probably the most ambitious. It is printing injectors for its LEAP jet engine, but not just as spare parts. Its plans are to print 35,000 a year by 2020. This takes the use of the technology to another level. One of the key benefits is the reduction in complexity. A GE 3D printed turboprop engine reduces the number of parts required from 855 to 12 – a fact that will have huge implications for the aerospace supply chain.

Construction

Many of the innovations that have occurred in the construction business have been in design, engineering and operations rather than in actual building and fabrication of materials. There are good reasons why 3D printing should be embraced by the construction industry, not least the worsening labour shortage as well as the huge level of waste that is endemic in the sector.

Chinese company Winsun, which specializes in advanced building products, printed 10 complete houses in 2014 and has since printed an office building in Dubai.

Since then many other companies have entered the market, often collaborating with start-ups, for example, concrete manufacturer LafargeHolcim and XtreeE.

In terms of the construction supply chain, 3D printing would mean reductions in:

- numbers of parts;
- complexity;
- number of deliveries to building sites;
- returns of misordered and damaged goods.

However, although the technology is available, it is still very expensive, which has inhibited its adoption.

Electronics

Consultancy firm EY (2018) believes that the electronics sector could be ripe for disruption by 3D printing, at least in the prototype stage. For example, the development and testing of printed circuit boards can take between 8 and 40 days and is often an outsourced procedure. With minimum runs required by the outsourced suppliers, which are likely to be based in Asia, this is often a costly as well as time-consuming procedure. 3D printing allows this to occur inhouse and, because no minimum run is required, is far less wasteful.

What does the future hold for the express and logistics industry?

Ultimately 3D printing could be a major threat to express and logistics companies should traditional tiered manufacturing and spare parts networks be swept away. There is no doubt this is a possibility, although it is unlikely to happen quickly, and the effects are more likely to be manifested as a headwind to growth rather than a 'cliff edge'. More likely the technology will bring about changes to supply networks rather than their elimination.

Scenario 1 (most likely)

3D printing becomes adopted widely for the production of parts in high-tech sectors such as automotive, aerospace, medical technology and electronics.

- The reduction of the amount of parts required in the assembly process means that supply chains become much, much less complex. This means that inventory storage requirements reduce at all supply chain levels.

- Manufacturing companies that were focused on the assembly of components (largely in China) invest heavily in 3D printing technology in order to capture higher levels of value-added. This means that 'tier' suppliers in Asia lose out and intra-Asian trade in intermediate goods falls.

- Global manufacturers no longer require large labour forces and can base their facilities anywhere. This means that manufacturers *with the capabilities* can re-shore production.

The outcome of this last point will be difficult to assess. Although 3D printing means that in theory manufacturers will be able to base their production facilities much closer to the end market, no longer dependent on low cost labour, the fact that generations of manufacturing know-how has been relocated to China casts considerable doubt as to whether there is the ability to redevelop sufficient manufacturing expertise in Europe or North America.

Therefore, in terms of impact on the logistics industry:

- Intra-Asian shipping and freight forwarding volumes will be adversely affected.

- Global movements of finished goods may not be affected, with the main origin still being China. Japan would be another beneficiary.

- Domestic movements of goods in developed markets may benefit if re-shoring takes place.

- Certainly, global inventories of spare parts will be reduced as parts will be printed close to demand. Still likely that the last mile delivery will be undertaken by an express company (from a forward location with industrial printing capabilities).

Scenario 2 (less likely)

Less likely is the scenario that manufacturing is consumerized, that is, 3D printing allows individuals to print products in their own homes. Although this is already possible for hobbyists, it is not likely that the type of industrial 3D printing machinery needed to produce most goods will be affordable.

However, if an element of 3D printing could be introduced to households:

- The movement of goods throughout the supply chain will become redundant.
- This will be replaced by the flow of materials that are required for use in the printers.
- Raw materials from predominantly developing regions such as Africa and Latin America will be refined into printer materials.
- The final movement (whether domestic or international) will depend on the location of these refineries.
- Large warehouses would be required to store these printer materials.

Investment by logistics companies

Recognizing the long-term threat of 3D printing, or more likely looking at the short-term opportunities that it provides to add value to their operations, logistics companies are investing heavily in the technology.

UPS

In 2016, UPS launched what it called a 3D printing manufacturing network. Working with SAP, it rolled out 3D printers to 60 UPS stores in the United States as well as a 3D printing factory in Louisville, leveraging what it saw as a need for 'manufacturing as a service'. Customers will place their orders centrally, and the part will be printed at the optimal location.

FedEx

FedEx has followed UPS's lead, and in 2018 it created 'FedEx Forward Depots', a business unit responsible, inter alia, for critical inventory and 3D printing. However, the product is still in an early stage of development.

DB Schenker

Schenker's customers can now upload a 3D template via the online portal, eSchenker, select materials and colour, consult prices, place orders and have the end product delivered.

At present, printing includes medical devices made from stainless steel, robot gripper fingers made from plastic, or customized packaging material.

DB Schenker organizes the printing and delivery via its data platform. The company does not have its own printers but uses a digital business model within a partner network of start-ups as well as established companies.

Summary

Although 3D printing has not caught on yet to the extent many people had expected, its implementation has been steady and its wider adoption would seem inevitable. 3D printing is being integrated within existing manufacturing processes, which will result in what could be termed 'hybrid' supply chains. Over time, increasing numbers of parts and sub-assemblies will be produced by 3D printing either within the final assembly facility, logistics centres, or in specialist plants.

This will mean that, eventually, there will be significant changes to supply chains. This may not be evident for many years, resulting perhaps in lower growth for the logistics sector rather than an overall reduction in market size. However, there is no good reason to expect the present system of globalized supply chains to remain set in stone, and technological development could well be the catalyst for transformation.

Not all changes will threaten logistics companies. As mentioned, 3D printing will provide the opportunity for more customization of parts and postponed manufacturing that will take place as far downstream as possible, for example at a logistics centre in a developed market.

It is clear that with so much uncertainty as to how fast and in which direction the technology will develop, all supply chain parties must remain prepared for the many opportunities and threats that 3D printing will inevitably provide.

Bibliography

Deloitte [accessed 10 August 2018] Exponential Technologies in Manufacturing [Online] www2.deloitte.com/us/en/pages/manufacturing/articles/advanced-manufacturing-technologies-report.html

Dohnalek, M [accessed 11 August 2018] 3-D and the Global Supply Chain, *Supply Chain Management Review* [Online] www.scmr.com/article/3_d_and_the_global_supply_chain#When:14:27:00Z

EY [accessed 10 April 2018] How Will 3D Printing Make Your Company the Strongest Link in the Value Chain? [Online] www.ey.com/Publication/vwLUAssets/ey-global-3d-printing-report-2016-full-report/%24FILE/ey-global-3d-printing-report-2016-full-report.pdf

Manners-Bell, J and Lyon, K (2015) *The Implications of 3D Printing for the Global Logistics Industry*, Transport Intelligence Ltd, UK

The disruptive potential of robots and automation

08

THIS CHAPTER WILL FAMILIARIZE THE READER WITH:

- the changing demand-side trends that have led to the increased need for automation in the warehouse;
- the type of robots being employed within the warehouse environment;
- the use of robots by companies such as Amazon and Ocado;
- how robots will lessen the need for labour while increasing efficiency;
- threats to logistics service providers from automation;
- how the use of robots in production processes may influence future supply chain structures.

The rise of the robots

Automation in the warehouse through the use of robots is gathering pace. Although robotic systems have been around for some time, a number of demand- and supply-side trends are driving their widespread adoption.

Not least of these is the e-commerce phenomenon that has led to many retailers adopting omni-channel and multichannel marketing and distribution strategies, transforming the characterization of supply chain volumes from unitized and quite predictable, to single item and volatile. According to a report by consultancy IDC, 'By 2018, 45% of the 200 leading global ecommerce and omni-channel commerce companies will deploy robotics systems in their order fulfilment warehousing and delivery operations' (2018). At the same time, many new entrants have emerged, challenging bricks and mortar incumbents through the ability to develop new distribution centres custom-built for the demands of e-retail customers.

A further driver is the increasing cost of labour and its shortage. Automation is being seen as a way of increasing efficiencies in the warehouse, reducing the need for human workers and at the same time providing more flexibility to fulfil peaks and troughs of demand using modular systems.

Apart from the labour cost element, automation also means lower real estate costs as a human-free environment allows greater density of storage, ie operating with narrower aisles (or in some cases, no aisles at all).

What is more, robot technology is becoming more robust and the cost per robot is falling, bringing them into the reach of smaller customers. Robotics-as-a-service solutions are being developed by some suppliers, which work on a 'pay-per-pick' basis, therefore taking away the large capital outlay formerly required.

However, automating such a labour-intensive sector as warehousing will have repercussions. These may well be at a macro level, affecting governments and policymakers due to the impact on employment. It will also be felt among logistics service providers (LSPs) whose revenues are largely made up by managing or providing labour forces.

Types of robots

Although there have been many developments in the automation sector as a whole (which includes a range of materials handling equipment such as conveyors and forklift trucks), robots are likely to have a transformative effect. There are several types of these already in use.

Material transport robots

- Autonomous Mobile Robots (AMR) – robots that move materials around the warehouse environment. They work alongside humans and forklift trucks using a pre-programmed warehouse map. They use sensors such as lasers and cameras to interact with their environment. Costs on average US $30,000 per unit upwards.

- Automated Guided Vehicles (AGV) – another type of material transport robot, but this time restricted to certain routes using wires, magnetic strips or sensors. Good for repetitive movements for high volume and consistent demand, but inflexible and unable to navigate obstacles.

While AGVs have been around longer, it is likely that AMRs will become the future of material transport robots due to their higher levels of flexibility, the fact that they can operate without special infrastructure being built for them, and their lower overall cost.

A hybrid system involves self-driving carts leading workers around the warehouse and telling them where to replenish stocks or when to pick an item to place in the carrier. One of the benefits of this system is the lack of investment needed in the warehouse itself and the lower cost of the robots.

Collaborative robots

Collaborative robots or 'cobots' as they are known for short are designed to help human workers in their tasks, usually deployed where a good deal of repetition is involved. It can be 'trained' by the worker to undertake a task and thereafter needs no further intervention (apart from maintenance). A distinction between 'collaborative robots' and 'industrial robots' is that while the former can be retrained, the latter is less flexible and set up for one role only unless reprogrammed (a more complex process). Cobots are often used for packaging functions such as wrapping, sealing and boxing, or 'pick and place'.

Automated picking

Robotic picking relies on the development of arms that are capable of grasping and manipulation. The ultimate aim for many companies is to eliminate human pickers completely. Two-armed robots, developed by Hitachi, use cameras to identify multiple items at the same time, which allows it to work more quickly than existing alternatives. These should be rolled out in 2020.

Robotics in logistics

Although most robots fall into one of these categories, the way they are used can differ significantly. Amazon uses robots to bring the picking face to the human pickers, rather than have staff walk up the aisles to the right picking location. Amazon now employs 80,000 robots at 25 fulfilment centres worldwide.

This automation has allowed Amazon to offer industry-leading service levels at a much lower cost than is the case with a wholly human solution. It is estimated that it allows workers to pick two to three times faster than conventional, manual systems. Amazon itself says that the average time it takes to fulfil an order has fallen from 90 minutes to just 15. In the United States, this has allowed it to push back two-day delivery cut off times from 3pm to midnight, achieving an impressive extension for this service option.

The solution still requires human participation: not only pickers, but the workers needed to unload trucks, unpack the boxes and place items in racks. These racks are then taken by robots to locations in a caged, 'non-human' area, awaiting collection by another robot. Amazon increased its number of employees by 13 per cent to 613,000 in 2018.

Amazon has adopted one particularly strategy, but there are many other manufacturers. The best known of these are Rethink Robotics, Locus and Fetch from the United States and Singapore-based GreyOrange, which is heavily focused on the Indian market. Alibaba uses a system that looks similar to Amazon's in that it uses robots to lift stacks of boxes that it then moves to the picker.

British company Ocado has been pioneering robotics for groceries for many years. The grocery e-retail sector faces different challenges to the relatively low number of items needed to be picked per shipment in the Amazon model. Ocado's management claims that its system, where robots swarm over a specifically designed (human-free) matrix, can pick 50 items for an order in a matter of minutes.

Logistics companies such as DHL have invested heavily in trialling different solutions, including the widespread use of cobots. For example, it has deployed Rethink Robotics' Sawyer cobots in packing contracts in the UK.

People versus robots

The number of people employed in the warehouse environment is still growing, but their role is already changing. Many of the most highly repetitive jobs are the best suited to be automated. This means that human roles can become more value adding with the benefit that they become more personally fulfilling. For example, human workers, whose role was once to stack containers, a physical and tiring but necessary function, now oversee robots who have taken over this function.

According to one US-based logistics company that has successfully trialled material transport robots, RK Logistics (2018), 'For the 4,500 deliveries that the robots have traversed our warehouse floor in the past six months, that's 1,000 kilometers our workers haven't had to spend time transporting items. By allocating mundane transportation tasks away from our employees to the robots, we are freeing up our people for higher value work'. Management says that ROI was within 'a few months'.

For the time being it would seem that human jobs are safe in the warehouse. The economic value that is being created by greater levels of efficiency has, so far, led to the need for more workers not fewer. In fact, jobs could be set to become less monotonous and physical, which labour organizations should welcome.

However, there are two clouds on the horizon. First, due to the fact that Amazon and other e-commerce companies have created efficiencies in the warehouse that allow them to out-compete many bricks and mortar retailers, the employees that they take on may be at the cost of employment in traditional retailing as well as their distribution systems. What this means is that there is a migration of jobs to the likes of Amazon rather than an overall generation. The logic (although this will be difficult to prove without more data) is that there must be a net loss in employment as many of the jobs that would have been created have been taken by automation.

Second, robots are getting cheaper, which will mean that eventually all segments of industry will be able to use them. At the same time as this, employing humans is becoming more expensive as governments around the world have made it increasingly difficult for companies to employ staff given the high degree of costs and regulation that is involved with each employee hire. Consequently robots, which don't require breaks, health insurance or holidays and can work round the clock at peak times, to mention just a few benefits, will be very attractive to many companies. How governments can deal with the social fallout from this and loss of tax revenue is another problem. Indeed, this is something that Amazon may have to address sooner rather than later. Given that it has received tax breaks from many US states eager to attract the e-retailer for the jobs it promised to create, administrators may want their money back if the investment results in 'jobless' warehouses.

To understand the economics of robots, and consequently how likely they are to replace humans, it is necessary to identify their cost. This is not easy as the price of a robot depends on:

- their complexity;
- their payload carrying ability and reach;
- the tools they use;
- the sophistication of the software required to run them;
- the 'teaching' interface.

Popular collaborative robot models cost approximately US $30,000, although this can easily rise to US $100,000 with customization. Although this might sound expensive, anecdotally one cobot can replace two human workers on a line and so the payback is fast and the economic case is obvious. ROI can be achieved in six months to a year.

Warehouse design and demand

As well as fewer workers being required, the use of robots can make the layout of a warehouse more efficient as aisle space can be narrower. The increased inventory density means that more products can be stored under one roof.

However, this is not as easy as it sounds. A recent report by real estate company, CBRE, says that in the United States the average age of a warehouse is 34 years old with many having low ceilings and uneven floors, conditions that are either sub-optimal for automated warehouse design or prevent the use of material transport robots of any type (CBRE, 2018).

This means that new warehousing is in great demand with one billion square feet of warehousing being developed in the last 10 years alone in the United States. However, CBRE estimates that this is just 11 per cent of the total warehousing inventory, and the lack of appropriate building has seen development land prices soar by up to a quarter since 2016.

What will be the future role of the LSP?

Increasing automation in the warehouse will change the role of the outsourced contract logistics provider. If there are no longer large labour forces to manage in the distribution centre, then what function will it perform?

It could be that the logistics provider becomes an additional source of capital for its customer, providing the robotics equipment, as DHL does with cobots for co-packing services. But it may well be that the customer actually has better access to cheap capital itself and may want to benefit from the tax breaks that are available in many markets for capital investment.

As mentioned earlier, robotics-as-a-service is now being offered by some robot manufacturers, which would also remove the LSP from the equation. This involves the integration of robots into the web and cloud computing environment. Data captured by the robot, such as number and location of items picked or remaining inventory levels, can be shared and retrieved as required. Data on the robot's performance itself can also be shared and fed into planned maintenance programmes.

The situation will be complicated by the new accounting standard IFRS 16, which comes into force in 2019 and may mean that leased robots have to appear on the lessee's balance sheet whether or not they are operated by an LSP. Much will depend on whether the robot is a shared or dedicated asset.

That contract logistics is very much a labour management operation can be seen by example figures based on actual P&L figures of a US $15m European distribution centre dedicated contract (not including transportation). Of the operating costs necessary to generate this revenue, payroll and benefits of the staff amounted to US $6.4m. Depreciation of equipment was just US $200,000 and occupancy costs were US $1.2m. In fact, looking at a wide variety of other logistics contracts, the proportion of staff costs to revenue for this contract was at the lower end of the spectrum: depending on the services being provided, direct labour costs can amount to two-thirds of revenues.

From a financial point of view, in the coming years the payroll and benefits P&L line looks likely to diminish, while depreciation of assets (such as robots) will increase.

It should be noted that this example is for a dedicated outsourced contract. The situation regarding the impact of automation is more complicated for shared-user contracts. While many, if not all, of the costs in a dedicated open book contract can be passed onto the customer, in a shared-user environment, the logistics provider is likely to bear more of the risks. It may be that it makes sense for an LSP to invest in robots in order to increase productivity across a variety of operations in a single distribution centre, especially where labour is in short supply and expensive. Therefore, they will bear the financial risk if volumes are lower than forecast, although the corollary is that they have a better upside.

However, whatever relationship the LSP has with its customers, the efficiencies gained in the warehouse will inevitably have a short-term impact on revenues for the sector as a whole. One US bank, Janney Capital Markets, has suggested that retailer fulfilment costs in the United States will fall by US $450m to US $900m – a third (Bhaiya, 2018). Logistics companies may still benefit in terms of margins, but to do so they will have to change their operating models substantially to focus on their value-added.

Robots in the supply chain

Logistics companies will also be affected by the increasing use of robots and automation in production processes. These could have as much an impact on logistics companies' businesses as the tactical use of robots in warehouses, not least due to the shift in global trade patterns that could result. If robots remove the need to locate production in low-cost labour markets, one of the key drivers for globalization will have been eliminated.

The economic use of robots in production lines is generally a trade-off between the time it takes a skilled human to train them, against the consistent, reliable output that results from the machine. In the past the dexterity of a low-skilled but cheap human has usually outperformed the robot.

As manufacturing has evolved, robots have become cheaper and more dexterous, while at the same time people have become more expensive. Consequently, more robots are being seen in production facilities, especially those of high-tech manufacturers.

As production lines and collaborative manufacturing networks emerge, intelligent devices and machines will be harnessed to support faster and more agile production runs. The communications networks supporting this activity will need to have sufficient capacity and operate at gigabit speeds in a very secure manner, all of which implies that the manufacturing landscape will be very different to that of today. Case Study 8.1 looks at the impact of robots on fashion supply chains.

CASE STUDY 8.1   Fashion supply chains set for disruption

The apparel sector currently embraces many innovations discussed in this book to compete in the e-commerce space. Nike, for instance, is one manufacturer who is using 3D printing to customize sport shoes for specific individuals. Adidas is also innovating in this area along with other major sports apparel brands. But it is not only technologies such as 3D printing that are being used. Robots, advanced smartphone apps and high definition optics are all being exploited by the fashion business.

One major Chinese contract manufacturer has built a plant in the United States with multiple production lines manned by 'sewbots'. These are robots that can manufacture clothing, in this case t-shirts for the German company Adidas, incredibly quickly. The 'bots' can cut and sew a new shirt every 22 seconds from very soft and flexible fabric. This was something that was impossible to conceive a few years ago. The designs can also be changed very swiftly according to market demand.

Amazon is reputed to have major plans in this area. The company is exploring customized clothes that can be manufactured to order using the techniques mentioned earlier. By using the high definition cameras and a related app on a smartphone, customers will be able to take precise images and measurements of themselves. This will provide very detailed sizing information. Any garments the customer selects from the online stores are then cut, sewed and finished for rapid delivery by the closest facility.

The implications for logistics companies are clear. This kind of innovation, if successful, would have a major impact on the flows of garments from Asia to Europe and North America, negatively affecting shipping lines and air cargo operators as well as freight forwarders. However, key beneficiaries will be the express and last mile delivery companies and, should manufacturing take place in distribution facilities close to the end-recipient, contract logistics providers.

Summary

Automation, and robotics in particular, will transform the warehouse environment by the mid-2020s. Although the sector is a long way from becoming 'jobless' there is no doubt that, as robots become cheaper and more ubiquitous, the role of the warehouse worker will change. It remains to be seen whether the economic value created by robotics will generate a net gain in jobs, but with many retail jobs being lost to more commoditized warehouse functions that are then at risk from automation, it seems inevitable that labour requirements will diminish. The quality of work for those left, however, will improve.

Although the role of LSPs will remain significant for years to come, the services they will be asked to provide will change. There will be more focus on the value they can bring to the overall supply chain as labour becomes less important. This will impact on gross revenues as well as change the character of LSPs' P&L accounts. More importantly it will also change the relationship they have with their customers.

Bibliography

Bhaiya, A [accessed 10 June 2018] Is Robotic Automation the Future of Ecommerce Warehouses? *Huffington Post* [Online] www.huffingtonpost.com/ amit-bhaiya/is-robotic-automation-the_b_12909658.html

CBRE [accessed 11 June 2018] Most U.S. Warehouses are Inadequate for E-Commerce Distribution, Despite Recent Construction Push [Online] www.cbre.us/about/media-center/cbre-most-us-warehouses-are-inadequate-for-e-commerce-distribution

IDC [accessed 11 June 2018] IDC Unveils its Top 10 Predictions for Worldwide Robotics for 2017 and Beyond [Online] www.idc.com/getdoc.jsp?containerId=prAP42000116

RK Logistics [accessed 10 June 2018] RK Logistics Increases Productivity with Robots [Online] www.rklogisticsgroup.com/robotics/rk-logistics-increases-productivity-with-robots/

Blockchain in supply chains

09

THIS CHAPTER WILL FAMILIARIZE THE READER WITH:

- what is meant by the term 'blockchain';
- the stages of the technology's development;
- the benefits that 'blockchain' will deliver to all supply chain parties;
- supply chain and logistics segments in which blockchain will be applied;
- case studies of how the technology is already being utilized;
- its role in facilitating smart contracts and what this means for industry;
- problems facing the adoption of the technology.

What is blockchain?

This chapter seeks to explain and clarify blockchain technology, what it is, how it functions and its potential for use in the logistics and supply chain management sector. As can be seen from a 2018 market survey by consultancy Transport Intelligence, more than half of the respondents believed the technology to be a 'game-changer' (Ti Ltd, 2018).

The blockchain is a permanent digital record (or ledger) of transactions that is stored across a distributed or decentralized network of computers. The 'blocks' that are chained together are cryptographically sealed records of transactions. The blockchain itself is not split across multiple computers but copied to every computer, and they all agree it is identical by consensus.

At the moment each computer stores the entire blockchain and this represents a limitation of the technology. However, a lot of research has

Figure 9.1   The importance of blockchain to the logistics industry

How would you rate the potential level of impact of blockchain in the logistics industry?

Much ado about nothing 3%

Too early to tell 11%

TI's global survey found that 56% of supply chain executives believed that the technology was 'a game changer'.

Game changer 56%

An interesting trend 30%

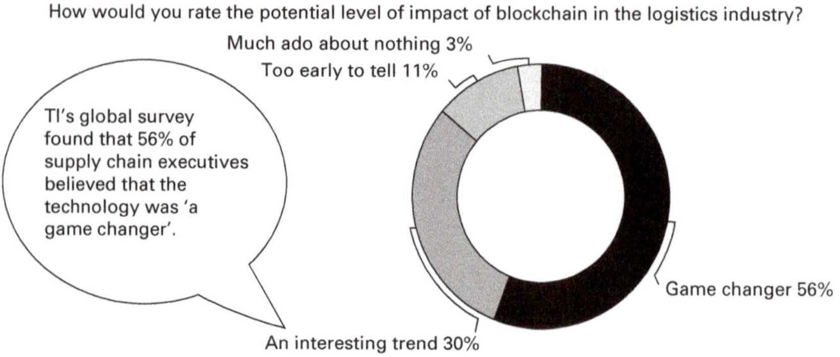

been done to develop solutions where computers do not store the entire blockchain, but they get challenged randomly to judge if a transaction is correct or not.

Although there is one clear master record, in a 'public' blockchain the computers involved are not owned or controlled by any single party or organization. The network of computers supporting the blockchain confirm, verify and record the transactions independently, providing trust through consensus. This is an alternative approach to the explicit trust that is provided by a third party sitting between all of the participants, for example, banks or market exchanges. This guarantees that transactions cannot be modified once confirmed in the blockchain unless every computer (node), or a majority of them in the network, all agree to do so at the same time. If the blockchain network involved comprises a random number of machines outside the control of any single party, this becomes impossible to subvert. The implication of this is that public blockchains are likely to be most trusted and implicitly more secure.

In contrast, 'private' blockchains require participants to be registered and conform to rules established by the owner of the blockchain. However, this poses the question of why a private blockchain would be preferred as opposed to a solution built around a centralized database. This is perhaps similar to the situation when the internet became generally available to all. Many companies used the technologies supporting the internet to build their own private intranets. After creating these walled gardens (often for perfectly valid reasons) they soon realized that the open (public) internet provided much more capability. The walled gardens soon opened up and these days, some companies only maintain their private intranets where industry legislation requires, eg banks.

There are now a number of very large organizations coming together to collaborate around blockchain developments across industries. The Linux foundation's Hyperledger Fabric, Corda from R3 and Coco from Microsoft are all examples of these, with Amazon's AWS about to enter the market as well.

Despite the emergence of platforms such as these, no comprehensive supply chain standards are currently in place for blockchain solutions or providers. This means there are no definitive solutions to questions relating to consensus on blocks and which encryption technology to use. A solid interoperability standard is very likely to emerge as the technology advances. An absence of such standards would add complexities, hindering supply chain applications due to confusing information exchanges.

Blockchain's timeline
Four stages of evolution of blockchain

1 Basic stage, or entry point blockchain, which is utilizing the technology's serialization capabilities. The life science industry is one of the most prominent use cases in which the technology is being used for audit tracking.

2 Application of blockchain to vertical solutions. One example would be the finance supply chain where the technology is being used to create new products and services that take cost out and remove friction.

3 Aggregating and augmenting the data that is being collected with blockchain and tying it with other data (eg inventory data) to drive better decision-making.

4 Blockchain in edge computing, which refers to the trend of reverting from the 'cloud-based' centralized solutions to 'computing on the edge' where businesses can create a massive amount of processing capability. The current cloud computing models are not designed to be able to handle the volume and velocity of data that the Internet of Things generates. This development requires a new kind of infrastructure.

Figure 9.2   Four stages of evolution of blockchain

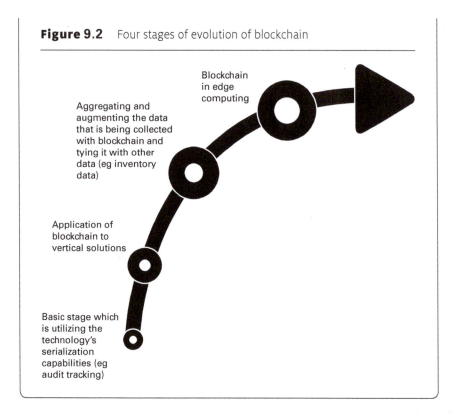

Blockchain
in edge
computing

Aggregating and
augmenting the data
that is being collected
with blockchain and
tying it with other
data (eg inventory
data)

Application of
blockchain to
vertical solutions

Basic stage which
is utilizing the
technology's
serialization
capabilities (eg
audit tracking)

Many companies are still gathering information about blockchain and its implications. There is also an acute shortage of real technical expertise, but this is changing rapidly due to the explosion in interest and pilot projects across the globe. Blockchain technology is still evolving, particularly the number of transactions that can be processed per second. This is a function of block size, storage and bandwidth limits. These should improve over time.

Potential areas of use in logistics and supply chain

Blockchain has applications in many parts of the logistics and supply chain sector. Not least of these is in cost saving. Current industry estimates indicate that 10 per cent of all freight invoices contain inaccurate data, including duplication, wrong freight mode charges and incorrect fees (Tanner, 2018).

This leads to disputes as well as many other inefficiencies in the logistics industry. One of the major advantages of the blockchain is that it can power leaner, more automated and error-free processes.

It will also have important implications for international trade. 'Smart contracts' are applications that are stored and executed on a blockchain depending on their embedded rules. These are agreements or contracts that have embedded business rules that can exist and operate independently of any centralized control. Once a contract is stored on a blockchain it becomes immutable and cannot be changed, embedding any flaws that might be exploited by hackers (see later and Chapter 15 for more detail).

Other examples of applications in the sector are:

- asset tracking;
- total visibility across and down into multiple tiers of the supply chain;
- accountability;
- process conformance;
- improved collaboration across the supply chain.

Examples of blockchain in the supply chain

IBM: asset tracking

IBM recognized an opportunity to improve its asset management system through the use of blockchain technology. A blockchain would capture all transactions and record changes that occur as the assets move from manufacturing to deployment, including those actions that occur outside of IBM's systems. Capturing this information in the blockchain would give IBM and its supply chain partners a 'single source of truth' with regard to core asset information. This way, no matter what happened to an asset as it moved through the supply chain, all stakeholders and systems would know its status.

Visibility: OriginTrail and Provenance

OriginTrail protocol enables exchange of different data sets between multiorganization supply chains. Input and sharing data is based on a common set of data standards that allow multiple organizations (companies involved in production, distribution or retail of goods) to exchange data.

Provenance provides transparency between manufacturers, sellers and buyers. The Provenance platform allows buyers to gain a transparent insight into the people, places and processes that have contributed to the creation of a particular product. Data verification allows for proven business and supply chain claims. This gives consumers trust in the company from which they are buying. Batches or even individual items are given digital passports, enabling buyers to follow a digitally verified journey from start to finish.

Improved collaboration across the supply chain

A leading logistics provider has built a platform that allows it to offer extended payment terms to its customer base. This is an area where the provider has seen an increased demand from customers and has worked with a blockchain provider to build the platform to obtain cheaper funding from insurers and banks for the extended payment terms. The use of the blockchain element offers more simplified administration procedure for the banks and insurers as well as a better audit trail and validation, which removes costs and ultimately allows them to offer cheaper funding rates to the logistics provider. At the moment, this solution is focused on receivables, but the company is hoping they can expand this relationship and broaden it out to include other types of data and customer information that would also be of value for banks and insurers and offer more security about the way they are lending.

Do you need a blockchain?

- DO NOT consider blockchain solutions as replacements for existing solutions that are built around a central database and that continue to work well and do not share data outside the organization.

- DO NOT consider blockchain as a solution component if you need to control/validate access from a known group of users that seldom change.

- DO NOT consider blockchain for data storage. Blockchain is a very inefficient database so if you need to solve a storage problem, blockchain is not the suitable solution.

- DO consider blockchain if you need to capture and/or share data from a variable number of suppliers, partners, customers. This is especially true if many of them do not know each other, are competitors and need to use a verified, immutable and accurate single version of the truth, eg operating in an industry that requires detailed traceability across extended supply chains.

- DO consider blockchain if you are thinking about establishing, reviewing or replacing an IT strategy for your organization.

How do blockchains work?

A blockchain is a distributed database of records that, as they are created, are individually time stamped and grouped in blocks that are linked to each other, as you would find in a chain. The data in the blocks cannot be altered retrospectively. Each transaction entered into the blockchain database is verified (authenticated) by the consensus of every computer across the network collaborating in this verification process.

Figure 9.3   How do blockchains work?

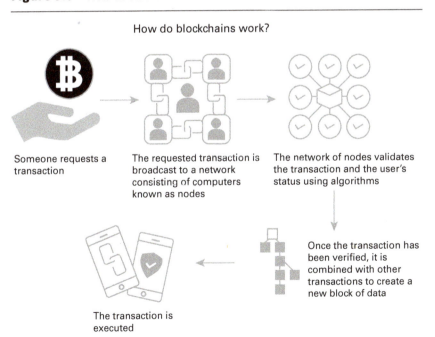

How do blockchains work?

Someone requests a transaction

The requested transaction is broadcast to a network consisting of computers known as nodes

The network of nodes validates the transaction and the user's status using algorithms

Once the transaction has been verified, it is combined with other transactions to create a new block of data

The transaction is executed

Authenticated means signed by a unique cryptographic key. As all transactions are authenticated in this way it is possible to view the state and status of any and all transactions at any point.

Any attempt to modify or change an existing transaction recorded on the blockchain would require a large number of the machines involved in authenticating the specific transactions to agree to do so. However, to maintain the integrity of the blockchain after the transaction has been modified, they would then have to repeat that process on every subsequent block in the chain before any new blocks are added. Given that the machines involved in verification are not under the control of a single authority (they operate by consensus remember) and that new transactions are being added to the blockchain continuously, it becomes an almost impossible task to change history.

To give this point some context, imagine an inventory management capability that only held data and information that was always a correct reflection of the real world, without duplications, erroneous or falsified information. Blockchain provides the capability to do this, not only for inventory but also for many other aspects of logistics operations.

Assuring supply chain integrity

Supply chains are constantly evolving and changing in response to the massive shifts in manufacturing and fulfilment. As e-commerce growth has accelerated and extended into numerous sectors, conventional supply chain structures are struggling to adapt. More significantly, the information systems supporting them cannot cope. Data remains in silos in a digital environment, and there is no real incentive to share it.

This results in disconnects in the information flows and missing pieces of data. In concert with this, huge volumes of data generated by mobile devices and sensors attached to inventory and assets as they move through the chain are ignored. This is because many of the operational systems underpinning the core supply chain operations were never designed to operate in an interconnected world where data was constantly being generated from every direction. This kind of fragmentation makes it difficult to attain whole supply chain visibility.

In many sectors, supply chains are becoming faster, more fragmented and often controlled by companies with whom the supply chain owner has no direct relationship. They are perhaps depending on the suppliers to the suppliers that may be many tiers down the chain. However, their performance has a direct impact on the efficiency of the chain. Blockchain is one way in which these participants can be held accountable for their actions both during and after the fact. This is because irrefutable transparency can be established if the information flow across the supply chain is recorded on a blockchain.

In China food chain transparency is considered a national priority, and there have been several pilot projects testing the appropriateness of such solutions. Many of these have moved into production processes. Consumers can access this information trail at any time by scanning product barcodes in the supermarket or local store and the information trail is revealed – literally a record of what took place on the journey 'from farm to fork'. Case Study 9.1 looks at some of the organizations involved in bringing blockchain initiatives to the food industry.

CASE STUDY 9.1   The food supply chain

Food supply chains are increasingly complex and dynamic, relying on a large number of suppliers, so transparency is essential to guarantee food quality and provenance to all consumers of food products. This is, however, not an easy task. In fact, it has become almost impossible for food producers and retailers to guarantee the provenance of their products. Indeed, according to the Lockton Food and Beverage 2017 Report (Lockton, 2018), 32 per cent of supply chain food executives stated they cannot vouch for authenticity of ingredients they put into end products.

Given these problems, it comes as no surprise that several blockchain initiatives have already been established in the sector:

- IBM and Walmart launched blockchain food safety alliance in China with JD.com. Ten food suppliers and retailers – Dole, Driscoll's, Golden State Foods, Kroger, McCormick and Company, McLane Company, Nestlé, Tyson Foods, Unilever and Walmart – signalled their intention to collaborate.

- Provenance tracks the origin and authenticity of products from origin to sale using the blockchain platforms of Etherium and Bitcoin. Currently working on fresh food trials with various retailers.

- OriginTrail developed the first middleware protocol based on blockchain that is purpose built for data exchange between organizations along the supply chain. The company started collaborating with scientific laboratories focused on verifying the integrity of food supply chains by analysing samples from batches of food using modern analytical and scientific technologies.

This access to the data generated at each stage in the supply chain process can reduce costs and provide a very rapid response to any problems that occur. Precise identification characterizes the value of transparency that blockchain can bring. This capability is usually only available through advanced track and trace systems, although these systems often only operate within the operational envelope of logistics services providers. They are frequently challenged when custody of shipments or inventory is passed across to another supply chain partner, who may only be transferring shipment IDs rather than a whole suite of additional information that provides vital context.

An appropriate blockchain-based solution can reveal all of the relevant information captured at every stage across the chain, irrespective of the parties involved and the myriad different systems each participant may be using. Indeed, it can be 'the single version of the truth' that supply chain managers have been seeking for decades.

Of course, there is the fundamental question of trust at the heart of any information-sharing exercise. This is particularly contentious where competitors contribute to the same supply chains or procure inventory from the same suppliers. Decentralized networks act as a neutral platform that incentivizes data exchanges while using cryptography to keep data both secure and accessible only by the parties authorized to do so.

Case Study 9.2 looks at how organizations are collaborating and implementing blockchain technology.

CASE STUDY 9.2   Examples of blockchain implementation

GS1 pilot project in the pallet network

In April 2018, GS1 Germany announced the launch of a large-scale blockchain pilot project in the logistics sector. A group of leading companies would test whether and how blockchain technology could be used to manage the exchange of Euro pallets in a digital, transparent and efficient manner. Participating in the initiative on the retail side are dm-drogerie markt, Kaufland, Lekkerland and MARKANT. Beiersdorf, Dole Europe, Dr. Oetker, Gärtnerei Ulenburg, Ringoplast and the Wernsing Food Family are involved on the manufacturing side. Key participants from the logistics sector include Container Centralen, Deutsche Bahn, the European Pallet Association e.V. (EPAL), PAKi Logistics and the Nagel-Group.

A.P. Moller–Maersk and IBM joint venture

A.P. Moller–Maersk and IBM have announced a joint venture to provide more efficient and secure methods for conducting global trade using blockchain technology. The aim of the new company will be to offer a jointly developed global trade digitization platform built on open standards and designed for use by the entire global shipping ecosystem.

The new company initially plans to commercialize two core capabilities aimed at digitizing the global supply chain from end to end. A shipping information pipeline will enable all actors involved in managing a supply chain to securely and seamlessly exchange information about shipment events in real time. The other core capability is paperless trade.

This will digitize and automate paperwork filings by enabling end-users to securely submit, validate and approve documents across organizational boundaries, ultimately helping to reduce the time and cost for clearance and cargo movement.

Unilever and Sainsbury's in blockchain trial

Unilever and Sainsbury's announced the launch of a trial to test whether blockchain technology can help unlock financial incentives that improve transparency and sustainability in supply chains. They are part of a group that also includes technology developers Provenance, Landmapp, FOCAFET Foundation and Halotrade as well as the Department for International Development, Sappi, Barclays, BNP Paribas and Standard Chartered. The year-long project will trial the concept by using a shared data system for tea farmers in Malawi that supply Unilever and Sainsbury's. The same system will also track the materials produced for the tea's packaging.

DHL trials blockchain in pharma supply chain to cut out counterfeit drugs

DHL is trialling blockchain technologies to try to address the distribution of counterfeit drugs in the pharmaceutical industry. The project should enable DHL to track the pharma supply chain, from the point of origin (for example, the factory where the drugs are produced), right through to the consumer, preventing the drugs from being tampered with en route. Using blockchain should also help eliminate errors in the processing of the freight, ensuring supply data is as accurate as possible. It uses a system of serialization across six territories, with the ledger available to share with stakeholders, which could be the manufacturer, originating warehouse, distributor, pharmacy, hospital or doctor's surgery and can process more than 7 billion unique serial numbers and 1,500 transactions per second (ITPRO, 2018).

Successful blockchain trial concludes in Singapore

Following the signing of the MOU in 2017, Pacific International Lines (PIL), terminal operator PSA International (PSA) and IBM worked on a Proof of Concept exercise, built on IBM Blockchain Platform. The exercise tested a blockchain-based supply chain platform to track and trace cargo movement from Chongqing to Singapore via the Southern Transport Corridor. Core objectives of the trial included real-time track and trace, transparent and trustworthy execution of multimodal logistics capacity booking, regulatory-compliant execution of the multimodal logistics capacity booking processes and permission access control for ecosystem participants. The trial has been deemed a success by the operating partners (Port Technology, 2018).

Developing trust

Trust is the glue that binds commercial relationships together. Across all manner of supply chains trust is enforced and assumed by a series of contracts and legislative convention. These trusted relationships and arrangements have been established over long periods of time and have been successful in providing a mechanism for compensation and dispute resolution. However, due to the fragmented nature of many of today's supply chains, and the velocity at which they operate, a new kind of trust model would be helpful.

Existing trust models are almost always constructed around a third party acting as the reference point. For example, a bank guaranteeing the transfer of funds between parties or foreign exchange markets using brokers to manage the transaction flows between buyer and seller. In these cases, the third party is required to validate and confirm the transactions. This has generally worked very well, but they also have drawbacks in terms of efficiencies and sometimes cost.

Blockchain protocols remove the requirement for a single third party to sit between all of the participants in a transaction chain. Therefore, in a commercial environment where there are numerous participants who need to establish relationships and transfer funds, often for the first time in a very compressed timeframe, blockchain can provide a trust mechanism to do this.

It does this through a consensus model that distributes trust across a network, using mathematics and cryptography to enforce the trusted environment guaranteed by the consensus of all of the participants. In effect, it is replacing the single intermediary/arbitrator that usually validates any transactions with a series of consensus rules. In short, the network provides the consensus.

One of the other factors of this model is that the identity of the party contributing data and information onto the blockchain is recorded. Thus, it is impossible to assert that, 'it wasn't me who did this' when assigning responsibility.

The blockchain trust model in many respects is the biggest innovation with this technology, as it is redefining what trust means and how it can work at scale across digital services.

In interviews conducted for a study for TI (2018), there was a consensus from all of the interviewees that blockchain will be able to resolve trust fears along the supply chain. According to IBM, 'the absence of a single controlling organization will encourage more participation and disputes will be minimized as the truth is distributed across the network'.

There are some good examples of pilots in the shipping industry (see earlier) exploring how blockchain-based platforms can reduce the number of documents and paper-based exchanges that take place. By streamlining many of the processes, there are efficiency gains and cost reductions that can be realized.

While the use of the technology can help reduce the number of paper-based exchanges along the supply chain, it is unlikely that the blockchain will make these processes completely disappear. While these manual processes are likely to persist, organizations might also be motivated to digitize their processes in order to monetize their data.

Blockchains and false data

The various parties that participate in the blockchain need to record their transactions. For instance, as soon as a carrier delivers a shipment to the warehouse, details about the shipment are recorded on the blockchain. Upon receiving the shipment at the warehouse, the warehouse recipient should record the same information. Neither of these parties can see what the other party has reported – it is the computers that verify that the information they have provided is identical. This is, in fact, one of the key aspects where block-chain can transform the supply chain – it allows supply chain stakeholders to identify any issues that may arise in the chain as everyone can see what is happening at all times. Overall, the more nodes, the harder it is to put false information onto the blockchain.

Moreover, the more automated the processes are, the more difficult it is to tamper with the data. By digitizing the supply chain processes, the relevant information is captured directly from sensors (eg sensors placed on trucks, temperature sensors, etc) and entered onto the blockchain. If a process involves lots of systems generating or sharing data, and that data originates from an established system, it is likely to be viable and trustworthy. According to Mark Parsons, former DHL Senior Executive and Supply Chain Innovator:

> False data usually occurs when plain text is used as the data point. While plain text is necessary, it should be used to augment data generated by a machine. The GS1 barcodes are generally found on most consumer products and there you have a very established dataset that can be trusted if used as the basis for correctly identifying products. So, if you accidentally describe a tin of beans as a can of hairspray in a text field and the barcode says beans, it is pretty clear what should be trusted. (Ti Ltd, 2018)

The more data that is captured from these kinds of systems, the better, as it should result in very accurate information. The 'farm to fork' food supply chain is an example.[1] Within that platform, there are so many checks involved and automated systems measuring the processes, that any attempts to insert false data would be very difficult. Similar rigour should spread to other supply chains as automation is increased across manufacturing and order processes.

Blockchain and smart contracts

One of the other aspects of blockchain technology is its ability to be used to define so-called 'smart contracts'. These are agreements or contracts that have embedded business rules that can exist and operate independently of any centralized control. They can act as the system of record confirming ownership, operational lifecycle and any related stores of value.

The principle behind them is that they are essentially 'self-executing' in that they are defined similarly to a computer application (or app). This means they are stored on the system and execute according to the various rules that are embedded within them. Because they are stored on a blockchain, it is very difficult (if not impossible) to tamper or subvert the transactions related to the contract.

One example of their use might be the registration of an asset identified by a smart contract. Depending on how the contract is defined, the contract will record how the asset is used and who rents it, and it can also deduct and store small amounts of value from each transaction. This provides the means to cover costs of repair or provide a return for the ultimate owners of the asset. Due to the decentralized nature of the smart contract, it is not 'owned' by any one party; its related information only exists on the blockchain.

In this regard and as an example, blockchain-based smart contracts might control fleets of autonomous delivery vehicles that are available for use in urban areas by anyone. They could be rented, operated and funded independently of any company, available on demand as a general resource. This approach echoes the rise of cloud computing environments that provide a general platform that can be rented and used as required.

Blockchain problems

While blockchain can certainly add value, every technology has its limitations, and such is the case with blockchain at the moment.

Latency and scalability

All blockchain solutions have scalability problems and limited transactional input. Latency refers to the time it takes for transactions to be confirmed on the blockchain (ie the creation of the blocks of data and their subsequent confirmation and verification in the blockchain). In 2018 this was around 10 to 15 seconds, albeit very variable depending on what was being done. The key point is that unlike conventional transaction processing systems used for credit cards and banking, adding records to a blockchain is more analogous to an airline reservation and other booking systems that commit orders to a database and may take several seconds. What is highly likely is that the speed of these systems will improve as technology advances.

Cost and energy usage

Presently, a huge amount of processing power is required to verify blockchains. This is a significant cost and explains why many of the large server farms that process these transactions do so in areas where energy is cheap and ambient air temperatures are as cool as possible, eg Iceland, Scandinavia, Northern Canada, Siberia, etc.

Lack of regulation

As with all emerging technologies, legislation is still very much a grey area in relation to blockchain. Some legal frameworks are emerging (eg Slovenia is seen as a pioneer in this area recording contracts subject to EU laws), but it will be some time before the situation is clear.

This implies that dispute resolution will be an issue for some time. This is not a reason to do nothing, but it is a reason to proceed with caution before any significant investments are made. As a reference point, exactly the same situation applies to autonomous/driverless vehicles and drone operations. Projects are still happening, but their legislative boundaries are constantly evolving.

Data quality

Ensuring data quality (ie the ability to capture the data as close to the source as possible and ensuring its accuracy) is a big challenge. Organizations and supply chain managers will need to undertake more audits of data quality, which is essential for many of the merging systems and technologies to work effectively. If random quality checks can be carried out on data across the supply chain at regular intervals, it should be possible to avoid the issue of false data corrupting trust in the information.

Lack of knowledge

As with all nascent technologies, related knowledge is confined to the early adopters. This situation will improve as the number of pilot projects continues to grow.

Fortunately, the developer communities are far more collaborative these days, and many of the key developments are 'open sourced' and shared across the community. This is very similar to the way the internet protocols and the world wide web spread across the globe rather than being under the control of a proprietary corporate regime. Of course, how organizations seek to exploit the technology for their own benefit may remain confidential, but the underlying technology will be publicly available.

According to a major logistics provider, in addition to the lack of knowledge, cultural awareness is another key determinant of blockchain adoption:

> When we can clearly articulate to our customers what the value proposition of blockchain is then the adoption is going much faster. So, ultimately, when companies will be able to quantify the value of the technology they will come onboard much faster. Time is another factor. Businesses are working on a number of initiatives to drive value in and deal with new technologies. Blockchain is just one of the initiatives on the portfolio, so the wider acceptance and implementation of the technology will take a little time, just like IoT is taking a little time. (TI, 2018)

Due to the points raised previously, it would be wise to proceed with caution and avoid making any significant 'bets' on the technology until smaller pilot projects have validated any assumptions. As more pilot projects take place using this technology confidence will grow and lessons will be learned.

Blockchain and General Data Protection Regulation (GDPR)

This is a conundrum at the moment and is a clear example of where well-intentioned regulation is challenged by technology that continues to advance/improve faster than legislation. One of the key elements of the GDPR is the 'right to be forgotten'. This means that personal data can be erased and prior copies cannot be disseminated or processed.

From a technical point of view, the design of a blockchain ensures it is immutable and cannot be changed. Therefore, due to the design of the technology it would be in breach of the GDPR, eg in relation to personal data.

Outlook

As blockchain and other technologies are adopted by organizations across the supply chain industry, their capabilities to streamline and accelerate information flows are hard to ignore. The general acceptance of a neutral third-party technology platform that is available to anyone, recording inventory, order and shipment transactions, will be the point of transformation. Any platform such as this that is not controlled by a single commercial entity and provides blockchain-based transaction records that are immune to tampering may very well lead to the restructuring of the industry.

Moving forward, while the use cases of blockchain along the supply chain will be plentiful, the most promising application of the technology would be the food, perishables and pharmaceutical sectors. Overall, the most valuable use cases of blockchain are likely to be in sectors that are prone to risks of counterfeiting.

Summary

The blockchain is a permanent digital record (or ledger) of transactions that is stored across a distributed or decentralized network of computers. This guarantees that transactions cannot be modified once confirmed in the blockchain unless every computer (node), or a majority of them in the network, all agree to do so at the same time.

Blockchain is not a silver bullet for any and all problems found with supply chain technology. It does have great potential to resolve some practical problems that have been around for years, eg supply chain visibility.

Blockchain provides:

- total transparency;
- immutability and transactional integrity across the supply chain;
- scalability – reliable and verifiable inclusivity from almost any number of participants in any location;
- the potential to dramatically reduce the cost of operations.

There has been an increasing interest in the technology, and various claims have been made regarding its potential for transforming businesses and their trading partnerships.

In many cases at present it may make no sense to implement blockchain technology, for example applications built around a centralized database and accessed by specific users. But where many companies need to share data between themselves, their suppliers, partners, customers and competitors, the most obvious being supply chain visibility, blockchain is an exciting option.

It should also be kept in mind that blockchain technology is still evolving and has a number of challenges ahead of it, not least performance. But this is the same for all technologies that emerge. The successful ones improve, adapt and evolve so long as they provide utility and value. Blockchain is at a very early stage in its evolution and as a reference point, how many people imagined what the internet would become when Tim Berners-Lee launched the world wide web from a server in his office in 1991?

Bibliography

ITPRO [accessed 23 July 2018] DHL Trials Blockchain in Pharma Supply Chain to Cut Out Counterfeit Drugs [Online] www.itpro.co.uk/Blockchain/30748/dhl-trials-Blockchain-in-pharma-supply-chain-to-cut-out-counterfeit-drugs

Lockton [accessed 18 February 2018] Lockton Food and Beverage 2017 Report [Online] file:///C:/Users/jmannersbell/Downloads/01253-foodbeveragereport-brochure_final.pdf

Port Technology [accessed 26 February 2018] Successful Blockchain Trial Concludes in Singapore [Online] www.porttechnology.org/news/successful_Blockchain_trial_concludes_in_singapore

Tanner, M [accessed 28 August 2018] Why China Will Drive Blockchain and Four Related Myths, *Forbes* [Online] www.forbes.com/sites/tannermark/2018/08/01/blockchain-china-misunderstandings/#a65d29213c85

Ti Ltd [accessed 28 August 2018] Why is Blockchain a Game Changer for Supply Chain Management? *Transport Intelligence Ltd* [Online] www.ti-insight.com/product/why-is-Blockchain-a-game-changer-for-supply-chain-management/

Note

1 The 'farm to fork' concept involves the regulation of every stage of the supply chain, and in the United States it is administered by Food and Drug Administration through legislation.

Digital logistics marketplaces   10

**THIS CHAPTER WILL FAMILIARIZE
THE READER WITH:**

- how levels of inefficiency in the road freight market have led to the development of new digital marketplaces;
- the different types of road freight platforms;
- the importance of scale to platforms and charging mechanisms;
- leading freight marketplace start-ups in Europe, North America and Asia;
- how 'shared economy' business models can benefit the warehouse sector;
- the benefits and disadvantages of 'on-demand' warehousing;
- two leading digital warehouse platforms.

Digital road freight platforms

As has been outlined in Chapter 2, disruption can occur in a sector where the incumbent players are failing to develop solutions to address industry inefficiency. In the road freight sector 'inefficiency' can be measured in terms of underutilized capacity, ie empty or part loaded running, although the industry also faces many other challenges including:

- levels of fragmentation;
- lack of collaboration between carriers;
- commoditization of products;
- lack of insight into prices and capacity;
- often low quality services;

- lack of investment in technology;
- manual processes;
- paper documentation;
- lack of real-time tracking.

In Europe and Asia, the problems are exacerbated by the numerous individual country markets that exist with a diverse range of regulations, cultures and languages to overcome. This is even the case on an intra-country basis in markets such as India and China, where efforts to integrate local, city and regional markets are ongoing.

Numerous new technology platforms have entered the road freight/trucking market, each promising to address many of the problems outlined here. However, their fundamental aim is to better match supply with demand, leading to fuller trucks for carriers and better rates for shippers. The merit of this premise and an analysis of the sector as a whole is discussed in more detail in this chapter.

Types of digital freight marketplaces

The taxonomy of the sector can be outlined as follows:

1 'E-forwarders', 'digital' or 'virtual forwarders' actively intermediate the process and take on execution and pricing risk. These can be categorized as:

  a 'Captives': DHL's Saloodo!; Drive4Schenker/Schenkereasy; UPS's Coyote.

  b 'Non-captives' or independents:

   i Europe: eg Instafreight, Freighthub, Transporteca, Loadfox, Convargo, Cargonexx, Colo21, Frachtraum, Ontruck;

   ii United States: eg UberFreight, FreightOS, FlexPort, Ontruck, Convoy, CargoMatic, Transfix, TruckerPath, 10-4 Systems, FreightGuru, Loadsmart;

   iii Asia: eg Blackbuck (India), Huochebang (recently merged with Yunmanman) (China).

2 'Load Boards' or 'marketplaces' provide an exchange between shippers and carriers but do not take responsibility for the successful execution of the transaction, eg TimoCom, Cargoclix, DAT, Truckstop.com. Some focus on 'shipper to carrier' relationships, helping locate available capacity in the market, for instance on specific routes. Others help carriers

collaborate among themselves ('carrier to carrier'). LoadFox and Teleroute are examples of the latter. Many of these exchanges have been around for decades and are now developing additional services such as 'digital warehousing'.

3 Tender platforms provide for longer-term relationships between carrier and shipper. These include: Transporeon (TIContract), Logistitrade, Tendereasy, TNX Logistics and Jaggaer (acquired Bravosolution in 2017 – a more general 'spend management' platform). In addition, they are able to provide value-added solutions, helping balance carriers' networks.

4 Data connectors/aggregators provide standardized connections between many market participants for purposes of pricing, freight allocation, visibility and/or payments: FourKites, project44, Sixfold, Transporeon, Xeneta.

5 Traditional freight forwarders, such as Kuehne+Nagel, are also targeting this market in the customer portal/quoting engine area.

'Quality' is seen as an important distinction between e-forwarders and freight exchanges. An argument employed by the former is that trust is essential to the process and that a forwarder is critical to ensuring the successful completion of the transaction.

In other words, 'relationship' is essential to the offering of the forwarder both in terms of customers and carriers. Customers develop trust with companies and individuals who hold responsibility should anything go wrong. Relationships are important for carriers too. They will trust a forwarder and build long-term partnerships to ensure consistent volumes at sustainable prices in return for a commitment to quality.

Although load-matching platforms may check the credentials of the carriers using their platforms ('curated'), ultimately the risk is borne by the shipper who may or may not have had any prior contact with the carrier.

As can be seen from the cross-section of e-forwarders and freight exchanges highlighted here, there are many options available for both shippers and carriers. The categorization above differentiates the players in terms of their varying business models. However, many platforms also differentiate themselves in the following ways:

- Geography. As discussed in more detail later, Germany is the biggest road freight market in Europe, and this has spawned the development of several large exchanges that have then expanded into other countries across Europe.

- International/national/local volumes. Whereas some platforms have specialized in cross-border movements (eg FreightEx – now Coyote), others are targeting local freight needs. An example of the latter is Ontruck, which focuses on more localized movements of pallets.

- Commodities. Transporeon has created a community of carriers and shippers specializing in the bulk sector, especially steel.

Charging models

A subscription model is often used by the marketplaces to generate revenue. For example, although Euro Freight Exchange offers users the opportunity to post cargos or trucks on its exchange for free, they charge for more value-adding services, such as adding regular routes, advertising or use of their transport management system. Premium membership is only €29 a month, indicating that freight exchanges need to be very competitive to acquire both loads and trucks for their platforms.

E-forwarders employ a more traditional form of revenue generation: buying and selling capacity via their platforms and retaining a margin. They can also perform many of the usual value-adding freight forwarding tasks such as document origination. Although it may be considered that digitization would remove the necessity for human interaction, this is not necessarily the case. An attribute of some of the successful platforms involves a strong sales process and account management team. This helps to keep the rates they charge higher than the market average while ensuring long-term partnerships with the carriers at lower input costs.

Digital marketplaces and brokerage

One of the big issues for many road freight marketplaces is that there is little to differentiate them from each other. Traditional 'freight exchanges' have undertaken load matching for some time and dominate the market in terms of scale. E-forwarders offer a different type of service, maintaining responsibility for the customer relationship, but they lack the presence of the marketplaces.

Whether e-forwarder or marketplace, in order to be successful, these businesses need to maintain both an effective service and a large supply of capacity (carriers). However, as competition commoditizes the basic load-matching service they provide, shippers risk receiving low quality service and carriers risk attaining low rates – it can become a race to the bottom based on price.

'Network effects', or demand side economies of scale, are critical to success in these platforms. These occur when a service becomes more valuable to its users as more people adopt it, creating barriers to entry for rivals and barriers to exit for users. Eventually, this can allow a single firm to dominate the market.

The successful companies building on the marketplace concept will integrate a range of technologies (including mobile) for their customers, not just a technological layer. Moreover, they will establish a strategic lock-in with both carriers and shippers by effectively serving the needs of both parties. While the potential advantages of a digital brokerage service are relatively clear to shippers (lower costs, flexible capacity, assets on-demand), many companies operating in this field have failed to articulate clear benefits to carriers, which has weakened their offering (see Case Study 2.1 'Palleter' in Chapter 2).

In this 'chicken or egg' dilemma, other businesses have established scale by focusing on providing useful services to carriers first, before subsequently introducing brokerage operations for shippers. Notably, the US start-up Trucker Path has gained traction among owner-operators by providing them with parking, navigation and financing services. Similar methods have been applied by companies in India and China.

Leading digital marketplace start-ups

Investment has poured into the sector since the mid-2010s. According to consultancy BCG (2018), venture capital funds invested $3.3 billion in digital logistics start-ups between 2012 and 2017 of which, it says, a significant proportion went to road freight marketplaces.

In Europe the market has come to be dominated by German platforms although it is noticeable across the region as a whole that there have been relatively low levels of funding compared to similar companies operating in the United States and Asia.

The large proportion of German start-ups operating in the road freight brokerage space is largely a product of the country's market size. Germany possesses the largest road freight market in Europe by some distance (particularly for international freight), and, as such, this overall scale makes it attractive. This is also evidenced by the market share of the top German firms operating in the European market (eg DHL, DB Schenker, Kuehne + Nagel, Rhenus, Dachser).

But why the funding disparity compared with other regions? With the exception of Ontruck, which raised $25m in 2018, no other company has attracted 8-figure sums from investors. This is in stark contrast to tech-based road freight companies in China, India and the United States (Figure 10.1).

Figure 10.1 Top 10 trucking start-ups by investment

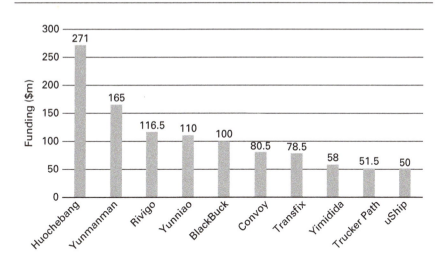

There are several reasons why this is the case. First, the market opportunity for a road freight platform start-up company in India, China or the United States is much greater than Europe. While the overall EU market as a bloc is the largest in the world, each of the European companies is restricted as a result of variations in language, legislation and culture, as mentioned earlier. This is not a complete block to expansion to adjacent countries, but it does make it more difficult for development.

Moreover, the growth opportunity in Europe is nowhere near as great as it is in India and China. In these nascent markets, large-scale traditional trucking operators have not been able to develop to the same extent as in the United States and Europe. Consequently, there are more opportunities for technology-based innovators to address weak service provision and a hyper-fragmented supply side.

In China, the two largest platforms agreed to merge in late 2017. Huochebang (also known as Truck Alliance) and Yunmanman have created an enterprise (Manbang Group) valued at $2 billion. The former has backing in part from Tencent Holdings Ltd, while the latter counted Alibaba's Jack Ma as an investor through his holding in Yunfeng Capital. With an estimated 8.8 million truck drivers and close to 2 million on the combined platforms, the company is investing heavily in AI to effectively deal with data flows. As with the US platform Truckerpath (see later), load matching is just one of the services offered. They both also sell carriers toll cards, fuel, tyres as well as second-hand vehicles. Manbang Group also has plans to invest in autonomous and alternatively powered trucks, following in the footsteps of Uber.

Competition between major European logistics companies

An important development for Europe's digital freight marketplaces has been the response of incumbent road freight companies. Specifically, three leading firms have attempted to protect themselves from the threat of disruption by buying into the space. They are:

- UPS (acquired FreightEx in January 2017);
- DHL (acquired Cillox in 2016);
- DB Schenker (invested in uShip during February 2017).

Each of these companies has taken a slightly different approach to entering the digital road freight brokerage market.

UPS

UPS does not have an asset-heavy road freight business in Europe analogous to UPS Freight in North America. The company has scaled up its European express operations significantly over time and is also recognized throughout the continent for its contract logistics activities, but it has always lacked a trucking business.

This changed following the company's 2015 takeover of Coyote Logistics. Set up in 2006, Coyote is one of a previous generation of digital brokerage firms in the road freight space and had grown steadily over time through an approach that combined traditional brokerage with proprietary web-based software to match freight with available capacity. By 2015, the company was growing rapidly, and UPS acquired it following three years in which it had contracted with the company for extra capacity during demand peaks.

With Coyote delivering strong growth within the UPS Supply Chain and Freight division, the company decided to replicate the model in Europe by acquiring a similar company, FreightEx, and establishing consistent technology and practices across both continents. UPS is currently in the process of integrating the two companies and installing unified systems. The takeover of FreightEx allows UPS to expand into the European road freight market without committing to the development of an expensive, asset-based network of operations.

DHL

In contrast to UPS, DHL Freight is well established as the second largest player in the European road freight market. The company has diversified its operations into a number of differentiated solutions, including its premium 24- and 48-hour Eurapid service.

As such, DHL did not need to buy an established brokerage company to establish itself in the market. Instead, the company acquired an early stage start-up, Cillox, in order to gain access to its technology and is in the process of scaling it up. Cillox was later rebranded to Saloodo! and has established a presence in Germany and the UK.

The technology behind Saloodo! was developed as a cloud-based application designed for use on various devices. The application matches shipments with capacity on-demand, manages documentation, payments and provides route information to drivers. The system is available in 13 languages with Portugal and Spain the two most recent markets in which it has been rolled out.

Saloodo! differs from the integrated approach of UPS/FreightEx in that it operates solely as a software platform, with no human intermediary overseeing the carriers. Saloodo! does offer DHL Freight shipment options as an alternative service when its platform cannot provide enough capacity on demand, but aside from this, the company offers no direct point of contact to oversee transportation operations.

DB Schenker

DB Schenker is the largest road freight operator in Europe, and as with DHL, is investing in the technology as a risk mitigation strategy, rather than in an effort to spearhead growth. Where the two companies differ is in their oversight of the respective digital brokerage operations.

DB Schenker has elected to take a hands-off approach. In February 2017, the company announced a $25m investment in the US freight matching platform uShip, having negotiated an exclusive licensing deal for the company's technology within Europe during 2016. uShip was established in 2003 and, as with FreightEx, this longevity demonstrates the viability of the business.

In addition to its capacity matching function, uShip provides payments and documentation management, insurance, messaging and tracking within its application. By incorporating the company's technology into its operations, DB Schenker will have access to capacity on-demand during peak periods, complementing its core assets.

Case Study 10.1 takes a look at Trucker Path, a US company offering crowd-sourced information together with factoring services to truckers.

CASE STUDY 10.1   Trucker Path

Trucker Path offers crowd-sourced guidance to truck drivers; this includes the nearest truck stop, weigh stations, hotels, diesel fuel and freight shipments.

Freight shipments are managed through a marketplace system for regional or long-haul business, where brokers submit shipments along with deadlines, destinations and other requirements, with parking and navigation information to long-haul truckers in the United States.

The company initially launched as a free information service app, before subsequently adding the freight marketplace. As such, the business had cultivated a community of users and has built out its marketplace as an additional service within a wider ecosystem.

Furthermore, Trucker Path has been successful in adding a payments service 'InstaPay'. This non-recourse factoring arrangement pays carriers immediately, issuing a one-time flat rate with no hidden fees, and addresses a major pain point among carriers who often wait 30 to 60 days before receiving payment.

In total, Trucker Path claims to serve 550,000 long-haul truckers in the United States, out of a total of roughly 1.6 million. The company's marketplace business, 'Truckloads', serves substantially less (around 100,000 with 3 million monthly load postings), but by gaining traction among the population of long-haul drivers in the United States, the company has established a defensible position.

Digitizing the warehousing sector

It is not only the transport sector that has the potential to be disrupted by the sharing economy. New companies are entering the warehouse sector with the same aim: allowing companies to connect with customers to leverage previously underutilized space.

Traditional warehousing market

In terms of LSP services, warehousing and distribution have long been characterized by a split between 'dedicated' contracts (where the customer pays for the costs of an entire warehouse operation) and 'shared'. In the latter instance, a proportion of racking is often given over to a customer inside a warehouse that caters for multiple other customers. This means that the costs are spread and are likely to be variable, depending on usage.

Although shared warehousing offers more flexibility than dedicated operations, it still will be subject to a contract, often of several years. There will often be minimum volume levels, which provide protection to the logistics operator but reduce customer flexibility. As such it could be described as long term and static.

Of course, many manufacturers, retailers and warehouse users choose to retain their logistics operations inhouse. This means that they will take on the responsibility for the warehouse lease, locking them into an agreement with a property company lasting much longer than the usual three- to five-year contract length with an LSP.

The structure of the property market is very traditional: landlords, developers and estate agents all have vested interests in agreeing long-term deals. In addition to this there has been very little visibility of available warehousing let alone visibility of availability of space within the warehouse.

A lack of a transactional market and the prevalence of ad hoc fees make comparison between warehouse operations difficult and pricing structures opaque. Obviously, it is in the interests of the LSPs involved in the process to limit the commoditization of the business, as high levels of competition already exist. This means that they will do everything they can to prevent unbundling of transport and warehousing services, which they describe as cherry-picking.

On-demand warehousing

The fundamental premise of on-demand warehousing is that what is already occupied can be utilized much more intensively. Much warehousing is not fully used: not only is the unutilized space not visible to other customers but, in many cases, there is no traditional method of making it accessible.

On-demand companies offer:

- search facility for suitable warehouse capacity;
- scalable warehousing solutions;
- efficiency of transaction;
- legally backed agreements;
- quality control/compliance accreditation.

Unlike a room-letting service such as Airbnb, the process offered by on-demand warehousing companies is not 'real time' as it involves an electronic tendering process. However, it is much faster than traditional transactions, perhaps taking a couple of weeks rather than several months. It also involves services as well as commoditized storage, as the product still requires put-away and picking among others.

Several companies have emerged offering to provide warehousing on-demand, by leveraging cloud computing to provide quick and flexible service solutions. Specifically marketed towards fast-growing businesses and SMEs with dynamic requirements, these companies leverage empty space in existing warehouses as well as providing integration of order management and inventory management tools as a bundle.

The enabler for such solutions is Software-as-a-Service (SaaS), a variant of cloud computing that enables companies to access software remotely through an internet connection rather than by locally installing the relevant systems. This also means that it is much easier to connect distinct software functions together; for instance, to connect a cloud-based warehouse management system (WMS) to a cloud-based transportation management system (TMS), the integration only needs to be achieved once and can be done remotely. Doing so with locally installed software requires the manual integration of operations throughout a company's entire network, which is expensive and time consuming.

The flexibility provided by software means that companies now have the option to fulfil orders from a single 'virtual warehouse', while their physical inventory is spread out over several facilities. Operations like this, once impossible, are proliferating, and the implications for industrial warehousing are a world in which space is used far more efficiently.

Meeting e-commerce needs

A common problem for growing e-retailers is the need to expand fulfilment to accommodate demand. Not only can this process be quite difficult, but in markets with large geographic scale, it can also cause considerable expense. Companies are often faced with the choice of charging customers for shipping or subsidizing shipping costs. A move towards a network of regional distribution facilities is often constrained due to the scale of initial investment and the commitment to long-term leases.

By adopting a more flexible warehousing approach, retailers can afford to test markets. Moreover, in a volatile environment, third-party logistics could theoretically balance fixed and flexible warehousing capacity in the same way that they balance their transportation fleet.

This represents an alternative to the common approach applied currently, whereby many retailers adapting to the omnichannel environment contract out their expanding need for e-fulfilment to LSPs. These logistics providers then deploy support through large-scale multi-client facilities, until such time as the client chooses to move on; for example, when the scale of their operation necessitates a dedicated facility. It is important to state that this story of expansion is by no means set in stone; both Walmart and Target are aggressively expanding their e-commerce capabilities through intensive investment inhouse.

Dealing with volatility

The modern supply chain is designed to be agile and flexible, dealing effectively with risks such as falling/increasing demand, trade wars, natural disasters or terrorist events. While many parts of the logistics process can be flexed to meet these changing demands, warehousing is often the exception. As discussed earlier, shippers frequently enter into long-term warehousing contracts, often based on inevitably inaccurate forecasts.

It is inconceivable that on-demand warehousing will replace the traditional warehousing market in its entirety. However, what it does offer customers is a way in which peaks and troughs of demand can be better balanced. Instead of buying or leasing enough warehouse capacity to deal with the peak of demand, as has often been the case, customers will be able to provision for what is called a 'baseload' demand and add in capacity to meet seasonal peaks throughout the year. That means that waste in the system is minimized. For those warehouse users with too much capacity, on-demand offers the ability to market the space, providing a revenue-generating opportunity.

Pros and cons of 'on-demand' warehousing

- On-demand warehousing turns a fixed investment into an operational cost, which will improve balance sheet strength.
- Large investments become much smaller and are spread over a longer time.
- It will allow customers to better meet peaks and troughs of demand.
- Warehousing capacity can be selected closer to end-user demand, making it quicker to serve customers.

- Risk is mitigated over many more locations.
- Users can hedge their warehouse needs against volatility.
- There will be a reduction in CO_2 in the supply chain due to distributed warehousing networks.
- Multiple warehouses can be integrated into a nationwide network while retaining a single point of contact.

One industry KPI puts warehouse utilization at around 80 per cent (Opsdog, 2018). This average figure could be viewed in two ways. First, it shows that there is still considerable spare capacity that could be potentially released onto the market. But second, it also suggests that this capacity is not necessarily enough to deal with a peak in demand, for example in the holiday season. Consequently, a warehouse user with an average of 80 per cent utilization may require shared warehousing to deal with overspill. (NB In the United States presently this may be an underestimate. The US economy is so buoyant that vacancy rates are now at only 5 per cent despite considerable speculative capacity having been added in recent years.)

On-demand warehousing could be described as a halfway house between warehouse ownership (or leasing) and outsourcing. However, the concept is not without its weaknesses. Beyond the major contract logistics providers, dedicated e-fulfilment providers (such as Ingram Micro's Shipwire) provide a compelling proposition, offering to exploit their access to global markets through freight forwarding, thus fulfilling cross-border sales that are currently unobtainable through the on-demand approach.

Another confounding factor is control. Although on-demand providers operate their own WMS, which can be integrated into client ERP systems, the actual fulfilment operations within the warehouses are controlled by the seller, not the buyer. This means that whoever owns the warehouse will be fulfilling the buyer's operations, regardless of their specific needs.

Environmental considerations

Better utilization of warehouse space has environmental implications as well as operational. The first is obvious. Building large warehouses has an impact on the local environment in terms of:

- land use;
- water run off;
- energy use;

- greenhouse gas emissions;
- pollution;
- embodied carbon (that emitted during the manufacture of the building materials);
- local environment and communities.

The better utilized a warehouse is, the fewer are required to be built. It is obviously very difficult to quantify the impact that on-demand warehousing could have on utilization, but the World Economic Forum (WEF, 2018) estimates that shared warehouse capacity could benefit society through a reduction in emissions of 1.3 billion metric tonnes.

If the 80 per cent average utilization figure is accepted and, for argument's sake, on-demand warehousing pushed this figure up by 5 percentage points to 85 per cent, this would mean that 350,000 square feet of the estimated 7 million square feet of new warehousing under construction in the UK in mid-2018 would not be required. This, of course, is very simplistic but perhaps provides an indication of the impact of this particular innovation upon the sector.

Second, distributing inventory at warehouse locations around a market has an impact on the transport required to move it to the end-user and hence the carbon emissions. Centralization of inventory has been shown to provide many benefits operationally, but if full visibility of inventory can be maintained while holding stock further downstream, this could potentially have positive environmental and supply chain benefits.

Case Study 10.2 looks at two on-demand warehouse providers – Flexe in the United States and Canada, and Stowga in the UK.

CASE STUDY 10.2   On-demand warehouse providers

Profile: Flexe

Flexe acts as a marketplace for warehousing space, connecting lessees and lessors with cloud-based software, and makes money by charging commission on top of the leasing fees set by the latter. The company's SaaS offering also provides a WMS, inventory management and billing services, which can be accessed and managed by customers through an internet browser.

Flexe operates in the United States and Canada, where its marketplace covers a network of over 550 warehouses. The average Flexe fulfilment customer operates from six to eight locations. The minimum utilization requirements for those looking to access warehousing space are a 30-day lease and at least 50 pallets of goods. However, once qualified, inventory owners have the advantage of a fast and flexible service, including software that was until relatively recently quite expensive to purchase.

The company offers a marketplace for asset-owners to rent out their warehousing for short durations, thus offering an option to companies that are not prepared for the financial investment of a long-term lease. For companies looking to scale up quickly or try out a new product line, on-demand warehousing could provide a useful solution.

Profile: Stowga

Stowga is a start-up B2B marketplace, based in the UK, which enables spare warehousing capacity to be matched with the short-term needs of customers. It has raised £1.8m in funding since its establishment in 2016. The company has more than 4,000 warehouses listed on its platform.

Rather than 'on-demand', Stowga describes its services as warehousing-as-a-service (WaaS). This is perhaps more accurate, as on-demand conveys an immediacy that is not part of the core attributes of this sharing economy innovation. Rather, the short-term and flexible nature is of more importance.

Stowga's management describes its WaaS as allowing customers to more effectively meet the peaks and troughs of demand. It counts UK drinks manufacturer, Nichols, owner of the Vimto brand, among its customers.

Summary

Theoretically, digital platforms have the potential to dramatically disrupt many of the world's least-efficient road freight/trucking markets. However, the extent of this disruption is far from clear. In Europe the opportunity may not be as big as many start-ups believe, and the market has already become crowded. To succeed, platforms will need to focus relentlessly on specific market segments and build targeted communities, integrated and served by exceptional technology and a range of services. China and India would seem to hold greater opportunities. In comparison with the relatively high quality road freight markets in Europe and North America, the industry is plagued by inefficiencies. The giant logistics platforms that have developed see themselves not so much as freight exchanges but as disruptive technology platforms that can transform the entire industry. In contrast, the role of the digital freight platform in Europe and North America will perhaps always be complementary to the dominant incumbent trucking operators.

Although the warehousing industry will never become 'on-demand' in the way that road freight transport may do, there are certainly opportunities to improve efficiencies in the sector. Of course, as with any disruptive technology or business model, there will be winners and losers. As the World Economic Forum (WEF, 2018) states:

> Shared warehouse agreements provide companies (customers of logistics companies) an opportunity to reduce their logistics costs by as much as 12 to 15%. We estimate that companies implementing these agreements could save close to $500 billion in operating costs, but this could have a negative impact to the tune of $35 billion in operating profits for logistics companies.

Bibliography

BCG [accessed 23 August 2018] Why Road Freight Needs to Go Digital – Fast [Online] http:// www.bcg.com/en-gb/publications/2018/why-road-freight-needs-go-digital-fast.aspx

Cushman and Wakefield [accessed 18 August 2018] U.S. Economy Positioned to Perform Well in 2018 [Online] www.cushmanwakefield.com/en/research-and-insight/2018/us-q4-2017-marketbeat

Jones Lang Lasalle [accessed 23 August 2018] JLL's Big Box Logistics [Online] www.jll.co.uk/united-kingdom/en-gb/Research/JLL_Big_Box_Infographic_July_2018.pdf?ab451d06-57e5-4c3a-a249-43ba81b97b89

Opsdog [accessed 18 January 2018] Warehouse Space Utilization [Online] https://opsdog.com/products/average-warehouse-capacity-used

WEF [accessed 23 July 2018] How Can Digital Help Logistics Be More Sharing? [Online] http://reports.weforum.org/digital-transformation/cutting-costs-through-sharing-logistics-assets/

On-demand delivery and crowd-shipping

11

THIS CHAPTER WILL FAMILIARIZE THE READER WITH:

- what is meant by the terms 'on-demand' and 'crowd-shipping';
- how these business models work;
- the economics behind their success and failure;
- the 'gig economy' and potential regulation;
- the opportunities for express parcels companies;
- a case study of GeoPost's acquisition of an on-demand platform;
- future prospects for these innovative models.

On-demand delivery platforms and implications for the last mile

The on-demand delivery sector has grown rapidly over the past few years. Developed as a way of enabling small food outlets and retailers to provide a home delivery service, on-demand providers have tapped into a latent source of consumer demand.

What is on-demand?

Dablanc *et al* (2017) provide the following definition for the on-demand concept: 'Instant delivery services provide on-demand delivery within two hours – by either private individuals, independent contractors, or employees – by connecting consignors, couriers and consignees via a digital platform'.

There are two key elements to this definition:

- On-demand has a timescale attached – in fact a very short timescale of below two hours.
- On-demand is facilitated by a digital platform that matches demand with supply, usually via a smartphone.

On-demand should not be confused with crowd-sourced shipping or 'crowd-shipping', which refers to the type of transport used rather than the service supplied. Crowd-sourced shipping often involves private individuals using their own or public transport to fulfil a delivery. This could be a subsection of the on-demand market, but whereas on-demand is growing quickly, crowd-shipping has yet to take off. This is discussed in more detail later.

On-demand has also been used interchangeably with other terms such as 'gig economy', referring to the use of self-employed contractors working on an ad hoc basis. This also is not strictly accurate as although many platforms' business models require flexible resources to deal with the peaks and troughs of demand, some on-demand retailers are starting to employ delivery agents directly. This is partly due to regulatory issues and pressure from labour organizations, but also due to issues of control and quality.

Instacart in the United States, for example, has recently started to hire many of its contractors as employees, which benefits the company by allowing it to train its workers (the US tax authorities use training as a way of deciding on the status of a worker). Better trained workers improve the customer experience, both in terms of picking goods from stores and the final delivery.

On-demand is perhaps most closely associated with the delivery of meals prepared by restaurants in a local area. However, it is certainly not confined to this sector, with some markets offering on-demand deliveries of:

- groceries;
- fresh food;
- alcohol;
- laundry;
- consumer goods.

Perhaps the most important trend driving the market is the concept of 'instant gratification'. Whether meals, products bought online or fashion items bought at a shop but delivered to buyers' homes, consumers increasingly want immediate access to their purchases. Whether a good thing or not, this is an unalterable part of modern life, which suggests that on-demand will be with us for many years to come.

Moreover, it seems inevitable that the market will continue to grow. Consultants BIA/Kelsey estimate that in the United States only 7 per cent of the addressable market is served (Paine, 2018), which suggests in other, less mature, parts of the world, the opportunities are even bigger. Other estimates suggest that the market for on-demand household services is growing at around 45 per cent a year in the UK, and at around 50 per cent a year throughout the rest of Europe (PwC, 2018).

How does on-demand work?

On-demand platforms do not regard themselves as logistics or delivery companies. Rather they see themselves as a matching service, allowing consumers to connect with retailers or restaurants.

Some, such as Just Eat or Delivery Hero, do not provide delivery capabilities, instead solely providing the software platform over which consumers can place their orders with restaurants. These are then fulfilled by the restaurants themselves. Others, such as Deliveroo, provide the delivery networks to restaurants that otherwise would not be able to offer home delivery. Even so the latter companies do not own assets, using the services of largely self-employed couriers.

The way these companies define themselves is important. In 2018 the European Commission decided that Uber – which regarded itself as a similar platform for personal mobility – was a 'taxi' service provider and should be regulated as such. On-demand platforms may face similar types of regulation in the future, especially if controversy continues over the treatment of sub-contractors.

Another issue that has yet to be fully addressed is the issue of insurance. A normal courier company would provide a range of insurances from public liability to goods-in-transit. Responsibility is potentially unclear in the on-demand chain if the on-demand company is variously regarded as either a restaurant provider, a grocery retailer, a delivery company or, as many would prefer, purely an online platform.

The on-demand business model

In order to attain scale and market leadership, which are essential attributes in the on-demand market, the platforms obviously need to build a strong marketing presence as well as being focused around price. This is only part of the equation, however. In order to retain both customers and couriers, on-demand providers have to achieve a competitive advantage by developing best-in-class functionality involving:

- efficient dispatch of orders to couriers;
- availability of good quality couriers;
- capacity planning;
- integrated relationships with consignors.

One critical question for companies providing on-demand delivery services is whether or not there is a large enough market to support them. In order to make a profit, on-demand businesses need to have a high frequency of orders within an operational area, and if this frequency drops below a certain rate, the unit economics of the service are unworkable.

There are two main underlying causes of this:

- The market was never large enough to support the service in the first place.
- Competition from rival service providers has diluted market share.

So long as competing start-ups possess the funding to expand their business, the latter issue can be addressed by pricing incentives for both couriers and consumers in order to build effective economies of scale. However, this inevitably results in financial losses, forcing start-ups in a competitive market to make tough choices when the money begins to run out.

The economics of an on-demand service provider are reasonably straightforward. Revenue comprises commission charged by the platform to the restaurant (perhaps 25 to 30%) and a delivery fee to the customer (typically around €2.50/£2.50 in Europe and the UK). Costs, on the other hand, derive from the fee paid to the courier (per job or per hour), plus overheads.

Therefore, revenues are driven by the value of the meal ordered, their volume and the delivery fee (if the market allows – 'free delivery' is becoming common). Running costs depend on the utilization rate of the courier, if paid by the hour, although this is not as important if paid by the job. This explains why on-demand companies rely heavily on the 'gig-economy' – the model is far harder to make work if the courier is an employee or a worker paid by the hour. Whether this is sustainable in the long run due to lobbying by unions and governments looking to garner labour taxes is yet to be seen. Of course, couriers have a choice not to work below a certain remuneration and will find better paying on-demand platforms. This will create a vicious cycle – the company will not be able to hire sufficient couriers, leading to longer delivery times and low customer satisfaction. With reducing volumes, more couriers will leave and so it goes on.

According to Adrien Roose (2018), co-founder of TakeEatEasy, an on-demand platform that shut down in 2017, 'Courier utilization is one of the most important metrics in our business. Assuming couriers need to make [a] minimum 15€ / hour not to churn, a low courier utilization (<1.5 deliveries / courier / hour) implies a negative contribution margin'.

Bluntly, if on-demand companies are not able to attract and retain good quality contractors they will quickly go out of business. Pay is crucial to this, but some companies are able to provide benefits such as supplementary insurance.

As the on-demand market consolidates, so does a finite supply of financing, and it becomes harder for even some of the larger providers to find more funding when they are losing market share and money. The demise of TakeEatEasy was blamed by senior management on such a situation when even one of its own investors decided to acquire and fund a better-placed rival.

Consolidation among the existing companies is inevitable, through M&A and bankruptcy. Due to the geographical nature of this market, it is likely that certain companies will dominate in certain countries.

Hong Kong, where Lalamove and GoGoVan are two of the market leaders, has seen the number of competitors shrink since the early 2010s from approximately 300 to just a handful. Commentators believe that, for this market at least, consumers on their own are not able to create a big enough market. There needs to be a business market as well, and these customers are driven by service and reliability rather than cost promotions that can build market share.

These two successful on-demand companies have attracted the most investment. Lalamove has recently been valued at US $1 billion and has raised US $100m with plans for an IPO by 2020. The money will be used to build out its international HQ in Hong Kong and help it reach 200–250 cities across China and South East Asia. GoGoVan says it wants to raise US $200m to allow it to develop operations around the world.

Interestingly, the market is moving so quickly that disruptors can themselves become the disrupted. Amazon, for example, in many markets can be regarded as the incumbent, and vulnerable itself to disruption by on-demand retailers. Instacart in the United States, by employing agents to pick from established bricks and mortar retailers, is able to provide consumers with one-hour deliveries and provide a very broad range of goods. In contrast, Amazon has a vertically integrated model, using national and regional distribution centres, perhaps similar to traditional retailers. Instacart can add an on-demand layer to existing retailers' capabilities, allowing them to participate in this sector and compete against Amazon.

Opportunities for parcels companies

Although on-demand is attracting huge attention from investors, the opportunities for express parcels companies to move into this fast-growing sector would seem limited.

On-demand services rely on a critical mass of users and drivers, but on a localized basis. This means that there are very few synergies to be had between the national, regional or global express parcels companies and on-demand operations that work on a city-by-city basis.

The likes of FedEx, UPS and DHL operate models that rely on the movement of vast volumes of parcels in order to maximize the utilization of national and international network infrastructure rather than the instant collection and delivery of an order within a limited area.

However, that has not stopped one major parcels company, GeoPost, from exploring the sector. The subsidiary of the French post office has acquired outright an on-demand operator, Stuart, in which it originally took a minority shareholding in 2015.

As is indicated in Case Study 11.1, although there will be a certain amount of integration with GeoPost, the operation will remain autonomous.

CASE STUDY 11.1   GeoPost and Stuart

Founded in 2015 by Clément Benoît and Benjamin Chemla, Stuart is a technology platform that connects retailers with a fleet of independent couriers to help business meet the delivery expectations of their end-customers. Following acquisition of a 22% share in 2015, major European parcels operator, GeoPost, subsequently bought the entire company in 2017.

Stuart has built algorithmic dispatch for both on-demand and scheduled jobs and integrated its API with leading multinational retailers across France, the UK and Spain. With 100 employees across technology, data, product, operations and business development, Stuart facilitates thousands of deliveries per day for more than 500 active customers including Carrefour, Franprix, Burger King, The Kooples, Pizza Hut and Cdiscount.

Paul-Marie Chavanne, GeoPost's CEO, stated, 'This decision logically follows our investments in Stuart over the past two years. Stuart completes our delivery service at a local level and embodies the future of express urban delivery, a rapidly expanding strategic activity for us'.

Stuart remains an independent brand and subsidiary in order to ensure the autonomy of its management team and its commitment to technological innovation. However, the company will be co-chaired by the management of Pickup, a start-up specializing in alternative delivery, which GeoPost acquired in 2009. Pickup's leaders will integrate Stuart within GeoPost in order to maximize synergies between the companies, including developing value-generating solutions for the Group's customers.

As well as operational, there are other reasons why other express parcels carriers may not be keen to buy into the market. In some quarters the sector is regarded as highly toxic due to the controversy over working practices and remuneration in the 'gig economy'.

If they were to consider entry, cost may also put them off. Acquiring an established player, such as Deliveroo, would be very expensive, with investors looking to realize highly inflated multiples. Instead, as with GeoPost, it is more likely that acquirers would look at an early stage start-up (like DHL did to develop their Saloodo! road freight platform) or develop the technology internally.

Just because there are few synergies between on-demand and express parcels networks does not necessarily mean that GeoPost's acquisition of Stuart should be viewed as an isolated acquisition. As the on-demand sector becomes more mature, more opportunities for express companies to become involved in the market may well present themselves. For example, the technology that underpins the platforms may well prove useful in B2B sectors such as Service Parts Logistics, providing a step change in the costs of fulfilling narrow delivery windows to meet service level agreements. The delivery of restaurant food may well be the start for many providers, but the future of on-demand may well be other business sectors that still remain untouched.

In the end, the market may just become too big for the express parcels giants to ignore. However, for the time being, the risks of picking the wrong on-demand provider are probably too great – it would seem more sensible to let financial investors bear the strain of building the necessary scale or indeed losing their stakes if they fail.

Start-up successes and failures

Start-up successes

- Shutl – Purchased by eBay for around US $100m. Previously raised US $8.69m from UPS, La Poste and others, in seven venture capital funding rounds. eBay continues to invest in Shutl. In September 2016 it announced a revamp allowing easier access for SMEs.

- Doordash – Received funding of US $186.7m in 5 rounds, from 16 investors. It gained US $127m in funding at a Series C round during March 2016, and expanded into Austin, Texas, in August of that year.

- Instacart – Received funding of US $274.8m in 5 rounds, from 12 investors. A new US $220m Series C funding round that valued the company at more than US $2 billion, was announced in January 2015. Instacart has expanded into cities in Massachusetts, Florida, Georgia, New Jersey, North Carolina and California.

- Roadie – Received funding of US $25.03m, in 4 rounds, from 8 investors. Gained US $15m in Series B funding during June 2016.

- Delivery hero – Backed by first-tier investors raising US $1bn. Launched in 2011, it operates food delivery services in 33 countries, employing 3,000 people. Pulled out of China, but is now seeking an IPO to raise 175 million euros to fund additional growth projects.

Start-up failures

- Tok tok tok – Gained US $2m in seed funding. Set up as a food delivery company. Lacked the resources and cost control necessary to scale. Sold technology platform to Just Eat in September 2016.

- Wunwun – Various institutional and individual investors raised US $23m. Closed down and acquired by delivery service Alfred in May 2015. Failed to scale enough to compete.

- VF – Subsidiary delivery arm of Delivery Hero, launched in 2015. Attempted to outsource delivery for fast food restaurants. Entered administration in April 2016 after failing to get costs under control. Scaled up too quickly and found acceptable margins unattainable.

- Foodpanda – Raised US $210m in 2015, including a US $100m injection from Goldman Sachs and a separate US $110m round. Has sold businesses in Mexico, Brazil and Indonesia and has laid off 15% of employees in India and Hong Kong. It is rethinking its South East Asia strategy. Only profitable in smaller markets of Saudi Arabia and Eastern Europe. Parent Rocket Internet has been unable to find buyers.

The 'gig economy' and the status of transport workers

Many logistics companies are rightly proud of the way they treat their workforce. Despite this, the business models and employment structures that many companies in the sector operate are coming under intense scrutiny due to the impact they have on logistics workers. Many of the issues relate to the highly sub-contracted nature of labour in the transport market.

The increasing use of owner-drivers

Although the use of owner-drivers (self-employed transport workers who also provide their own vehicle) has been widespread for several decades, the demand for such workers has soared in the recent past, not least due to the spectacular growth of e-retail-related deliveries. While much of the logistics market has seen weak growth, the volume of home deliveries has increased dramatically. This has brought a welcome source of revenue to many express parcels operators while at the same time raising a number of significant challenges.

Volatility in the market with frequent peaks and troughs has meant that the vast majority of parcels carriers have adopted an outsourced model, in effect de-risking their own operations. Sub-contractors bear not only the cost of investment in transport assets but also carry the risk of revenues by being paid 'by the drop' or by the mile.

The e-retail market is such that so-called 'free shipping' is a major selling point for many companies. The costs of this marketing device are pushed onto the carrier making the delivery, resulting in ultra-low rates of remuneration.

This has raised ethical concerns. The low barriers to market entry and a plentiful supply of people willing to take on a low-skilled job have meant that the amount paid by some carriers is barely enough to cover the cost of running a vehicle. There have been allegations that to some carriers their sub-contractors are 'disposable'. They can be utilized for a period of time at an unsustainable rate, knowing that they will eventually be forced to give up due to the lack of economic viability. The carrier will then replace the owner-driver from a plentiful pool of new market entrants.

Of course, many would argue that this state of affairs is merely derived from the healthy operation of a free market. In the developed world, many owner-drivers are migrants who have been attracted by employment opportunities and wages much higher than those in their own countries. By providing a large pool of new migrant capacity, the developed countries' economies have benefited through a lower cost base. If this labour pool were reduced, then inevitably supply chain costs would rise throughout the industry.

At the same time, the status of owner-drivers provides them with fewer entitlements than those who are legally defined as employees. For example, they have none of the protection rights of employees: sick pay, maternity/paternity leave, pensions, etc despite fulfilling a role that could be argued is identical to that of an employee. Also, due to the likelihood in the parcels sector that the owner-driver will be providing and driving a van rather than a large goods vehicle (LGV), they do not have to comply with European drivers' hours legislation, placing a limit on the length of time for which they can drive. Consequently, work load and hours are often very long and, as already mentioned, rates of pay are very low.

The on-demand economy – unethical or new employment model?

The development of the so-called 'on-demand' business models of delivery companies has brought the treatment of sub-contractors under even more scrutiny from labour organizations and policymakers.

Start-up restaurant meal delivery company Deliveroo is facing challenges to its sub-contracted labour model from both regulators and the sub-contractors themselves. The company has a network of drivers and riders across many countries who collect and deliver meals from a range of food outlets that do not have their own delivery capabilities.

In the UK, in 2017, the company paid its sub-contractors £7 an hour, plus £1 per delivery. However, management introduced a new pay structure that resulted in unrest among its drivers. The company wanted to change the remuneration to a simple £3.75 per delivery. Although this could result in higher payments during peak times, overall there was concern that the new system would result in contractors receiving less than the minimum wage across the day as a whole (Wallace, 2017).

Rival start up, UberEats, is facing similar dissention among its contracted workforce. The casual basis of employment for couriers means that although the opportunities to earn around £9 an hour are available, on some occasions few, if any, jobs will be allocated. However, management counter that couriers don't have set shifts, minimum hours or delivery zones that they must keep to. Many have other jobs as well.

Although some of the sub-contractors may see the on-demand model as unethical, many are suited by the arrangement. After all, both Deliveroo and UberEats have attracted many thousands of couriers to sign up to their business models.

However there have been legal challenges to whether self-employed workers should be given access to the same rights as other employees. In the contract that Deliveroo requires its drivers to sign, contractors must sign away their right to challenge their status, although legally this may be unenforceable.

In a case related to the sacking of two workers by private hire company Addison Lee, the legal company of Union GMB commented:

> Employers cannot be allowed to have all the financial benefits of employees and none of the responsibilities to these people's livelihoods. The attempt to reframe normal employment as part of the gig economy is a serious threat to the financial security of thousands of hard working people and will end up costing the tax payer huge sums whilst companies take all the profit.

One of the main issues, it would appear, is that the cultural barriers to less formal employment will need to be overcome if the on-demand economy is to become mainstream. It is likely that employment status will become even more contentious in the future as labour organizations try to prevent the prevalence of more informal working structures and governments try to mitigate the loss of tax receipts. Both sets of vested interests are likely to be left behind by developments in the sector.

Crowd-shipping

The smartphone phenomenon has effectively democratized technology. All companies (not just large) and individuals have high levels of computing power available to them, which in turn has encouraged technical innovation to flourish. No longer do very large computing companies monopolize the development of software; rather, everyone has the opportunity to conceive and develop new technological solutions as well as distribute them to a mass market. This has led to disruptive, agile and continually evolving applications.

One of the benefits of these network-connected devices is that they provide the means to combine users into virtual communities. This power has been utilized by disruptors such as Uber to challenge regulated sectors such as personal mobility – but now also transportation.

Running in parallel with the distribution of computing power and hardware throughout the population has been the generation of massive amounts of data. This can inform decision-making opportunities that can bring significant benefits, either economic, societal or environmental.

Technological innovation, democratization and the ubiquity of low-cost sensors have combined with an important cultural shift to create the 'sharing economy'. Whereas asset ownership was once seen as highly important, a new generation is happier to forego the status that this once bestowed in return for greater levels of efficiency or service. Many see that cars will become shared assets in the foreseeable future with a focus being on 'on-demand services' rather than a way of increasing self-esteem through association with a brand. This is due partly, it must be said, to economic necessity, which puts many assets (housing, transport, etc) out of reach of many so-called 'millennials'.

Crowd-shipping is also part of this broader trend. The leading academic, Professor Alan McKinnon (2016), says crowd-shipping 'effectively turns ordinary citizens into couriers, creating new informal logistics networks for the local distribution of small items ordered online'. The concept involves ordinary individuals taking parcels with them on an existing journey and stopping to effect the delivery en route.

The benefit of this process is that the delivery can be made with low marginal costs in terms of both the financial and environmental implications. It also means that the person carrying out the delivery can be reimbursed for their time and effort, creating value from an essentially non-value-adding exercise. As McKinnon (2016) has also commented, 'The growth of crowd-shipping is an example of people using social networking to behave collaboratively and share services and assets for the greater good of the community'.

Although the term crowd-shipping originally referred to the practice as undertaken by ordinary individuals, some of the platforms that have been established, such as Zipments, are used predominantly by professional couriers. Some, such as Deliv, are focused around the delivery of goods purchased in shopping malls. Deliv (part owned by UPS and operating in the United States), for example, says it seeks to bridge the gap between multichannel retailers and their customers. DHL was one of the first companies to trial crowd-shipping as an addition to its existing service.

Whether or not crowd-shipping is undertaken by an individual, on their way to work, for example, or by a professional courier, is an important issue. Although it may not matter to the end-recipient, the shipper or for that matter the platform, there are implications in terms of road use, congestion and environmental impact. Professional couriers may travel much longer distances to collect and deliver shipments, making dedicated journeys for each consignment. By substituting a low-cost alternative to formal delivery networks traditionally involving the consolidation of parcels in vans, the result may be higher levels of congestion and emissions. Certain popular high density delivery locations, such as an urban area, may attract large numbers of professional couriers from outside, exacerbating already overcrowded roads.

The benefits to shippers of crowd-shipping in its purest, original form are evident from the illustrative graphic in Figure 11.1, which is based loosely around the UK market.

In the current scenario, a shipper has the option of using a relatively small number of major carriers. Using new technology, a shipper now has the opportunity of bypassing these carriers to establish its own distribution solution, using local partners. This is exactly the strategy employed by one of the biggest shippers in the market, Amazon, through its subsidiary, Amazon Logistics. Using crowd-shipping technologies, a shipper would then be able

Figure 11.1 Crowd-shipping: giving shippers access to enhanced supplier pool

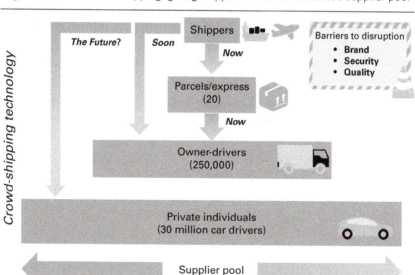

to directly access a large number of owner-drivers and, beyond this, a larger number of individual drivers. In fact, this number would be of an even higher magnitude as it could include train and bus passengers, especially those who could deliver small packages very easily to an inner city destination.

There are, however, risks involved with 'disintermediating' established carriers. Not least of these are the issues of quality and security. The major express parcels operators have been successful over the years partly due to the brands they have established, and a large factor in this has been the guaranteed levels of service and trust. Although these carriers may charge their services at a premium, many shippers, especially those of high value goods, may be willing to accept these if they know that their goods will be moved securely and will be well taken care of.

There have also been worries by regulators that crowd-shipping services may be vulnerable to misappropriation by terrorist or criminal gangs. If a crowd-shipping platform is completely 'open', perhaps resembling a social networking site such as Facebook, it is possible that, inadvertently, a courier may be asked to deliver illicit goods or even explosive devices. Although even the major global network providers are not immune to such acts, the bad public relations that would result may put a halt to the development of these services.

Case Study 11.2 looks at how Walmart is testing various crowd-shipping options, and Case Study 11.3 reviews the latest innovations in last mile delivery.

CASE STUDY 11.2   Walmart testing crowd-shipping options

Walmart, the giant US retailer, has been at the forefront of the crowd-shipping trend, testing out various options since the early 2010s. In 2013 the company trialled using customers to collect orders when they were in-store and deliver them to other customers on the way home. In 2017 the company examined an alternative, asking its warehouse employees ('associates') to undertake the delivery of orders on the way back from work.

As Walmart commented in a blog, 'Not only can this cut shipping costs and get packages to their final destinations faster and more efficiently, it creates a special win-win-win for customers, associates and the business'.

The model being trialled would involve the delivery of an e-commerce order to a store located closest to the customer where the associate would collect it and deliver it at the end of their day. The employee would set the parameters of their delivery capabilities, including the number of packages they could deliver as well as the size and weight limits. Walmart has stores within 16 kilometres of 90 per cent of the US population and over a million employees, which makes the concept feasible.

Three test stores are being trialled, but the company says response from staff has been positive not least as the GPS functionality of the app that Walmart has provided enables associates to find faster ways home using their smartphones.

One further advantage that overcomes the argument that crowd-shipping could lead to more vehicle miles and emissions rather than less, is that the employee starts off at the same origin as the shipment (the store) and it is delivered en route.

CASE STUDY 11.3 Last mile innovation
Address mapping

Many companies are trialling new solutions by which parcels can be delivered effectively and cheaply to customers. A number of start-ups are now focusing on how to deliver to e-commerce customers in emerging markets, where formal addresses do not exist.

Markets such as China and India are attracting huge interest from e-retail companies, due to their large and growing middle classes. However, much of the Middle East and Africa also suffer from the issue of having limited or no addresses. Large proportions of these populations live in rural areas where addresses, let alone postcodes, are few and far between. A home might have no identifier beyond a street name, or even just a part of town.

On major Asian e-commerce sites, such as Alibaba Group or Flipkart, customers who do not have formal addresses instead enter their name, town and phone number on the checkout screen. They may also include a local landmark as part of the address. Parcels are then either delivered to a convenient collection point, or the delivery drivers call the customer for specific directions as they near the 'vague' location.

Companies are now developing solutions to make deliveries to these more remote locations easier by using technologies ranging from mobile apps to bespoke global mapping systems. Surprisingly, instead of using traditional geographical coordinates, such as latitude and longitude, these companies have opted to develop their own coordinates, creating unique 'address codes' for every spot on the planet, using designations that are shorter and simpler than latitude and longitude.

Companies in this area include Fetchr and what3words. Fetchr has developed an on-demand delivery app that uses a customer's mobile phone as the postal address. The delivery company, which operates in Dubai, Bahrain, Saudi Arabia and Egypt, has raised US $12.5m in funding.

what3words assigns a unique series of three words to every 10 ft by 10 ft square of the earth's surface. It claims that this approach is far more accurate than a postal address and is much easier to remember than a set of coordinates. Aramex recently invested US $3m in what3words to effect e-commerce deliveries in the Middle East, Africa and Asia.

In addition, Nairobi-based OkHi Ltd has raised US $1.1m for its technology that creates an 'address' via a mobile app, using an amalgamation of the geographic location and a photograph of the customer's house. The company's founders say they have reduced e-commerce delivery times by as much as 50% as a direct result of this technology.

Summary

On-demand delivery and crowd-shipping are two innovations most closely associated with 4IR. Of the two, on-demand has been the most successful, with the model adopted primarily for the delivery of food. It has provided cafes and restaurants (as well as some retailers) with the ability to provide a home delivery service that previously was the preserve of only much larger competitors. However, political pressures may result in more restrictive regulation of this sector, particularly concerning the potential for large employers to exploit their workforce. As with zero-hour contracts, this will be a contentious point of debate.

In contrast, it is still to be seen whether crowd-shipping will be the game changer that many believe. In theory the value that will be released by sharing previously underutilized transport assets should be huge. However, significant barriers will need to be overcome before the model can be more widely adopted.

Bibliography

Dablanc, L, Morganti, E, Arvidsson, N, Woxenius, J, Browne, M and Saidi, N (2017) The rise of on-demand 'instant deliveries' in European cities, *Supply Chain Forum: An International Journal*, **18** (4), pp 203–217

McKinnon, A (2016) *Crowdshipping: A Communal Approach to Reducing Urban Traffic Levels?* Kuehne Logistics University, Germany

Paine, J [accessed 26 January 2018] $57 Billion Dollar Opportunity: The State of the On Demand Economy in 2017, *Inc.* [Online] www.inc.com/james-paine/5-stats-to-know-about-the-on-demand-economy.html

PwC [accessed 26 January 2018] UK's Key Sharing Economy Sectors Could Deliver £140 Billion by 2025 [Online] http://pwc.blogs.com/press_room/2016/06/uks-key-sharing-economy-sectors-could-deliver-140-billion-by-2025.html

Roose, A [accessed 25 January 2018] From 0 To 1,000,000 To ? [Online] https://medium.com/@adrienroose/from-0-to-1-000-000-to-ecb4e2f863c7

Wallace, T [accessed 5 November 2017] Deliveroo Offers Workers Pay Per Trip in Bid to Defuse Self Employment Row, *Daily Telegraph* [Online] www.telegraph.co.uk/business/2017/05/31/deliveroo-offers-workers-pay-per-trip-bid-defuse-self-employment/

Autonomous vehicles and delivery robots

12

THIS CHAPTER WILL FAMILIARIZE THE READER WITH:

- the reasons behind the development of autonomous vehicles;
- the barriers to their adoption;
- the levels of vehicle autonomy;
- what is meant by 'platooning' and its benefits;
- the prospects for the future of 'drones';
- the development of autonomous ships and their prospects;
- 'delivery robots' and their potential role in last mile delivery.

Introduction

With technology giants such as Google and Uber and vehicle manufacturers investing heavily in 'autonomous vehicles', it is only a matter of time before they are seen on roads around the world. In fact, many 'assistive' technologies (such as help with parking) are already being used. Vehicles now have the capability to interact not only with other vehicles around them but also with highway infrastructure.

While the headlines have mostly focused on cars, automotive manufacturers, both incumbent and start-up, have invested billions in developing autonomous trucks. Significant progress has already been made. For example, a Mercedes Benz prototype truck has driven autonomously on an autobahn in Germany, successfully navigating a junction in real-life driving conditions.

Being able to communicate with each other, there is also the possibility of 'platooning'. Trucks (and even eventually cars) will be able to travel in convoys along the motorway, drafting the vehicle in front. According to the US Department of Environment, this can create fuel cost savings of between 8 and 11 per cent (Lammert *et al*, 2014).

It is also increasingly possible to 'harvest' a huge amount of data from vehicles, both cars and trucks, which if analysed in a proper and timely way will result in efficiencies, mostly related to the avoidance of congestion. These data can be generated either by traffic authorities (such as municipalities or highway agencies), by private companies that provide information to users on speed of traffic, or, more recently, mobile applications that allow individuals to log incidents as they observe them. The latter can theoretically mobilize thousands of drivers who act as monitors of traffic situations in areas that no other organization could reach.

The forces behind autonomous trucks

Increase in efficiency

One of the foremost reasons for the investment in this technology is the potential increase in transport efficiency that could be achieved. With congestion forecast to rise substantially in the near future, there is a need to break the link between economic growth and vehicle movements. German authorities predict that truck transport volume will increase by 39 per cent by 2030 unless steps are taken (Newbold, 2018). Construction of new roads is unpopular from an environmental perspective, and many countries in Europe just don't have the money available to make the sort of investment required. Major trunk road networks in Western Europe have barely grown since the late 2000s. Therefore, it becomes essential to utilize existing road capacity more efficiently, and new technologies can aid in this goal.

Cost savings

In many countries in Europe, it is estimated that around 45 per cent of total cost for road freight operators is related to the driver. Eventually removing the driver (although no one is suggesting this is likely for many years) would obviously then have an enormous impact on road freight costs, profits and margins.

Another issue is the looming driver shortage crisis. Many people are increasingly unwilling to commit to a career as a driver given the hours away from home, the relatively low pay and the conditions. This will eventually translate into higher costs for road operators and their customers. By taking away much of the stress from driving by leaving most of the important decisions to a computer, working conditions will become more attractive. There may also be the opportunity for the role to become more value-adding as the driver will have the time and connectivity to undertake an enhanced role, perhaps in transport management activities.

In summary, vehicle manufacturers believe that the efficiencies the technology will deliver will come in the form of:

- reduced fuel consumption – the computer will drive the vehicle more fuel efficiently;
- reduced emissions – for the same reason;
- 100% connectivity and location services that allow for 'perfect' route planning;
- diagnostic services that ensure correct maintenance and fewer breakdowns;
- emergency braking will ensure fewer accidents, gaps between vehicles will be adhered to;
- routes can be re-planned around known areas of congestion;
- accidents caused by human error (through tiredness, for example) will be considerably reduced;
- communications can be shared with customers to provide visibility of delivery times, changing in line with the traffic situation.

Barriers to autonomous driving

The United States is leading the way in the development of autonomous vehicles, although other jurisdictions have not been slow to catch on. As of 1 May 2018, 29 states had enacted legislation allowing for autonomous vehicle testing and operations. This jumped from just 11 at the start of the year. In Europe, Spain, Italy, Finland and Greece have also passed some form of legislation.

However, at this stage, removing drivers from trucks is still a very long way off and will face huge challenges, not only from labour organizations but also safety and regulatory bodies and even the wider population. A cursory look at the railway industry throws up some of the barriers faced.

Although the technology has existed for many years for driverless trains on rapid transits, very few are in service. In theory, the highly controlled environment of a railway should lend itself ideally to such technologies. In fact, given the congestion that exists on many parts of a rail network and the expense of building new infrastructure, it would seem obvious that autonomous driving should have been adopted several years ago. At the very least plans should be in place to implement these technologies. However, this is not the case, and this perhaps hints at the problems such initiatives in the road freight sector will face.

It is for this reason that vehicle manufacturers such as Mercedes Benz (Daimler) are being very careful with the language they use, unwilling as they are to upset vested interests. For the foreseeable future the technology they are developing will assist the driver rather than take over the driving. A comparison perhaps would be with airline pilots who use an autopilot once they have taken off and only return controls to manual when they are about to land. This is despite the fact that at many airports some newer airliners are quite capable of landing themselves. Other barriers relate to data security, insurance liability, and driving and resting times.

Technology progress

Vehicle autonomy will not advance to its greatest extent overnight. Instead, through a series of incremental improvements, manufacturers will introduce a range of enhancements that eventually combine to provide high levels of autonomy. The Society of Automotive Engineers categorizes these levels as shown in Table 12.1.

Level 3 and above are described as autonomous. Lower levels are already being adopted by truck manufacturers. For example, Autonomous Emergency Braking Systems (AEB) have been a mandatory feature for new heavy goods vehicles (HGVs) deployed in Europe since November 2015.

At present, the most advanced autonomous driving system commercially available is Tesla's Autopilot feature, which is classified as Level 2 autonomous by the National Highway Transportation Safety Administration (NHTSA). First made available in October 2014, Autopilot provides drivers with forward collision warning, automatic emergency braking, adaptive cruise control and automatic steering. Together, these features allow the system to match the vehicle's speed to traffic conditions, stay within a lane, change lanes, transition between motorways, exit the motorway and self-park.

Table 12.1 Levels of autonomy

Level	Type	Example
0	No driving automation	–
1	Driver assistance	Adaptive cruise control or lane centring
2	Partial driving automation	Adaptive cruise control and lane centring
3	Automated driving (conditional)	Automated driving at low speeds
4	Automated driving (high)	Automated driving within city centre
5	Automated driving (full)	Automated driving everywhere

SOURCE Society of Automotive Engineers

Human supervision is still required in order to operate these features, as there are instances where manual control is necessary. This was highlighted in May 2016, when a Tesla Model S driver died after his vehicle collided with an articulated truck. The Autopilot system had been operational at the point of impact, and it later emerged that the car had failed to differentiate the trailer of the truck from the sky as it approached.

The legality of Autopilot varies by country, though it is likely that most will update their legislation to permit it, along with similar systems provided by other manufacturers. For example, German lawmakers updated their rules to permit certain types of vehicle autonomy in May 2017 with a view to normalizing the use of such systems.

Level 3 autonomous driving, whereby vehicles can operate without driver intervention in certain situations (semi-controlled environments such as motorways), is technically feasible for the majority of manufacturers exploring the technology. Audi has equipped its 2018 A8 with such capabilities, while Volvo deployed 100 Level 3 XC90s with Level 3 autonomy in West London during 2018 as part of its Drive Me programme. HGV manufacturers possess the same technology, but due to the dangers of operating such large and heavy vehicles, Level 3 road trials have been largely restricted.

Platooning

Classified as a Level 2 automation technology, a platoon is classified as a group of two or more vehicles driving in concert as part of a convoy.

When linked together by machine to machine (M2M) communication technologies, a local network can be formed between the vehicles, allowing them to act in concert. Thus, when the first vehicle brakes, each of the other vehicles in the platoon also brakes at the same time, with no delay.

As a result of this technology, vehicles in a platoon can drive much closer to one another than would be safe based on human reaction times, consequently benefiting from significant reductions in drag. According to ERTICO, this leads to a reduction in fuel consumption ranging from 1 to 8 per cent for the lead vehicle, and 7 to 16 per cent from trailing vehicles (Winder, 2018). In practice, each driver retains independent control over their vehicle and can disengage from the platoon where necessary, such as on approaches to motorway ramps and other points where traffic merges.

Following the Amsterdam Declaration on 14 April 2016, the EU established a roadmap for the steps necessary for the development of self-driving technology within its jurisdiction. The Declaration focused on the implementation of multi-brand platooning in Europe before 2025, and consists of a set of trials for manufacturers, adaptation of the regulatory framework governing vehicle autonomy, and the development of incentives to encourage the uptake of the technology.

As part of this plan, several semi-automated platoons of trucks drove across Europe in 2016, arriving in Rotterdam from Sweden, Denmark, Germany, Belgium and the Netherlands as part of a challenge coordinated by DAF, Daimler, Iveco, MAN, Scania and Volvo. The report on the trial, by the Dutch Ministry of Infrastructure and the Environment, found that truck drivers regarded merging traffic and on/off ramps as the most challenging elements of platooning in practice. Issues here centred on the policy of decoupling on the approach to motorway ramps, with one instance suggesting that maintaining the integrity of a small platoon may prove safer in practice than if two or three trucks decoupled (MIE, 2016).

While certain questions need to be answered, such as the maximum number of vehicles per platoon, standardization of communications technologies and driver training, the report provides a useful summary of the state of platooning in practice. The platooning challenge was not a scientific trial, and its results are therefore inconclusive, though the event demonstrates the concept in action and will inform further platooning trials.

In summary, vehicle platooning is a technology that is likely to become adopted within commercial road freight operations in the near future. The business case is solid, and the technology is approaching the stage where it is safe enough to become accepted by regulators. Issues on both aspects still need to be worked out, but the prospects for adoption are substantial.

Prospects for full autonomy

Although significant progress has been made, the likelihood of full autonomy – or 'driverless trucks' – is still some way off. Current programming techniques employed in AI are unable to provide a computer with the ability to infer potential actions in an unfamiliar situation. Hence, without access to any data relating to a similar situation, none of today's autonomous systems are able to determine how to respond to extremely low probability events.

Moreover, conceiving of such events in order to simulate an AI response is challenging in and of itself. As such, the physical safety of autonomous vehicles is incredibly difficult to determine because it is essentially impossible to test exhaustively.

Some companies, such as the Swedish start-up, Einride, have proposed remote operation as a partial solution to this problem. The company aims to produce vehicles capable of fully autonomous driving on motorways where environmental conditions are easier to control, while human operators will handle the vehicles within, and on approach to, urban areas.

Unfortunately, this solution presents manufacturers with a different set of problems. With an increasing reliance on connectivity over distance, the physical threat of cyberattacks increases significantly. In 2015, hackers exploited a 'zero-day' vulnerability (a system vulnerability unknown to the vendor), which allowed them to take full control of a Jeep Cherokee by connecting to its entertainment system over the internet. While the attackers in this instance were demonstrating the vulnerability in order to assist Fiat Chrysler with security, their success highlights a substantial problem for all manufacturers. Although security vulnerabilities are not a problem specific to autonomous systems, the increasing reliance of these vehicles on external connectivity, as with platooning operations for instance, means that they are worryingly susceptible to intrusions.

It should be noted that the above is merely an appraisal of autonomous vehicles as they exist in 2019. The rapid development of AI research and development since the early 2010s, enabled in part by the commoditization of advanced hardware developed for gaming, conveys incredible potential.

Other autonomous vehicles

Although the development of autonomous trucks has, by far, the largest potential to disrupt transport systems, opportunities exist for other modes, not least, of course, unmanned aerial vehicles (UAVs) or as they are popularly known, 'drones'. However, technology is also being developed for guiding crewless ships and, of course, autopilots have been in use for aircraft for many decades.

Unmanned aerial vehicles (UAVs) or 'drones'

In terms of attracting media attention, drones have been hugely successful. In reality, though, they will never be able to replace the utility of trucks and vans that deliver many millions of parcels across the world each day. Drones, which can only carry one parcel at a time, simply cannot compete in terms of speed and efficiency, at least in the mainstream market.

Challenges that still need to be overcome include:

- Range and payload

The maximum payload for most drones being developed is around 3 kg although JD.com's drone can carry up to 15 kg. Largely as a result of the payload issue, however, the drone systems have a short battery life. This is a potentially significant hurdle to commercial operations for obvious reasons, most notably delivery range. Of the delivery drones currently being trialled by Amazon, DPD (produced by Atechsys), Flirtey and Matternet (all of which are powered by lithium-ion batteries), none has a top range of more than 30 kilometres. JD.com is trialling a drone with a range of up to 50 kilometres.

- Safety and regulatory

Battery life and the associated scenarios accompanying a loss of power are other major issues. The implications of a power loss mid-flight over a crowded public area, for instance, are severe. There has also been much concern about drones flying into other users' airspace such as an airport or military zone.

- Security

The security of the drones, and the products they are carrying, is another concern undergoing rigorous testing. Companies such as Matternet, which is partnering with Swiss Post on its drone programme, advocate the use of a network of secure landing pads to protect (and recharge) the vehicles. Nonetheless, physical security is not the only issue under scrutiny here. The potential to jam radio signals or hack into drones is a real and significant threat.

- Noise and privacy

If drones were to become widely used for delivery of parcels, the air would become congested. This would create considerable noise pollution as well as visual intrusion.

- Delivery practicalities

There is also the problem of how drones would practically deliver to many residential or office locations if there were no landing areas.

Suitability for niche sectors

A preoccupation with e-commerce deliveries (precipitated originally by Amazon's marketing department) has diverted attention away from a role that drones can play much more effectively. Leveraging their ability to move quickly over terrain that may have little or no transport infrastructure, drones are already proving to be well suited to the transport of urgent shipments in remote locations. Examples of successful trials include:

- DHL drones delivering medications from the German mainland to the North Sea island of Juist in 2014;
- Zipline's drone-based transportation of medical supplies throughout Rwanda since October 2016;
- Matternet's operational network serving hospitals throughout Switzerland, transporting blood and pathology samples between hospital facilities on-demand.

What makes each of these business models viable is the absence of transport infrastructure. The mountainous terrain of Switzerland constitutes one of the few areas in Europe where the delivery of medical samples cannot be executed rapidly through conventional channels, while the underdeveloped road network in Rwanda is more representative of its region.

While conditions in Europe and Africa appear amenable to the niche use of drone delivery systems in support of medical operations, the vast geography of China makes the application of drone technology more appropriate for e-commerce packages.

Both SF Express and JD.com are deploying drones in order to fulfil e-commerce deliveries throughout rural areas in China. The former has been running limited drone delivery operations in Beijing, Sichuan, Shaanxi and Jiangsu since 2016 and sees the technology as a competitive advantage over e-commerce rival Alibaba.

Speaking to CNBC, JD.com's CEO, Richard Liu, said the cost of serving rural areas, 'will drop down at least 70 percent', with the use of drones as opposed to cars or vans. JD.com runs a more vertically integrated business than rival Alibaba, in which it owns and operates its own logistics infrastructure to serve customers. By being able to serve rural customers more rapidly than its rival, the company may be able to expand its market share.

The conclusions to be taken from recent activity are clear; drones used for logistics in Europe and North America are likely to provide deliveries in niche, time-critical areas where no other suitable options exist. In China, India and other emerging markets, however, it may be that drone delivery will serve as a leapfrogging technology, allowing the expanding e-commerce industry to overcome substantial infrastructure deficits to reach consumers.

Autonomous ships

Many in the shipping industry believe that autonomous ships will eventually totally replace the crewed alternative. There are good commercial arguments for this belief:

- lower labour costs due to the removal of crew;
- lower fuel costs due to the removal of accommodation (perhaps 6 per cent lower);
- lower construction costs and more room for paying freight;
- lower insurance for accidents involving humans.

However, the cost situation is not completely positive. As there would be no crew on hand to carry out repair and maintenance, there will need to be considerable redundancy built in to the ship's design, which will push up construction costs. Although some insurance may go down, the crew's existing role in mitigating accidents at sea involving other ships or port infrastructure has yet to be fully assessed.

Given that a ship's life may extend to 25 years, there is also a considerable disincentive to take a risk on complete redesigns should they prove to be uneconomic. This has meant that smaller investments in short sea shipping are occurring first as shipping lines test the market with the new technologies.

An example of this involves two Norwegian companies that are developing what they claim would be the first fully electric and autonomous container ship. The task is being undertaken by Yara International ASA, an agricultural and chemicals company, and Kongsberg, a high-tech systems manufacturer for the merchant marine, defence, aerospace and offshore oil and gas sectors.

Their project, the Yara Birkeland, is a US $25m undertaking that is scheduled for deployment in late 2018. It will transport fertilizer 60 kilometres in Norwegian waters from Yara's production port in Larvik to Brevik. The ship will have a capacity of around 100–150 TEU and will be fully run on a 3.5–4 MWh set of batteries. In its original stages, the operation will be manned, but by 2020 it will be fully autonomous.

The initial cost is high as it incorporates the costs of GPS, lidar, infra-red and high resolution cameras needed to operate this new type of vessel. However, its operating costs are likely to be dramatically lower than a normal container ship. Reports suggest annual operating costs could fall by up to 90 per cent, with no fuel costs or seafarers to pay for (Paris, 2018).

There are a variety of other developments within the sector too. Kongsberg in fact is in a separate undertaking with UK-based Automated Ships Ltd and French offshore services company Bourbon Offshore, in which they are developing an autonomous prototype vessel for servicing the offshore energy, hydrographic & scientific, and offshore fish-farming industries. Rolls Royce Holdings meanwhile is leading a project called the Advanced Autonomous Waterborne Applications (AAWA) initiative, which works with other companies and universities to develop new solutions in the area. One Baltic operator involved in AAWA, Finferries, is utilizing a variety of sensors and thermal cameras, alongside its manned operations in its Stella Ferry. These are said to be improving safety, by increasing awareness of the environment and making it easier for crews to navigate. According to Mikael Mäkinen, President, Marine, Rolls Royce, 'Autonomous shipping is the future of the maritime industry. As disruptive as the smartphone, the smart ship will revolutionize the landscape of ship design and operations'.

The success of such projects thus far has shown the strength of the concept. Petter Ostbo, Yara's head of production, told the *Wall Street Journal* that the company hopes to invest in larger autonomous ships for even longer routes and 'maybe even move our fertilizer from Holland all the way to Brazil' when international regulations for crewless vessels are set (Paris, 2018).

The International Maritime Organization (IMO) has also announced that it would launch a study into amending laws to permit the use of unmanned vessels. However, it is likely to be some time before any full regulations are set.

As with autonomous cars, it is likely that regulation will delay the deployment of fully autonomous ships. However, the accompanying technology used already has a part to play in aiding maritime transport by cutting fuel costs, increasing safety and helping navigation. In the short term, these developments will complement manned operations on vessels, though in the long term they may replace them altogether.

Delivery robots

An alternative to drones is self-driving robots. These navigate along paths rather than fly and, as a result, lack many of the problems associated with UAVs. The delivery robots travel at walking pace on pavements and in pedestrian zones, navigate autonomously to their destination, and avoid obstacles and danger points automatically. They have a load capacity of up to 10 kg and can transport goods over a distance of around 6 km.

Since 2016, Swiss Post has been conducting tests with self-driving delivery robots, provided by Starship Technologies, to assess their suitability for goods delivery over the last mile. In specific terms, Swiss Post envisages using this solution for special items that need to be delivered flexibly, quickly and inexpensively in a local neighbourhood. Some of the applications include same-day and same-hour delivery, grocery deliveries or even home deliveries of medical products.

Just Eat is also trialling these robots in the UK, Germany and Switzerland. The trial also includes Hermes, Metro Group and London food start-up Pronto. As part of the European programme, dozens of robots will be deployed in five cities to run test deliveries and introduce the devices to the public. The robots have been developed for delivering packages, groceries and food to consumers in up to a 5 km radius.

As with drones, it is too early to judge whether this delivery system will be a success or not. Many barriers to adoption exist, not least issues such as return on capital compared with employing a courier; security considerations; practical issues such as obstructions; and, critically, how the consignment is delivered from robot to house.

Summary

The acceptance of autonomous vehicles will likely increase steadily over time, as various levels of autonomy are adopted. For example, the platooning of vehicles on motorway systems and low speed movements of robotics systems such as Starship Technologies' delivery robot. The automation of transportation systems will reduce labour costs significantly and, along with the rise of on-demand services, will likely promote asset-sharing. Drone-based deliveries in areas where infrastructure is weak and populations dispersed will connect previously uneconomical delivery areas to mainstream services.

However, whether road, air or sea, it will be many years before autonomous vehicles become the norm. Regulatory barriers, security and safety concerns, not to mention commercial realities, will prove sizeable delays to the adoption of the new technologies that, for the time being, will assist human drivers and crew rather than replace them.

Bibliography

Lammert, M, Duran, A (National Renewable Energy Laboratory), Diez, J, Burton, K (Intertek) and Nicholson, A (2014) Effect of platooning on fuel consumption of Class 8 vehicles over a range of speeds, following distances, and mass, *SAE International Journal of Commercial Vehicles, 7* (2), doi:10.4271/2014-01-2438

MIE (2016) *European Truck Platooning Challenge 2016*, Ministry of Infrastructure and the Environment, the Netherlands

Newbold, R [accessed 23 June 2018] Five Driving Forces Behind Driverless Trucks [Online] www.inboundlogistics.com/cms/article/five-driving-forces-behind-driverless-trucks/

Paris, C [accessed 23 June 2018] Norway Takes Lead in Race to Build Autonomous Cargo Ships, *Wall Street Journal* [Online] at www.wsj.com/articles/norway-takes-lead-in-race-to-build-autonomous-cargo-ships-1500721202

Winder, A [accessed 23 June 2018] 'ITS4CV': ITS for Commercial Vehicles, *ERTICO* [Online] http://erticonetwork.com/wp-content/uploads/2016/09/ITS4CV-Report-final-2016-09-09.pdf

A guide to alternative propulsion systems

13

THIS CHAPTER WILL FAMILIARIZE THE READER WITH:

- why alternatives to diesel and petrol powered engines are being developed;
- how adoption of alternative fuels will depend on issues such as range and payload;
- the types of alternative fuels that are being developed and their benefits and disadvantages;
- which fuels are being adopted and trialled in the fleets of major operators;
- how hybrids work and their effectiveness;
- the choices facing fleet managers;
- the development of charging networks to meet the needs of electric vehicles.

Introduction

It is clear from the environmental and public health policies being adopted by most administrators and regulators around the world that diesel powered vans and trucks will make up a much smaller proportion of the commercial vehicle fleets in the years ahead. It is also clear that, despite a wide range of alternatives, not one single form of fuel or technology will be able to replace diesel across the board.

This chapter will summarize some of the main alternatives to diesel powertrains, highlighting their strengths and weaknesses. It will discuss briefly the initiatives taken by commercial vehicle manufacturers, their claims and the reality. It will also look at the role of some of the largest fleet owners and operators in providing a market for the vehicles and the input they have had in the development of alternatively powered vans and trucks.

Different powertrains for different needs

The demands placed on commercial vehicles are very different, not least due to the diverse functions that these vehicles undertake, the weight of freight they move, the number of stops they make and the range they require.

Light commercial vehicles (vans), for example, are likely to make multiple drops, work within urban areas and carry lighter loads. Heavier goods vehicles, in contrast, need greater range, will stop fewer times and obviously carry heavier loads. One of the main advantages of diesel power is its versatility; it performs well in multiple roles. This is certainly not the case for alternative powertrains – at the moment, there is no single technology able to supersede diesel (or for that matter petrol) powered engines. As ACEA Secretary General, Erik Jonnaert, stated, 'different transport needs require different transport solutions' (ACEA, 2018). Policy must recognize and support this market-based approach.

Another issue for industry is that without government support or, indeed, environmental regulation, alternative propulsion systems are unlikely to have been developed. The overwhelming operational advantages and the scope for making diesel technology even more efficient would have provided little impetus for investment in sub-optimal technologies. This is important because it has led to the trial of a proliferation of technologies, often subsidized, many of which are highlighted in this chapter. For a fleet procurement manager, the choices used to be much simpler, based on efficiencies, power and cost, with all van/truck manufacturers providing similar products. Now the landscape looks set to become much more complex with not only competing manufacturers but competing technologies against a backdrop of shifting government regulation and subsidy.

Although there is no overwhelming consensus on which technology is necessarily right for which vehicle, it seems clear that electric or electric hybrid technology is being favoured for vans, especially for intra-urban deliveries, although hydraulic hybrids are also being developed (see later for explanation of terms).

The advent of electric-powered heavy goods vehicles (HGVs) is much further off, despite work being undertaken by manufacturers in the United

States such as Tesla. Indeed, the UK's National Grid takes a very negative view of the potential for electrically powered HGVs. It says that, 'Currently the electrification of heavy goods vehicles is not considered viable and other fuel types are considered more likely for these larger vehicles'. It believes that natural gas will be the fuel of choice (National Grid, 2017).

This is not a view shared by all. Pasquale Romano, President and CEO of ChargePoint, has commented, 'The drivetrain debate has ended and electrification has won out as the propulsion method of choice across transportation categories, as evidenced by the growing interest in electrifying semi-trucks, aircraft and beyond' (Behr, 2018). This would suggest he believes that advances in technology will reduce the size and weight of the batteries while still providing the power to carry large payloads over long distances (as does Tesla).

It is useful to categorize commercial vehicles in order to assess their needs and consequently the likely most appropriate alternative powertrain. For this purpose, the International Energy Agency suggests three classifications (IEA, 2018):

- heavy freight trucks (HFTs) (those with a gross vehicle weight (GVW) of more than 15 tonnes);
- medium freight trucks (MFTs) (those with a GVW of between 3.5t and 15t);
- light commercial vehicles (LCVs) (GVW of less than 3.5t).

HFTs account for the majority of road freight activity not least due to the level of intensity of their use. The IEA (2018) estimates that they account for 70 per cent of road freight activity and 50 per cent of truck energy usage.

LCVs (which also include passenger) have seen the highest level of growth since the late 2000s as a result of the surge in e-commerce deliveries. Also, the more regulation of HFTs, the greater the increase in lighter vehicles.

It is also useful to examine the make-up of the global fleet of commercial vehicles to assess the market size for the most appropriate forms of propulsion (Table 13.1).

Table 13.1 Structure of the global commercial vehicle fleet

Vehicle type	Number
LCVs	130 million
MFTs	32 million
HFTs	24 million

SOURCE IEA

A model developed by the IEA (Figure 13.1) suggests that there is considerable variance in the distance travelled by the different classifications of vehicles across regions. This is due to the impact of factors such as:

- quality of roads and networks (developing countries have a larger proportion of MFT to HFT due to poor roads);
- urbanization (more vans);
- geography (large countries with longer distances between cities favour more HFTs).

One of the key issues affecting the adoption of alternative powertrains is their range. By using IEA figures related to the total annual travel of a vehicle and dividing them by the number of working days in a year, a simple average daily range can be calculated (Figure 13.1).

This suggests:

- HFTs travel over four times further a day than LCVs and around 1.5 times further than MFTs.
- Daily distance travelled by commercial vehicles in China is much lower than in Europe or the United States.
- An average daily distance travelled by an HFT in Europe is 281 km and in the United States, 346 km. This has implications in terms of the range of the vehicles and the capabilities of the engine technology required (and potentially for charging station infrastructure, if electric).

Figure 13.1 Daily commercial vehicle travel

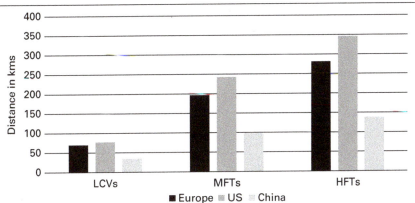

Distance in kms

■Europe ■US ■China

- For China the distance travelled by an HFT is much lower (138 km on average daily), so consequently this might not be such a problem.

- LCVs (vans) have an average daily travel of 69 km in Europe, 77 km in the United States and just 31 km in China. This would seem to be well within the range of electric options, which can presently provide 100–150 km before the need to recharge.

Obviously, this is a very simple exercise designed to demonstrate the contrast between vehicle needs against just one metric, range, across a number of geographies. It does not take into account weight of components, such as batteries, which reduces payloads, or the cost of the technology. Neither does it take into account the fact that many vans will require the capability to travel longer distances, for instance deliveries to semi-rural and rural areas. However, it provides some insight into the problems that manufacturers face when developing vehicles for a certain geography or sector. Unlike diesel technology, one size does not fit all.

Return on investment also varies by size of company. Research undertaken in the United States (Schoettle *et al*, 2016) suggests that small companies with fleets of between 1 and 20 vehicles will only invest in technologies with a payback of 6 to 36 months (average per year). Larger companies may consider a long payback period (18 to 48 months), averaging two years. Investment in vehicles using new propulsion systems will therefore be constrained by the levels of fragmentation in the industry. The fact that many logistics providers sub-contract to owner-drivers means that levels of adoption will be further supressed or delayed either from the more limited payback horizon or due to a lack of capital.

Consequently, some believe that the structure of the industry requires government intervention. If the 'cargo-owners' are not willing or are unable to force adoption of alternatives to diesel then a combination of regulation and subvention is needed. These include higher diesel taxes, higher vehicle duties for the most polluting, and potentially increased tolls (when within a government's remit). These can be combined with scrappage schemes for older vehicles and support for the purchase of new ones through subsidy of the retail price.

Types of alternative fuel

Governments and companies around the world have invested heavily in alternative fuel strategies with the aim of replacing some or all carbon-based fuels with sustainably produced substitutes. However, using alternative fuels in engines designed for oil-based fuel is not straightforward. For example, if bioethanol makes up more than a certain percentage of the fuel by volume, its corrosive nature means that engine components must be replaced more regularly. Costs of conversion and fuelling infrastructure can outweigh the cheaper costs of the alternative fuels (such as natural gas) within the total cost of ownership equation.

Presently the overwhelming demand of final energy by commercial vehicles is provided either by diesel or petrol (96.6 per cent). The alternative fuel portion is shown in Table 13.2.

Biofuels

The development of biofuels, that is fuel that has been derived from organic matter or animals, is becoming increasingly important not only for commercial vehicles but as a replacement for bunker fuels for ships or aviation gas. They can be used on their own or mixed with diesel (so-called 'dual fuel').

Biodiesel

Biodiesel is made from plant or animal oils. The main source of these oils varies from region to region depending on crops that suit local growing conditions. In North America, soy bean oil is preferred, while in Asia the greatest source is palm oil. In Europe, however, rape seed oil is most popular.

Bioethanol

Bioethanol is produced from any feedstock that contains sugars such as starch. This means that crops as diverse as wheat, corn, willow and sugar cane can be used.

Table 13.2 Breakdown of alternative fuel use

Fuel	Percentage use	
Biofuels	2.2%	
Of which	Biodiesel	1.6%
	Bioethanol	0.6%
	Biomethane	< 0.01%
Natural gas	1.2%	

SOURCE IEA

There are problems with the sustainability credentials of biofuels. First, studies have shown that although carbon monoxide, hydrocarbons and sulphur dioxide emissions can be reduced, other pollutants such as nitrous oxide and volatile organic compounds increase. Evidence on carbon dioxide emissions is ambiguous depending on the lifecycle assessment used. Obviously, there are considerable carbon emissions involved in the growing, harvesting, production and transport of biofuels.

Biomethane

Biomethane can be produced by the anaerobic digestion of organic material and can be generated by the diversion of landfill waste to biogas plants. However, there is unlikely to be enough biomethane generated from this source alone to meet the demand for alternative fuels.

Natural gas

Natural gas is an alternative source of methane but can only be transported in the form of compressed natural gas (CNG) or liquified natural gas (LNG). This provides enough 'volumetric energy density' for it to be used in trucks.

One of the operational disadvantages of the fuel is that fuelling stations need expensive and complicated equipment (such as cryogenic storage tanks), adding to costs and availability. In addition, twice as much LNG is required as diesel to travel the same distance.

One of the major disadvantages of natural gas is its environmental credentials. As a fossil fuel it is considered 'unclean'. Methane (one of the most frequent gases uses) has a global warming potential of 21 times that of carbon dioxide (McKinnon *et al*, 2012). Part of the reasons for this is that some methane remains unburnt after the combustion process and re-enters the atmosphere.

Natural gas does have its advantages, though. There are around 220,000 medium and heavy duty trucks powered by natural gas in the world, their popularity driven by low emissions of nitrogen oxides and particulates. They are also quieter than equivalent diesel-powered engines, which makes them well suited to urban deliveries, in particular.

Many analysts believe that biofuels and natural gas will eventually become the fuels of choice, especially in the MFT and HFT sectors. There is a long way to go as presently natural gas powered trucks account for only about 1 per cent of the world's total truck fleet.

Fleet adoption update

When diesel prices were rising strongly in line with the cost of oil, many fleet operators were tempted to look at cheaper alternative fuels, especially natural gas. The fall in the oil price has meant that enthusiasm ebbed, except in certain specialist niche segments such as refuse collection.

UPS   UPS operates 4,400 natural gas vehicles in the United States, and in 2017 it announced it was adding six new CNG fuelling stations to its network, plus 390 new CNG tractors and 50 LNG vehicles. Speaking to Automotive Fleet, UPS Director of Fleet Procurement Mike Casteel said:

> We are not changing from diesel to natural gas; we are adding natural gas trucks and stations to our fleet. In some cases, these trucks are purchased instead of diesel as older diesel trucks are removed from service. In some cases, the natural gas trucks are being added as part of fleet growth. But in all of our locations so far where we have built natural gas stations, we continue to run diesel and gasoline vehicles as well. (Cullen, 2018)

For UPS, as for some other operators, this is a long-term play, not dependent on the price of oil, although fewer cost benefits will delay adoption. A quick return on investment is not necessarily so important for the company as it typically uses vehicles until the end of their lives, rather than looking for resale value after a shorter period.

FedEx   As part of FedEx's EarthSmart programme, the company has recently invested in more than 100 new tractor-trailers that run on CNG as part of a test at its freight hub in Oklahoma City. FedEx said that while CNG tractors were more expensive than traditional diesels, they had a similar range (1,200 km), and driver certification was the same. It uses a 'time fill' option to refuel the vehicles. This fuels more slowly generating less 'heat of compression' and allowing for more CNG to be placed in the tanks, thereby increasing range.

Wrightspeed   Wrightspeed, a US truck manufacturing company, has working prototypes in operation powered by natural gas turbines. The company has entered into an agreement with a New Zealand bus company to repower its engines.

Hydrogen fuel cell

Hydrogen has the potential to be a completely clean form of energy in terms of tailpipe emissions. Electricity is produced from the chemical reaction between hydrogen and oxygen leaving only water vapour as the waste residue. The electricity is then used to power the vehicle, and in this respect the technology competes with other energy storage options, such as batteries or hydraulic (see later).

This is very much a technology in development although it is favoured particularly for use in urban environments due to the lack of pollutants.

However, hydrogen is not the answer to all pollution problems. The element has to be produced, and, depending on the energy source used (coal or gas, for example), there could be high levels of carbon emissions involved. Another issue will be the development of a hydrogen refuelling network in order to prevent 'range anxiety' dampening the technology's adoption.

Fleet adoption update

UPS   UPS has deployed a prototype extended range fuel cell electric vehicle (FCEV) in its Rolling Laboratory fleet of alternative fuel and advanced technology vehicles. UPS is working with the US Department of Energy and other partners to design a zero tailpipe emissions, Class 6 medium-duty delivery truck that meets the same route and range requirements of UPS's existing conventional fuel vehicles.

The vehicle will use the onboard fuel cell to generate electricity to propel the vehicle. The first FCEV prototype will be deployed in Sacramento, where UPS will validate its design and core performance requirements by testing it on the street. All of the trucks will be deployed in California due to the ongoing investment in zero tailpipe emissions transportation and the instalment of hydrogen fuelling stations around the state. According to Mark Wallace, UPS Senior Vice President, Global Engineering and Sustainability:

> The challenge we face with fuel cell technology is to ensure the design can meet the unique operational demands of our delivery vehicles on a commercial scale... This project is an essential step to test the zero tailpipe emissions technology and vehicle on the road for UPS and the transportation industry. (UPS, 2018)

Each FCEV produces electricity that continuously charges the batteries, thereby providing additional power and an extended range of 200 km. The UPS trucks are equipped with a 32 kW fuel cell coupled to 45 kWh of battery storage and 10 kg of hydrogen fuel. The drive train runs on electricity supplied by batteries. This will support the full duty cycle of the truck, including highway driving.

FedEx   FedEx, in partnership with vehicle manufacturer, Workhorse, is trialling an electric vehicle in New York charged by a Plug Power ProGen hydrogen engine. The hydrogen-powered electric delivery van is one of the first of its kind to operate in a standard commercial environment and is deployed on a standard delivery route for FedEx.

The Workhorse EGEN class 5 zero emission delivery trucks are designed to meet the needs of daily delivery duty cycles, as well as save delivery fleet buyers fuel and operational costs, reducing total cost of ownership over the lifetime of the vehicle.

The vehicle refuels using a hydrogen fuel station located in Latham, New York, one of the first hydrogen refuelling stations on the East Coast for on-road vehicles.

Nikola   US-based start-up manufacturer Nikola Motor Company has opted to develop a hydrogen-powered truck that it claims will have zero emissions. It says it will be able to achieve this goal because it plans to build its own solar farms to produce the clean energy required to generate the hydrogen from electrolysis of water.

In addition to this it will develop its own network of 50 hydrogen stations across the United States. Each truck will have a range of 1,900 km. The company says that in addition to the hydrogen cell, each truck can be powered by a 320 kW lithium-ion battery, although the hydrogen cell will be the main source of power. Other claims made by the manufacturer include:

- trucks will have half the operating costs of the diesel equivalent;
- 15 minute refill time;
- 1,000 horsepower;
- 20 mpg.

Brewing company, Anheuser-Busch, placed an order for up to 800 hydrogen-electric powered semi-trucks in May 2018. The zero-emission trucks are expected to be integrated into Anheuser-Busch's dedicated fleet beginning in 2020. Nikola has US $9 billion in pre-order reservations.

Electric vehicles

Electric vehicles have attracted much of the publicity in recent years as 'zero-tailgate' emissions have become the political imperative. From an operational perspective, the main challenges facing electric van and truck manufacturers are the range (dealt with earlier in this chapter) and that the batteries required to power freight-carrying vehicles are relatively large and heavy. This means that the vehicles are only appropriate for certain sectors, such as city logistics. Hybrid vehicles, which use a combination of diesel fuel and electric, have, however, become more widely adopted.

The advantage of electric vehicles is that there are virtually no emissions from the exhaust pipe and they are also very quiet. While local pollution may be eliminated in terms of carbon emissions, the sustainability of electric vehicles is reliant on the type of fuel used to generate the electricity that charges the batteries. If power stations supplying the grid are oil or gas based, vehicle emissions are in effect being transferred upstream. However, if the ultimate power source is either nuclear or from renewables, electric vehicles become much more sustainable.

Tesla and other auto manufacturers are investing huge sums in battery technology, and it seems inevitable that by 2025 it will become feasible for even the largest trucks to be powered by electricity. Up to then, electric vehicles will probably be restricted to urban deliveries, although given the growth of cities and mega-cities, this is an important sector in its own right.

Fleet adoption update

Tesla Tesla has opted for an all-electric option using the technologies it has developed for its automotive models. Details on the new 'Tesla Semi' are sparse, but plans have attracted scepticism as critics believe the batteries required will be too big and heavy. Tesla, however, claims a range of 500 or 800 km depending on the model purchased. With a Tesla Semi potentially costing up to double that of an orthodox truck, the operational savings will have to be considerable over a long time period to make the economics work.

Despite this, UPS has placed a reservation for 125 of the Tesla Semi. Tesla expects to begin production of the vehicles in 2019, and UPS will be among the first companies to put the vehicles into use. Other customers to pre-order include:

- Walmart;
- Pepsi (100);
- FedEx (20);
- Sysco (50);
- DHL (10);

- Ryder;
- JB Hunt;
- Flexport (1);
- Fercam (1);
- Girteka Logistics (1).

Daimler   Through its size and capabilities, Daimler Trucks is perhaps best placed to deliver a new generation of trucks. With its proven track record as one of the world's most successful vehicle manufacturers, its ambition to launch a range of 'eTrucks' by the beginning of the next decade must be taken seriously. Based on an existing model, the conventional drivetrain has been replaced by an electrically driven rear axle with electric motors directly adjacent to the wheel hubs. The power is provided by a battery pack consisting of three lithium-ion battery modules. The range of the truck is up to 200 km, long enough, the company says, for intra-urban deliveries.

DHL Freight has deployed two of Daimler Trucks' FUSO eCanter vehicles, which are to undergo a 24-month test phase in the Berlin metropolitan area. Wholly electric, the 7.5-tonne FUSO eCanter is, in terms of total costs of ownership, more cost efficient than conventional diesel-driven vehicles, it claims. The vehicle has a range of about 100 km with a maximum commercial payload of 3.5 tonnes.

The two trucks will mainly be used to deliver to businesses and private customers in Berlin city centre. The trucks will be on the roads delivering less-than-truckload shipments weighing over 35 kg, such as electric or large home appliances, to private customers. DHL Freight will be using the eCanter both for pick-up and delivery, with the aim of reducing pollution for first and last mile services in the road transport business.

In addition to the two vehicles for DHL Freight, DHL Parcel has also officially taken over four electric trucks for the Berlin region. DHL Parcel will use the four trucks in the central downtown area of Berlin for supplying companies and major customers. The electric trucks are fully integrated into the operational process and replace the vehicles previously used. The aim of the test is to gain more information about the use of e-trucks for company deliveries.

BMW   BMW deploys a fully electric truck to move goods between distribution facilities. The vehicle has a range of 100 km and can be charged in three to four hours. According to the company, it will save 11.8 tonnes of carbon dioxide a year compared to its diesel equivalent.

UPS   UPS has announced it plans to deploy 50 plug-in electric delivery trucks that will be comparable in acquisition cost to conventional-fuelled trucks. The company is collaborating to design the vehicles 'from the ground up', with zero tailpipe emissions.

EV manufacturer, Workhorse, claims these vehicles provide nearly 400 per cent fuel efficiency improvement. Each truck will have a range of approximately 160 km between charges. UPS will test the vehicles primarily on urban routes across the country, including Atlanta, Dallas and Los Angeles. Following real-world test deployments, UPS and Workhorse will fine tune the design in time to deploy a larger fleet in 2019 and beyond. Since most of the maintenance costs of a vehicle are associated with the engine and related components, UPS expects the operating cost of the new plug-in electric vehicle to be less than a similarly equipped diesel or gasoline vehicle. UPS's goal is to make the new electric vehicles a standard selection, where appropriate, in its fleet of the future. UPS has approximately 35,000 diesel or gasoline trucks in its fleet that are comparable in size and are used in routes with duty cycles, or daily kilometres travelled, similar to the new electric vehicles.

Deutsche Post DHL Group/Ford   Deutsche Post DHL Group and Ford have collaborated to produce the 'StreetScooter WORK XL', an electric delivery van based on a Ford Transit chassis. The vehicle is fitted with a battery-electric drivetrain and a body designed and built to Deutsche Post DHL Group specifications.

In total Deutsche Post DHL Group, StreetScooter and Ford plan to build 2,500 e-vans by 2019. Like StreetScooter's existing electric models – the WORK and WORK L – the WORK XL could be also sold to third-party customers.

The WORK XL will have a load volume of 20 cubic metres and provide stowage space for over 200 parcels. The e-van is fitted with a modular battery system delivering 30 to 90 kWh of power, giving it a range of between 80 km and 200 km. With a charging capacity of up to 22 kW, the average charging time is three hours.

Hybrid electric vehicles

Hybrid vehicles use either a petrol or diesel engine, but they are augmented by an alternative propulsion system.

Petrol or diesel/electric hybrid

These vehicles have been around for some time and a common choice in the passenger sector (Toyota Prius, for example). A normal engine is augmented by an electric battery that can also be charged through regenerative braking as well as by charging stations. The electric battery is typically used at low speeds and, when the speed increases, the petrol/diesel engine takes over.

One of the advantages is that the petrol/diesel engine can be small (as it is augmented by battery power) and so has lower emissions. One of the problems of such vehicles is the weight of the battery and the other components required. They are not necessarily as eco-friendly as perhaps might be first thought. For example, their batteries, containing toxins, need to be recycled. As well as this, at higher speeds, the petrol/diesel engines emit more pollutants than some of the most advanced fuel-efficient diesel/petrol alternatives.

Hydraulic hybrid vehicles

There is another alternative under development: hydraulic hybrid engine systems. The petrol/diesel engine is assisted by a system that works solely through regenerative braking. The kinetic energy powers a pump that when under braking moves fluid under pressure from a reservoir to an 'accumulator', which acts as a battery (inasmuch as it stores potential energy). The US National Renewable Energy Laboratory (NREL) states that up to 70 per cent of kinetic energy can be captured for deployment (NREL, 2017). The accumulator also holds nitrogen, and this pressurized gas can then be used to either power the transmission or wheels directly. The fact that energy is harvested and stored during braking makes these systems ideally suited for package delivery vans due to the stop-start nature of their operation. UPS has been testing such systems in the United States since 2012.

There are two types of hydraulic hybrid vehicles – parallel-hybrids and series-hybrids:

Parallel hydraulic A parallel-hybrid allows the battery to provide power to the vehicle through the transmission when it is accelerating but will not work independently. This means that the conventional engine can never be shut off completely. Despite this it can deliver up to 40 per cent in fuel economy.

Series hydraulic A series-hydraulic hybrid transmits power directly to the wheels rather than through a transmission. This means that it is more efficient (savings of up to 60 to 70 per cent) and can work when the ICE has been shut down, making it zero emission.

Fleet adoption update

Ford   Ford has plans to launch 40 electrified van models by 2022, which will include 16 full electric types. A series-hybrid prototype is being tested in London and Valencia before going into full production. The battery drives the four wheels of the Ford Transit at all times and is recharged by the petrol engine, which has a capacity of 1 litre. This means that the van won't generally be zero emission although its benefit is that the driver won't have any 'range-anxiety' – the worry about where to recharge the vehicle's batteries. However, it will have the capability of running for some kilometres direct from the battery (Ford suggest 50 kilometres at present, although this is likely to increase), which means it will be compatible with any future zero-emissions zones.

In total the van has a range of 570 kilometres and a payload of 1,000 kg – more than other pure electric rivals as it carries less weight in batteries due to its hybrid nature. Twenty Ford Transits are being deployed in the trial (including DPD), supported by Transport for London, and the data collected will be analysed to work out the most effective balance between battery and petrol engine.

The cost of the van will be much more expensive than a traditional diesel, although no figures have been released on its total life costs, and at present hybrid vans are eligible for government subsidy. Ford is also working with DHL to develop a larger commercial vehicle that will be fully electric.

UPS   UPS is expanding its hybrid-electric fleet and in 2015 purchased 125 new technology hybrid-electric delivery trucks. The new trucks provide significant fuel economy equivalency gains – up to four times the fuel economy of a diesel-powered vehicle, compared to a 10 to 15 per cent improvement with previous hybrid designs. They rely on a small internal combustion engine and lithium-ion battery to deliver an 80 to 100 km per day range.

FedEx   FedEx operates one of the largest fleets of commercial hybrid trucks in North America, consisting of more than 330 hybrid-electric trucks in addition to 19 all-electric trucks in Los Angeles, London and Paris.

Choices for fleet managers

From Table 13.3 it is obvious that in terms of most metrics, diesel power is by far the obvious choice (presently) for fleet managers. However, of course, in terms of political importance, tailpipe emissions are taking priority over

Table 13.3 Fleet choice matrix

	Range	Payload	Total cost of ownership	Tailpipe emissions	GHG emissions	Charging/fuelling infrastructure
Diesel	Yes	Yes	Yes	No	Yes	Yes
All electric	No	No	No	Yes	Dependent on source	No
Electric hybrid	Yes	Weight of battery issue	No	Some emissions	Some emissions	Yes
Hydraulic hybrid	Yes	Yes	No	Some emissions	Some emissions	Yes
Hydrogen fuel cell	Yes	Yes	No	Yes	Dependent on source	No
Natural gas	Yes	Yes	No	Yes	No	No
Biofuels	Yes	Yes	No	Yes	No	No

many other considerations. Diesel bans in cities are an inevitability that all the major manufacturers and truck/van owners are taking into account in their long-term strategies.

Meeting the challenge of charging electric vehicles

The charging challenge

A fundamental question for the electric vehicle sector is whether enough electricity can be generated to cope with the vast numbers of cars and trucks that are being forecast. One piece of research undertaken for power network provider, National Grid (2017), forecasts that an additional 18 GW of demand would be created in the UK alone by a take-up of electric vehicles (both cars as well as commercial vehicles) by 2050 – almost a third more than the peak power required in 2017. Cars and electric vehicles will be competing with industry and domestic requirements for power. However, National Grid asserts, the demand from electric vehicles could be dramatically reduced by the use of smart technology (discussed later). The National Grid research uses four scenarios to set out possible futures: two degrees (high economic growth and meeting climate change targets committed to by national governments); slow progression (low economic growth and policy interventions limited by affordability); steady state (low growth rate and austerity); and consumer power (high economic growth rate and consumer-led society).

Although the research relates to consumer behaviour and its effect on demand, it is relevant in terms of attitudes to business as well. It shows that power demand will be at its highest if consumers (and businesses) charge their vehicles at peak times – a real challenge to the grid in developed countries and perhaps overwhelming in many countries with less-developed generation capacities. However, the best case scenario suggests that if consumers and businesses charge at off-peak times, the peak demand will be much more manageable.

To spread demand there will need to be a combination of tariffs to encourage efficient charging behaviour by consumers and businesses, and smart technology that identifies the best time to charge vehicles.

Charging options

One of the most important factors inhibiting electric vehicle uptake has been the lack of confidence by drivers that they will be able to find a re-charging point, especially if they are undertaking journeys outside of urban areas. As we will see, this has prompted huge investment by a large range of different players, encouraged by government subsidies. The extent to which this impacts on parcels delivery companies is not so clear. Many vans will be recharged at a depot overnight, and the charge may be sufficient to last for a day depending on routes and loads, in which case, charging 'on-the-go' may not be so important, at least for urban deliveries.

Consequently, in addition to national networks of charging points, a pro-portion of infrastructure investment will need to be focused on centralized recharging hubs where the demands of charging considerable numbers of vans over a short period of time will place considerable strain on local power networks. Of course, not all parcels companies will operate on this basis. In a sector that is increasingly dominated by the use of owner-drivers (the so-called 'gig economy') many drivers take their vehicles home at night and will therefore be charging their vans from a domestic charging point. This will spread the intensity of demand over a larger area, although it will not, of course, reduce the overall demand placed upon the power generation companies.

Charging in the depot

As highlighted earlier, there are challenges related to charging large numbers of electric freight vehicles. When announcing a recent partnership with UPS related to a project undertaken in a London depot, Tanja Dalle-Muenchmeyer, Programme Manager Electric Freight at Cross River Partnership, said:

> Our previous work on electric freight vehicles has shown that local grid infrastructure constraints are one of the main barriers to their large-scale uptake. We need to find smarter solutions to electric vehicle charging if we want to benefit from the significant air quality and environmental benefits these vehicles offer. (Middleton, 2018)

Upgrading the external power grid to a depot is a very expensive undertaking that would put off many companies from adopting electric freight vehicles. However, the UPS smart grid solution uses a central server that is connected to each electric vehicle charge post as well as the grid power supply and the on-site energy storage. This has allowed the company to increase the number of trucks it charges from 65 to 170 by spreading the charge throughout the night, in tandem with the other power requirements of the building, without exceeding the maximum power available from the grid.

The smart-grid solution will be rolled out in conjunction with other innovations. These include conventional power grid upgrade, smart grid, on-site energy storage with batteries and local power generation (using, for example, solar energy generated on facility roof tops).

Also in the UK, London-based delivery company Gnewt Cargo, with EO Charging, has installed what it believes to be the UK's largest single-site electric vehicle charge point location with a total of 40 new EO smart-chargers at Gnewt Cargo's depot in Bow, London. A further 63 smart-chargers have been ordered. Gnewt claims that it has the world's largest fully electric delivery fleet in the world at around 100 vehicles. It delivered in excess of 2.6 million parcels in London in 2017.

In the United States, Italian energy company, Enel, has acquired eMotor-werks, smart technology that allows charging stations to be controlled remotely for what is termed 'grid balancing' purposes. This decides the best time for connected vehicles to be charged. The stations also have a storage element that can be charged at off-peak times and can then be used to charge the vehicle once connected.

'On-the-go' charging

Away from the depot, investment is gathering pace for the development of charging stations. At present the major investments have come in Europe, the United States and China. The key difference between domestic charging and public points is the speed of charge. Rapid charge points can charge an electric vehicle battery in 20 to 30 minutes. This will be essential for the fast-moving parcels sector where time is a critical commodity.

Europe

Many believe that a huge increase in charging points is needed in Europe if the infrastructure is to support the forecast number of electric vehicles. The bank Morgan Stanley estimates that 1 to 3 million public charging points will be required in Western Europe by 2030 compared to the present number of around 120,000 (Nishizawa, 2018).

Although most parcels companies will be rolling out fleets of electric vehicles in urban areas where 'on-the-go' charging is not so much a problem, it will mean, eventually, that with the improvement in battery technologies, fleets may go fully electric rather than a mix of both diesel and electric.

Figure 13.2 includes all charging positions, the majority of which are under 22 kW – it is estimated that only 6 per cent are 'fast'. The new 'Type-2' charging connections are much faster, but much fewer in number. 'Type-2' has been adopted by the European Commission as the standard and will become ubiquitous over time. These points are being supported by both public sector subsidy and regulation as well as private sector investment.

Recent European initiatives include:

- In November 2017, Shell formed a partnership with IONITY (a group consisting of BMW, Ford, Volkswagen and other vehicle manufacturers) to develop a high power charging network across Europe.

- BP has invested US $5 million in FreeWire Technologies, a US manufacturer of charging systems for electric vehicles. FreeWire's electric vehicle charging systems will be added to filling stations in the UK capable of fully charging an electric vehicle in 30 minutes.

- Not to be outdone in terms of diversification from its core energy business, Shell has acquired NewMotion, a company that specializes in building fast charging public electric vehicle stations. As with BP, they have started rolling out charging points in the UK with plans to expand in other locations in Europe. This will operate alongside Shell's network of points at its forecourts. With access to more than 64,000 public charge points, NewMotion has the largest charge network in Europe covering Belgium, Germany, the UK, France and the Netherlands.

Figure 13.2 Europe: charging positions 2017 by leading country

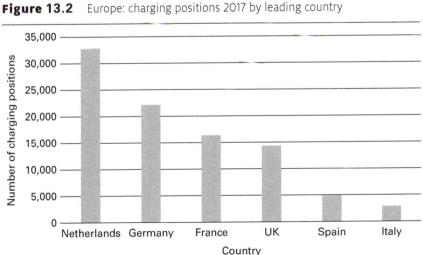

- Another collaboration between US ChargePoint and French company Engie is also planning to build a pan-European network of high-voltage fast-charging stations.
- Chargepoint is part owned by BMW, Daimler and Siemens and it has entered into a partnership with French-based TSG (previously owned by Tokheim), which provides maintenance services to filling stations in France, Germany, Ireland, the Netherlands and the UK.

Outlook for charging networks

Investment is pouring into the electric vehicle charging station sector. Government regulations and incentives will encourage consumers and freight operators to adopt electric vehicles over a relatively short time frame, and the infrastructure will need to be in place to support this growth.

Despite the rush to build large numbers of charging stations, a more focused response would be to develop fewer, but faster charging points. This would encourage consumers and companies to charge during the day rather than at peak times, such as the evening. Smart technologies that 'grid-balance' will become important, especially in parcels depots, to decide on the best time to recharge vans.

Among the parties involved are:

- oil companies looking to diversify from fossil fuel dependence;
- power distribution companies seeing the market as a major opportunity;
- automotive companies who need dense recharging networks in place in order to encourage consumers to buy electric vehicles;
- the technology hardware and software companies developing the charging stations;
- facilities management, retailers, filling station forecourt owners, etc, looking to leverage the location of their assets;
- governments and local authorities developing public policy for climate change and public health.

Summary

Public policy is demanding that alternative propulsion systems must be developed to reduce the impact of transport on the environment and public health. Many of the world's largest manufacturers and fleet operators have willingly invested in the new technologies that will ultimately supersede diesel power. However, to date, no technology is able to match diesel in terms of its all-round utility.

Consequently, it seems probable that instead of all-out bans on diesel and petrol-engine vehicles, more sensible targets will be set for the industry, taking into account advances in technology and encouraging investment.

As well as supporting the development of new technologies and fuels, governments will continue to facilitate the investment in charging and refuelling stations as well as ensuring that electricity supply is plentiful enough not only to charge vans and trucks but also the numerous electric cars that will appear on the roads.

As Preston Feight, President of DAF Trucks and Chairman of the ACEA Commercial Vehicle Board said:

> The affordability of alternatively-powered vehicles is key, as operators simply have to make money with their vehicles. Taxation policies, incentives and public procurement can be useful tools to stimulate sales of alternatively-powered vehicles. But it is crucial that there is sufficient clarity, harmonization and long-term stability in this regard. (ACEA, 2018)

Bibliography

ACEA [accessed 21 September 2018] What Will Power Our Trucks, Vans and Buses in the Future? *European Automotive Manufacturers Association* [Online] www.acea.be/news/article/conference-what-will-power-our-trucks-vans-and-buses-in-the-future

Behr, M [accessed 19 September 2018] ChargePoint Develops 2-MW Charger for Electric Aircraft, *Electrans* [Online] www.electrans.co.uk/chargepoint-develops-new-high-powered-charger/

Cullen, D [accessed 19 September 2018] Why Some Fleets Still Like Natural Gas, *Automotive Fleet* [Online] www.automotive-fleet.com/157688/why-some-fleets-still-like-natural-gas

IEA [accessed 25 September 2018] The Future of Trucks, *International Energy Agency* [Online] www.iea.org/publications/freepublications/publication/TheFutureofTrucksImplicationsforEnergyandtheEnvironment.pdf

McKinnon, AC, Browne, M and Whiteing, A (2012) *Green Logistics: Improving the environmental sustainability of logistics*, Kogan Page, UK

Middleton, N [accessed 18 September 2018] Switch to Smart Grid to Enable All-Electric Fleet at UPS, *EV Fleetworld* [Online] at http://evfleetworld.co.uk/switch-to-smart-grid-to-enable-all-electric-fleet-at-ups/

National Grid (2017) *Future Energy Scenarios*, July 2017, National Grid, London

Nishizawa, K [accessed 15 January 2018] The World Must Spend $2.7 Trillion on Charging Stations for Tesla to Fly, *Bloomberg* [Online] www.bloomberg.com/news/articles/2017-10-11/tesla-ev-network-shows-a-2-7-trillion-gap-morgan-stanley-says

NREL [accessed 1 November 2017] Hydraulic Hybrid Fleet Vehicle Evaluations, *National Renewable Energy Laboratories* [Online] www.nrel.gov/transportation/fleettest-hydraulic.html

Schoettle, B, Sivak, M and Tunnell, M (2016) *A Survey of Fuel Economy and Fuel Usage by Heavy-Duty Truck Fleets*, University of Michigan, US

UPS [accessed 19 September 2018] UPS Unveils First Extended Range Fuel Cell Electric Delivery Vehicle [Online] www.pressroom.ups.com/pressroom/ContentDetailsViewer.page?ConceptType=PressReleases&id=1493730807330-217

The digitization of international freight forwarding   14

**THIS CHAPTER WILL FAMILIARIZE
THE READER WITH:**

- the more positive progress towards digitization in international trade and freight forwarding;
- what digitization will mean for the industry and threats for the incumbents;
- the rise of digital freight platforms;
- the digital offerings of the main freight forwarders;
- what digital freight forwarders, such as Flexport, have to offer customers;
- how forwarders will adapt and survive in the new digital environment.

The importance of digitization

Despite an increasing trend towards digitization, many of the processes managed by freight forwarders remain manual. Reliant on email and telephone communications to contact carriers and establish quotations and bookings, many freight forwarders are, correctly, perceived as low tech and unresponsive by their shippers. As a result, the advent of cloud-based instant quotation and booking systems, such as Freightos and Cargobase, has led some to question the utility of traditional freight forwarders, who lack the speed and visibility provided by the new platforms.

Reinforcing this point, Freightos conducted a study in 2015 that found that the average quote time from a freight forwarder was 90 hours (Walters, 2018). The quickest response took 30 hours, while the slowest was 840 hours. Surprisingly, only five companies followed up after providing the quote in order to attempt to secure the business. Freightos also found that there was a 41 per cent difference between the lowest and highest prices. This lack of consistency paints a picture of poor visibility, which a number of companies are attempting to overcome. Such efforts are, however, held back by the slow adoption of new technology by companies locked into legacy systems.

A notable example of this is the system of air waybills (AWB): documentation that represents the contract of carriage between the shipper and the carrier for air transportation. Since 2010, the International Air Transport Association (IATA) has encouraged carriers and forwarders to adopt electronic air waybills (eAWB), to speed up the process of exchanging and sorting documentation through electronic data interchange (EDI). Though certain trade routes, such as those governed by the Warsaw regime, require the submission of physical documents, some 80 per cent of global cargo volumes travel on routes compatible with eAWBs. Nonetheless, uptake of the system has been slow: according to IATA, eAWB penetration only reached 39 per cent of viable shipments during May 2016 (ACN, 2018). Moreover, as the AWB represents only 1 of 30 paper documents that are required to conduct air freight transportation, there is some way to go before a complete e-freight system is in place.

The slow uptake of the eAWB system is at least partly derived from a lack of flexibility within the internal systems of forwarders and carriers themselves. As with many companies throughout the supply chain, carriers and freight forwarders tend to run expensive and complex, locally installed, enterprise resource planning (ERP) systems. At the upper end of the market these tend to be set up by enterprise software leaders such as SAP, Oracle and Epicor. ERP systems manage the internal data flows of an organization, integrating and automating back-office functions throughout the enterprise, including procurement, human resources and customer relationship management. These systems are effective in this function but are highly rigid and are difficult to adapt to new external requirements. They therefore limit an organization's ability to match changing customer needs. As a result of this difficulty, alterations are often also prohibitively expensive, which suppresses the incentive of organizations to change.

An example of the complexities of adapting an ERP system is DHL Global Forwarding's attempted 'New Forwarding Environment' (NFE) project. NFE was conceived as a means of enabling improved global shipment visibility and a reduction of paperwork through greater use of a document management system, among other upgrades. A significant driver of the project was the understanding that improved visibility throughout the organization would allow DHL to apply its enormous economies of scale more effectively. This was not to be, with increasing lead times, implementation errors and spiralling costs leading to the suspension and eventual cancellation of the project.

Given these issues, a number of software companies, providing services built upon a cloud architecture, have stepped up. By using 'Big Data' analytics, these companies sort through data aggregated from forwarders and, in some cases, carriers in order to automatically map industry spot rate fluctuations in real time. These companies have the advantage of being able to facilitate real-time quotation and booking services, based on the spot rate data, and have attracted attention for shining a light on a volatile market.

The implications for freight forwarders

The overwhelming takeaway from this is the dramatic improvements brought about in booking, quoting and price visibility. As regards implementation, many of the largest freight forwarders have developed their own online systems such as Kuehne+Nagel, DHL and Agility. Many other forwarders have elected to license this technology from the SaaS platforms. SEKO is a customer of CargoSphere, and notable customers of Freightos include Hellmann Worldwide, Nippon Express and CEVA. Meanwhile, Cargobase claims to serve 10 of the top 25 air freight forwarders. These platforms are more significant facilitators than they are competitors for freight forwarders.

The cost for companies not adopting a uniform, company-wide platform, on the other hand, is stark. Regardless of whether or not forwarders buy or license the means to operate company-wide data platforms, we may see an industry-wide decoupling between these data-unified companies and the less profitable data-fragmented ones, in which the former exercise a significant advantage over the latter. Examples of potential winners in this scenario include Expeditors International and Kuehne+Nagel.

For companies that may see themselves as the losers in this scenario, their position may be somewhat ameliorated by the fact that the adoption of new cloud-based services comes at a much more reasonable price than implementing on-site enterprise software. As a result, smaller companies may find that they are actually in a position to achieve data unification. Meanwhile, larger incumbents maintaining expensive legacy systems may find it more difficult to make the transition.

The threats for industry incumbents

A seemingly inevitable threat for freight forwarders at the theoretical level has been forwarder disintermediation, ie shippers booking direct with asset-owning carriers. In sea freight, many more shippers will book direct with the shipping line, but there is no incentive to do this for smaller companies, as they are more likely to benefit from the buying power offered by a freight forwarder. Some do choose to go through the SaaS companies, although, as mentioned, these businesses often operate with forwarders, rather than against them.

Within air freight, a prominent case study in disintermediation comes from Dutch carrier KLM, which attempted to institute a direct sales approach in 1999. The carrier was explicit in stating that the business drivers behind the plan were to compete with low-end forwarders only and were not intended to cut forwarders out of the loop entirely. Regardless, this manoeuvre unsettled the forwarder community enough for many to move their business to other carriers, which resulted in a damaging loss of cargo volumes for KLM, as well as the resignation of the executive who had driven through the project.

Though most have observed this incident as a cautionary tale, the increasing digitization of the air freight process may encourage one of today's carriers to take the chance once more.

The big three express integrators (UPS, FedEx and DHL), along with a new generation of Chinese companies (SF Express, YTO Express and more) are also entering the fray. They present forwarders with a more significant issue than carrier disintermediation in that they represent more attractive partners for shippers concerned with high-value goods. These clients deal with products that are typically shipped just-in-time, such as certain pharmaceuticals and automotive/manufacturing components, and offer high margins.

Having direct ownership of the entire door-to-door shipping process allows the integrators to maintain and share a 'single version of the truth' and also exercise a much greater ability to directly intervene when problems arise. Though carriers and forwarders alike will benefit from increasing tracking and visibility capabilities, express integrators will always have an advantage in the upper echelons of the market, due to their direct control over the assets involved.

While this high-value express segment is large and growing, it has its limits, with the rest of the market served by forwarders and carriers. Therefore, the advent of cross-border B2C e-commerce represents both an opportunity and a major threat for freight forwarders, with a new generation of providers entering the market. This group of companies includes those who have a technology background, such as Amazon and Alibaba's Cainiao, as well as smaller forwarders who have transformed their internal operations from the ground up.

The essential threat to established companies is summed up nicely by Flexport CEO Ryan Petersen, when discussing DHL's issues with NFE:

> There are two ways logistics companies can attain scale: Through acquisitions or with technology. Technology might limit how quickly you can grow because you can't acquire your way to scale. On the other hand, scale eventually becomes a hindrance to the acquirer as it struggles to tie together legacy platforms. (Petersen, 2018)

Digital freight forwarding platforms

Given that 'broking' (ie buying and selling carrier capacity) is such a big part of a freight forwarder's business, it would be imagined that they should be quick to recognize the threat from the rating/spot pricing platforms. Indeed, the larger forwarders who have long-standing relationships with their clients and various carriers, do use technology extensively. But as the margins in the forwarding business are generally low, across the board levels of investment in technology have also been low. This has been a major problem.

Established forwarders invested heavily in technology 10 to 15 years ago and many continue to use those systems. Although they are by now embedded into the core of the organization, they are unwieldy, difficult and expensive to maintain. As a result, clients demanding more information and more agile IT solutions become dissatisfied, and the forwarders are usually forced to introduce external solutions from the 'cloud' that are not integrated with their core systems. Ironically, the new entrants into the market can take advantage of the newer solutions at much lower cost, because they don't have to worry about integration with older legacy systems.

As with all of these things, any solutions they introduce must add value for the customer. Just introducing a standalone rate selection engine will be pointless, unless it is combined or integrated with an order and shipment management system to seamlessly flow information directly from the client to the carrier.

In short, there are lots of solutions that solve a specific problem, but unless the forwarder can introduce them into a coherent IT solution set, they may be wasting their money. Established forwarders have to deal with the challenge of updating legacy systems while maintaining service levels and reducing cost. This is expensive and will get more expensive as time goes on and ultimately will become unsustainable. It is easier to do a wholesale replacement exploiting a lower cost cloud service, but that requires skill and expertise to pull off. It is also massively difficult politically to sell internally, especially if senior management was responsible for the initial investment.

Survey: the use of online platforms

Results from a Ti (2018) survey contained in the *Global Freight Forwarding* report 2017 show a growing interest in the use of online quotation and booking tools to increase the ease and speed with which customer interactions can be conducted (Figure 14.1).

Half of the respondents have trialled the use of such platforms. Of those, 64 per cent went on to adopt or develop such a system for use as a permanent solution within their organization.

However, overall this indicates a moderate uptake, at least at this stage of the technology's development. One reason for this, given by the responses to a follow-up question, was the performance of the technology (Figure 14.2). Of those survey participants who had experience of an online quotation and booking platform, 61 per cent noted that performance was mixed. Only 14 per cent of respondents found that the platform delivered solid functionality.

Figure 14.1 Survey: use of online freight platforms

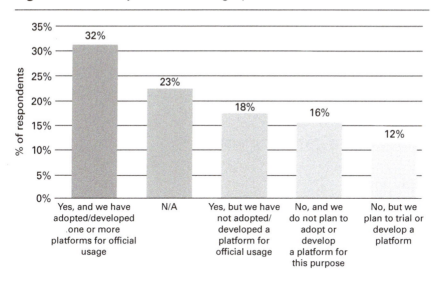

Figure 14.2 Survey: quality of online freight platforms

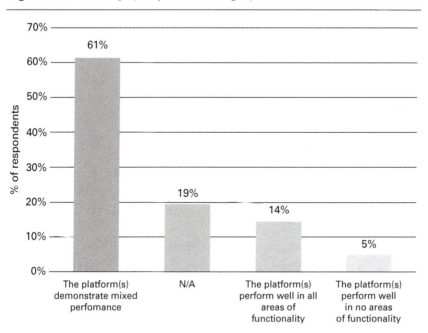

Looking at these results, some users may feel that the quotation and booking platforms presently on offer do not offer value for money. Nevertheless, many others are clearly willing to embrace the potential of these systems, even if this may only apply to certain shipments on certain routes. As time goes by, these systems will inevitably become more comprehensive and robust.

Selected digital forwarders

Flexport

Flexport has raised US $201.6m from the following investors: Y Combinator, First Round, Founders Fund, Felicis, Google Ventures, Box Group, Bloomberg Beta, Susa Ventures, Yuri Milner, Ashton Kutcher, Peter Thiel and Joe Lonsdale.

Flexport is a digital freight forwarder powered by unified, structured data, interfacing with clients through APIs. It does not offer customers instant quotation or pricing transparency but does provide end-to-end forwarding services including customs clearance. The company is primarily focused on the Eastbound Trans-Pacific trade lane, from Asia to the US West Coast, but also has operations in the Netherlands.

Flexport's software can provide pallet-level visibility over shipments, which it is building into its customer API. The company also runs software for compliance, a platform for asset-owners (principally road freight companies) and can facilitate the integration of shippers and carriers through its purchase order management software. While other companies can offer these services (for example, Damco performs the latter), they are often based on older technologies and come at a greater cost. Significantly, Flexport has built all of its applications from the ground up as part of a unified software platform, which avoids the integration issues larger forwarders experience as a result of siloed business units or M&A.

This backend allows for far easier interfaces for shippers and carriers, and the company's self-service web interface is a big draw for SME customers, which represent a large portion of Flexport's customer base. According to its CEO Ryan Petersen (2018), this is principally made up of three types of customer: small companies selling on Amazon; large, traditional businesses interested in both air and sea freight (including Bridgestone Tyres); and fast-growing e-commerce companies that have not had time to develop their logistics capabilities (including Harry's Razors).

FreightHub

The following companies are investors in FreightHub: Northzone, Global Founders Capital, Cherry Ventures, Cavalry Ventures, Saarbruecker21 and La Famiglia. The company has raised a total of US $43.23m in funding.

FreightHub is a digital freight forwarder providing a web-based system for freight quotes, booking and tracking, and aims to differentiate itself from peers through cost transparency. It is a full-service forwarding company, offering global full container load, less than container load and air transportation backed up by logistics specialists. FreightHub is primarily focused on the Westbound Asia-Europe trade lane.

Following a Series A funding round of US $20m during December 2017, FreightHub CEO Ferry Heilemann stated:

> With this funding, we will continue to deliver on our growth plans, and open new hubs in Asia and the USA... We are delighted that our investors will support us, not only with capital, but also with their international networks, as we look to build the digital backbone of the logistics industry.

The company operates in Germany, from offices in Berlin and Hamburg. FreightHub has a customer base of around 650 businesses, including Home24, Lesara, Franke and Viessmann.

iContainers

The following companies are investors in iContainers: Kibo Ventures, Serena Capital and GrupoRomeu. The company has raised US $8.33m in funding.

iContainers provides a marketplace platform for international sea freight. The company offers a quotation and booking services for the movement of goods on selected trade lanes. While the company has a digital-first approach and an emphasis on automation, shipments are also supported by dedicated sales and operations account managers.

iContainers operates a cloud-based marketplace platform, which matches customer shipments with appropriate carriers, based on defined preferences. The company's services cover 500,000 different shipping routes. In addition to providing shippers with quotation and booking services, iContainers also provides users with shipment tracking, one-click reservations, price alerts and customs requirements.

The company operates globally, with offices in Miami, Barcelona, Rotterdam and Santo Domingo.

Selected freight forwarders' digital offerings

Shipa Freight (Agility)

Beta-tested by Agility since 2017 and launched formally in April 2018, Shipa Freight provides an instant, no-obligation rate quote platform from the countries that account for 95 per cent of global trade. It allows users to manage their international shipments with a simple tool accessible by desktop, laptop, tablet and mobile app.

The platform is initially aimed at SME businesses providing transparency, flexibility, competitive pricing and customer service, which Agility believes has to date only been offered to multinationals and high-volume customers. The digital platform allows users to complete a shipment online including shipment booking, a range of payment options and online tracking.

The rate element of the offering is updated by country operations throughout Agility's network using dynamic pricing that can change by the hour, although rates are valid for two to four weeks. According to management, it has access to hundreds of thousands of trade lanes although it has yet to indicate capacity available. It does, however, have a compliance tool that provides details of necessary documentation as well as a history of previous quotes.

FreightNet (Kuehne+Nagel)

Swiss-based forwarder Kuehne+Nagel introduced its digital forwarder KN FreightNet for air freight in 2014, with LCL sea freight following a year later. Using KN FreightNet, customers can obtain instant quotes for export and import shipments online and place their orders. No pre-registration is needed to access the platform.

Quotations are based on simple shipment details such as place of origin, final destination, weight and volume. Users receive a structured overview of the all-inclusive door-to-door price including all applicable surcharges, as well as the estimated transit time. It is planned that a booking can be made or the offer, valid for 30 days, can be saved for later use. Users can also use the KN Login iPhone app to determine the status and transportation details of the LCL shipment while the shipment is in transit.

In 2017 Kuehne+Nagel entered into an agreement with Alibaba.com that will allow paid members in China to obtain quotations and book pick-up and destination delivery services for air freight and LCL consignments via the FreightNet platform. The offer is aimed at Chinese SME customers, enabling them to capitalize on cross-border trade opportunities.

Panalpina

In late 2017, Panalpina started trials of its own online instant quotation and booking portal. The initial development took nine months, but it is envisaged to be part of a much longer three- to four-year project to replace its legacy IT platform. Trials commenced with selected air cargo customers for door-to-door shipments. The rate 'engine' does not interact directly with carriers' own rate portals, but this will be the eventual aim.

Like other forwarders, the platform is aimed primarily at SMEs rather than global shippers that already have contracts in place.

Freightquote (DHL)

DHL Global Forwarding launched its online quotation and booking service in late 2017. Of the major forwarders, DHL is one of the last to provide such a service perhaps due in part to the well-documented problems it had with its internal information systems.

As with other quotation platforms, the new system provides customers with the opportunity to get a price and a contract immediately. DHL describes it as being able to rapidly create 'competitive customer quotations based on door-to-door all-in rates and transit information'.

The quotation and booking service connects to DHL Interactive, DHL Global Forwarding's online customer portal, where it additionally provides shipment tracking and the creation and distribution of customized shipment reports. The service is available in over 40 countries, covering most key lanes and point pairs globally. The quotation and booking service provides an immediate price for general cargo air freight up to 2,000 kg per shipment and offers two speeds of service.

Twill (Damco)

A digital 'start-up' owned by Maersk's freight forwarding unit Damco, Twill was launched in spring 2017. According to management its aim is to provide services to existing Damco customers including instant quotation, integrated document handling, milestone transparency and proactive exception management. It is focused on sea freight and uses major shipping lines, including non-Maersk. However, it has a focus on technological development, which is one of the reasons it is not headquartered in the same building as that of Damco.

Twill currently serves full container load, ocean services from port to door, importing from China (including Hong Kong and Taiwan territories), India, Vietnam and Indonesia to the UK, Spain, Poland or the Czech Republic.

The service commenced on Asia-Europe routes, specifically the UK, but it plans to include mainland European ports, most notably Rotterdam. In early 2018, Twill expanded to India, taking its first export booking, and it hopes to include the market as an import country on the platform.

Selected digital marketplaces

Freightos

The following companies are investors in Freightos: GE Ventures, Aleph, Annox Capital, ICV, OurCrowd, MSR Capital and Sadara Ventures.

Initially starting out as a marketplace platform for international freight movements, Freightos has established two main service platforms: Freightos Accelerate and Freightos Marketplace. The Freightos Marketplace platform represents an online spot market portal through which shippers can purchase freight forwarding services. Freight forwarders send Freightos their data on carrier contracts in Excel files (over 1,000 per week), which are automatically absorbed into the Freightos database. By aggregating this data and averaging out spot prices on various routes and modes of transport, Freightos is able to instantly automate spot quotations for shippers.

Freightos Accelerate is a rate management platform used by forwarders to manage buy rates and automate selling. At present, most of the companies that purchase this service use it to automate buying and selling processes inhouse, though an increasing number are using it to sell directly online. Accelerate tracks freight rates on all modes of transport.

Following Freightos's acquisition of WebCargoNet in August 2016, the company has been able to improve the performance of both its Accelerate and Marketplace platforms. WebCargoNet is a database of air cargo prices, retrieved directly from cargo airlines, which Freightos purports to be the largest of its kind in the world.

In total, 23 of the top 25 forwarders are customers of Freightos in some geographies or modes. This includes Hellmann, Panalpina, CEVA and Nippon Express. At present, the company's marketplace platform is available in the United States and the UK.

Cargobase

The following companies are investors in Cargobase: 500 Startups, Bukit Timah Capital and Ivan Yeo. The company has received US $1.3m in funding.

Cargobase provides an online marketplace for the quotation and booking of freight, with features for reporting, tracking and payments. The platform supports spot market bookings for air, sea road and parcel shipments, which allows users to compare offerings across different modes of transport. In July 2016, the company added features to support pre-negotiated forwarding contracts within its platform, allowing users to choose between spot market options and existing contracted providers, depending on the situation.

Cargobase runs a cloud-based SaaS platform, which supports a spot market exchange for cargo. The platform is connected to over 300 logistics service providers, such as Kuehne+Nagel, Expeditors, DSV, FedEx and DHL. In addition, data from 350 commercial airlines is also fed onto the platform. The platform initially focused on air freight (aircraft charters, on-board couriers, next-flight-out, regular air freight) and road freight. Ocean freight was added in November 2016, with parcels added in July 2017.

Cargobase launched a mobile app, 'On The Go', in April 2017. The mobile application allows users to book, approve and track shipments, as well as interact with logistics service providers.

Why freight forwarders will adapt and survive

As has already been mentioned, there is the risk that freight forwarders could be 'disintermediated' by shippers and carriers, going the same way as many travel agents in the air passenger sector. However, this will not be the case.

In addition to aggregating shipments in order to negotiate bulk prices from carriers, most freight forwarders also handle goods in warehouses at origin and destination centres. Furthermore, they offer transportation to and from these facilities, sometimes managing the entire end-to-end process all the way to a customer's doorstep.

What is clear is that freight forwarders have much more to offer than just the facilitation of point-to-point transportation. By comparison, this is all that is provided by the current generation of SaaS platforms, as well as the carriers they serve. This means that a shipper still has to deal with getting their shipment to and from the port or airport facility, a service that freight forwarders will offer as standard.

An additional advantage for freight forwarders, especially when considering the potential threat from Amazon or Cainiao, is that their businesses function as impartial intermediaries between two partners. While the likes of Amazon represent an entire, vertically integrated operation that many shippers may find themselves in competition with, forwarders are entirely independent. They can therefore exploit this position of neutrality to act as a partner to all agents throughout the supply chain – indeed, this is the reason freight forwarding was established in the first place.

The key to success is genuine collaboration. Freight forwarders in the information age have the potential to drive network effects by sharing information more freely with their clients. By deploying cloud-based network solutions, which engage every stakeholder in a supply chain, forwarders can build upon their current position as intermediaries in the transportation process.

With such transparency comes a broadening of scope, as the forwarding process comes to integrate more deeply with other business functions. By integrating the forwarding process with that of other supply chain information systems, such as demand sensing, it appears likely that freight forwarders are moving towards becoming fourth-party logistics providers (4PLs).

Often referred to as lead logistics providers, 4PLs perform a coordination and management function, sitting above the third-party logistics providers operating as part of a client's supply chain. By contracting out a supply chain to a 4PL, a company is essentially handing over their entire operation to an external provider, who, with expert knowledge and technology, offers cost savings and efficiency improvements.

The nerve centre of a 4PL operation is often referred to as the 'control tower' (see Chapter 6). Control towers facilitate the collection and analysis of data from their agents, customers and trading partners, enabled by specialist supply chain management software that allows interoperability between the diverse systems utilized by network partners. With the manipulation of the supply chain's entire information flow, the control tower is able to maintain security, optimize efficiency and execute interventions to ensure the process runs smoothly. By properly applying this model to their operations, freight forwarders can ensure that they remain not only relevant, but indispensable, in their function as supply chain intermediaries for the 21st century.

The fundamental potential of the 4PL model could be even greater, however. For a freight forwarder, the ultimate significance of acting as a platform in this manner is the ability to oversee an entire supply network, not just a collection of individual supply chains. While individual shippers are only concerned with their own operation, a forwarder facilitating partnerships throughout an entire supply network would have the capacity to encourage 'horizontal collaboration' (see Chapter 1) among nominally competing supply chain actors, in a scenario in which all benefit. The basic logic is this: if several retailers source from the same supplier, why not collaborate on transport and logistics if it can improve efficiency and save money for all involved?

Summary

There is no doubting that the freight forwarding sector is undergoing a digital revolution. A new breed of digital forwarder, such as Flexport, is entering the market and successfully taking share from bigger and slower-moving incumbents. However, the future is certainly not bleak for the existing freight forwarders. Those that are able to adopt the technologies that are under development and build upon their position as supply chain coordinators have the opportunity to propel themselves into a much higher value business than formerly.

What is more, freight forwarders are ideally placed to coordinate and manage complex, global flows of data, finance and goods in future supply chains, ensuring that they will adapt and survive for many decades to come.

Bibliography

ACN [accessed 2 August 2018] E-AWB Penetration Continues to Rise in May, *Air Cargo News* [Online] www.aircargonews.net/news/technology/e-air-waybill/ single-view/news/e-awb-penetration-continues-to-rise-in-may.html

Petersen, R [accessed 4 August 2018] DHL Global Forwarding Failed on Software, and That's Why It's Being Sold So Cheaply, *Flexport* [Online] www.flexport.com/blog/dhl-global-forwarding-sale-software/

Ti Ltd [accessed 2 August 2018] Global Freight Forwarding Report 2017, *Transport Intelligence Ltd* [Online] www.ti-insight.com

Walters, W [accessed 16 July 2018] Forwarders 'Failing Online Freight Sales Test', *Lloyds Loading List* [Online] www.lloydsloadinglist.com/freight-directory/news/Forwarders-%E2%80%98failing-online-freight-sales-test%E2%80%99/63182.htm#.W214iuhKiUk

Disrupting trade finance 15

Blockchain, banks and freight forwarders

THIS CHAPTER WILL FAMILIARIZE THE READER WITH:

- the importance of trade finance to international supply chains and how it works;
- why the sector in its traditional form is failing shippers in many parts of the world;
- the opportunities this has provided for innovators and new technologies;
- some of the market entrants that are developing new trade finance products and platforms;
- blockchain and the role of 'smart contracts';
- opportunities for freight forwarders in their role as supply chain intermediaries.

Introduction

Trade finance is one of the most essential aspects of international commerce. For many centuries, letters of credit, insurance and guarantees have facilitated cross-border trade by assuring that the necessary levels of trust exist between parties within supply chains, backed in the main by banks and their correspondents. In other words, the system gives exporters the assurance that they will be paid by customers who could be located anywhere in the world. Buyers have a guarantee that goods will be delivered when and where the exporter says they will.

Despite the model seemingly working well over the years (after all, it enabled globalization), the sector is on the verge of a revolution, set to become a key competitive battleground shaken up by new technologies. There is also the hope that this disruption will provide an opportunity for freight forwarders to cash in on their role as intermediaries in the supply chain, allowing them to break out of their present low margin business model. For although trade finance works well for multinationals (which generate the majority of global goods flows), many SMEs, especially in the developing world, are being increasingly excluded.

It is for this reason that organizations such as the World Trade Organization, World Economic Forum and International Monetary Fund are encouraging changes to the system. This chapter explores the reasons why and the opportunities it will create.

What is trade finance?

Trade finance is often described as the 'lubricant' of international commerce due to its role in bridging the gap between importers' and exporters' expectations on when payment for goods should be transferred.

Trade finance typically falls into two categories: inter-company credit and bank-intermediated finance.

Inter-company credit

This type of relationship involves the advance of credit by either the buyer or seller who effectively takes on the risk of the transaction. If there is complete trust between the parties, then transactions could be settled on an 'open account' basis. Although figures are hard to come by, it is thought that this type of arrangement accounts for 40 to 50 per cent of agreements (WTO, 2018a).

Bank-intermediated finance

When such levels of trust do not exist, intermediaries become involved to facilitate the transaction, and typically 'letters of credit' are used to specify the terms of the contract. The 'letter of credit' sets out a commitment by the buyer's bank to pay for the purchased goods if a number of obligations are met by the seller. These can include the conditions of delivery and the relevant documentation. Banks can even go further and provide finance to the exporter, which allows it to buy goods from its suppliers and progress the order. This type of finance perhaps accounts for a similar proportion of the market as inter-company credit – around 40 per cent.

Although statistics vary, the World Trade Organization estimates that up to 80 per cent of global trade is supported by finance or credit insurance, the rest being comprised of 'cash-in-advance' (WTO, 2018a).

Why does the sector need shaking up?

According to a report by the Asian Development Bank, 'where trade finance functions well, it enables firms which would otherwise be considered too risky, to link into expanding global value chains and thus contribute to employment and productivity growth' (WTO, 2018b).

However, it does not seem to be working well everywhere. This is a conundrum for many in the industry as trade finance is seen as a particularly low-risk form of finance. The International Chamber of Commerce asserts that the default rate is only 0.021 per cent, of which over half is recovered by the sale of the asset on which the bank has a call, ie the merchandise (ICC, 2018).

According to the World Economic Forum, problems accessing trade finance are a consequence of the 2009 financial crisis, which led to increased levels of risk assessment and enhanced due diligence. This has been compounded by diverse terrorist threats, which have led to tightened regulations (WEF, 2018).

The upshot of this is that the lack of trade finance is one of the main barriers to international trade particularly affecting emerging markets in Africa, the Caribbean, Central Asia and parts of Europe. The International Monetary Fund believe that this is due in part to money-laundering regulations and the cost of compliance, which make financing trade deals unattractive to many commercial banks. It says the withdrawal of these banking services, '[could] disrupt financial services and cross-border flows, including trade finance and remittances, potentially undermining financial stability, inclusion, growth and development goals' (IMF, 2018). The WTO also says, 'in the post-financial crisis era global banks are less inclined to invest in many developing countries' (WTO, 2018a).

What is more, there is a perception that this squeeze on trade finance reinforces the competitive advantage of the larger shippers due to their preferential access to banks and intermediaries. Another problem is the administrative burden.

SMEs in developed as well as developing countries are hampered by the levels of bureaucracy involved, or, at least, are less able to deal with it. The WTO (2018a) says that half of all trade finance requests from SMEs are rejected by banks compared with just 7 per cent of multinational companies.

This has led to what is called a 'financing gap', which has proved to be a headwind for the growth of global trade. The gap is particularly evident in Africa and other developing regions, although it is very difficult to put an actual figure on its scale.

Trade finance innovators and disruptors

The mismatch between supply and demand that these systemic problems have caused has created an opportunity in today's digital world. However, first the paper-heavy trade documentation systems have to be digitized. If the process underpinning bills of lading and letters of credit can be made more efficient and faster, then meeting the needs of regulations such as 'Know your customer' and anti-money laundering can be more easily met. An electronic audit trail is fundamental to ensuring effective compliance.

If the high level of shipment data that is generated can be harnessed, risk levels can be assessed, and this allows companies to innovate, not least in the provision of trade finance.

Creating supply chain visibility through layers of software also has other benefits. The trust it can engender in the transaction has led to the development of derivative products in the trade finance sector, building on the concept of invoice factoring. Investors can pool their capital into an asset class, which can be provided to SMEs to help fund their exports.

In an increasingly crowded sector, there are several examples of trade finance innovators.

essDocs

essDocs provides SaaS fintech and supply chain technology solutions for the export, trade and logistics industries with a goal to enable paperless trade. Solutions are provided through its CargoDocs platform, which digitizes the creation and approval as well as exchange of electronic original documents and also enables users to apply for, sign, stamp and receive back original certificates required for global trade. CargoDocs combines title, quality, condition, location and other key data to reduce risk and improve visibility and control. Key electronic documents covered include: bills of lading, warehouse warrants, certificates of origin, commercial invoices and inspectors' certificates.

Bolero

Bolero has been around since the 1990s and is another solutions provider working to digitize the sector. In conjunction with an enterprise software company, R3, it has embarked on a new electronic bill of lading (eBL) service that it says will connect multiple trade networks. Relevant parties will be able to endorse and verify an eBL's title without needing to revert to paper.

Interlinkages

Interlinkages is based in Hong Kong. It describes itself as:

> [a] cross-border trade finance-bidding platform that endeavours to democratize the international trade finance marketplace by providing the most efficient, cost effective and bank-neutral solutions for trade finance transactions of corporates and SMEs.

The platform matches 'buyers' (those with money to lend) with 'sellers' (those who need to borrow to finance their trade deal) using an 'eBay model' (as described by the founders). It allows lenders to reach markets in which they might not have a physical presence and allows exporters and traders to access funds that otherwise would not be available to them. The platform matches supply and demand but does not bear the risk of the transactions.

Chained Finance

This is a recent joint venture between a subsidiary of manufacturer Foxconn and online lending marketplace Dianrong. In its launch communication it said its aim was to 'meet the hugely underserved needs of supply chain finance in China' (Dianrong, 2018). The company went on to say that it believed that the existing trade finance arrangements only served about 15 per cent of suppliers needing financial resources affecting 40 million Chinese SMEs. Its focus will be on electronics, automotive and fashion manufacturing sectors, and its platform will employ the latest blockchain technology thereby eliminating many of the trust issues faced by counterparties and deliver automated execution.

In Europe banks are also stepping up their presence in this sector. Eleven banks, including Deutsche Bank, HSBC, Rabobank, KBC, Commerzbank and Société Générale have asked IBM to build a platform that will provide similar services to Chained Finance based on blockchain technology and aimed at European SMEs. The consortium has been named Batavia. Speaking to the *Financial Times*, Rudi Peeters, CIO of KBC, commented that blockchain was the obvious technology for trade finance as existing processes were paper-based, complex and expensive (Arnold, 2017). He said that initially the banks would target cross-border road-based trade routes although the product would subsequently be expanded to inter-continental shipping routes. The platform will be accessible to shippers and freight forwarders as well as other banks and credit agencies, allowing SMEs to track shipments and use smart contracts that trigger payment when invoices are raised or delivery completed. Other banks are establishing similar platforms.

It is interesting that IBM initially plans to focus on European cross-border trade, with plans to expand internationally at some point after that. This approach might appear unduly conservative in a sector where venture funded start-ups are known for their ambition and desire for scale. Obviously IBM is a well-established enterprise that understands the consensus building approach and has to be deliberate in building alliances that do not conflict with their existing commercial arrangements. But they are disadvantaged when trying to compete in the same pool with smaller companies who do not have those concerns.

As an example, it is instructive to look at the number of cross-border digital payment companies that have come from nowhere since the mid-2010s and evolved into significant forex players before being acquired for billions of dollars by established banks. The established technology companies could match them with technology but could not keep up with their aggressive and agile business development approach.

Blockchain and 'smart contracts'

The concept of 'smart contracts' has been around for much longer than blockchain technology. A smart contract has been defined by lawyers, Allen and Overy (2018), as 'a set of promises, agreed between parties and encoded in software, which, when criteria are met, are performed automatically'. They don't exclusively involve trade finance contracts, but due to many of the issues set out earlier (trust, complexity, time and paper-based inefficiencies), the benefits that smart contracts can deliver to the sector are substantial. As the legal company asserts, blockchains conveniently provide an underlying trusted network conveniently and efficiently.

By 'hardwiring' the financial transaction process into software code, certain events can be triggered at specified milestones. The most obvious of these is at the point when the goods have been delivered. When the final delivery is made and a scan or electronic proof of delivery is generated, a signal can automatically be sent back up the supply chain, authorizing, for example, the release of funds to the exporter.

This all assumes that the smart contract works in the way that both the exporter and importer intended. While they may reduce human error by eliminating human intervention, this is not to say that errors cannot be made in programming the hard code in the first place. How this plays out in legal terms has really yet to be seen. According to lawyers, there is a reversal of the burden of litigation, with the exporter having to pursue a claim for damages, as the shipment will have already been delivered and the importer will be in possession of the merchandise. At present it would fall to the importing party to pursue a claim for damages if delivery had *not* been made under the terms of a contract.

In addition, there are legal question marks over what happens when the smart contract becomes impossible to perform or there is misrepresentation or illegality. In some cases a smart contract may not be a contract at all, as it might not be recognized by certain jurisdictions.

However, more positively, the way that blockchain works in creating a single and unalterable record means that documentation duplication and even fraudulent invoice financing will become impossible.

The new competitive battleground for freight forwarders?

Freight forwarders are critical parties in the international supply chain process, and so it would seem obvious for them to be at the forefront of the trade finance revolution. In 2009, DHL, in partnership with Standard Chartered Bank in India, provided a first step in digitizing trade documents by scanning them in specially equipped courier vans and sending them digitally to the requisite bank, reducing the time it took to courier these documents physically.

But it is new market entrant Flexport that is now capturing the headlines. Part of its investment plans include rolling out a new trade finance offering to its customers. It believes that the huge amount of supply chain data it is able to generate and analyse will allow it to assess the risk of making temporary loans to many manufacturers and other exporters. This would be a step change in the level of sophistication of services available through forwarders to SMEs and a huge competitive advantage.

If this additional product were rolled out, it would allow freight forwarders to increase their value-added by leveraging their own balance sheets. Forwarding is a low margin business, and operators in the sector are always looking to increase profitability, some more successfully than others. If they are to achieve this goal, however, forwarders will have to move fast and partner with companies that have the appropriate levels of expertise. There is no reason why trade finance could not become a powerful USP for forwarders, not only generating a new revenue stream but also attracting the volumes of higher margin SMEs. If they do not move quickly, it will be left to the many other trade finance innovators to disrupt the market and gain this particular prize.

Summary

The trade finance sector is being shaken up by new technologies such as blockchain, which will provide greater levels of trust between supply chain parties. This will have highly positive implications for exporters in many parts of the developing world that struggle to access competitive sources of finance. Trade finance will also prove to be an important competitive battleground for freight forwarders. The new breed of digital forwarders has an advantage in that the data they can collect on shippers' behaviour will enable them to make loans to SMEs, providing an important new revenue stream.

Bibliography

Allen & Overy [accessed 15 January 2018] Smart Contracts for Finance Parties [Online] www.allenovery.com/publications/en-gb/lrrfs/cross-border/Pages/Smart-contracts-for-finance-parties.aspx

Arnold, M (2017) European Banks to Launch Blockchain Trade Finance Platform, *Financial Times*, 26 June

Dianrong [accessed 15 January 2018] Chained Finance: First Blockchain Platform for Supply Chain Finance, *Dianrong* [Online] www.prnewswire.com/news-releases/chained-finance-first-blockchain-platform-for-supply-chain-finance-300418265.html

ICC [accessed 16 January 2018] New ICC Report Confirms Trade & Export Finance Are Not Risky Business, *ICC* [Online] https://iccwbo.org/media-wall/news-speeches/new-icc-report-confirms-trade-export-finance-not-risky-business/

IMF [accessed 15 January 2018] The Withdrawal of Correspondent Banking Relationships: A Case for Policy Action, *International Monetary Fund* [Online] www.imf.org/external/pubs/ft/sdn/2016/sdn1606.pdf

WEF [accessed 14 January 2018] The Role of Law and Regulation in International Trade Finance: the Case of Correspondent Banking, *World Economic Forum* [Online] www3.weforum.org/docs/WEF_White_Paper_The_Role_of_Law_and_Regulation.pdf

WTO [accessed 13 January 2018a] Trade Finance, *World Trade Organization* [Online] www.wto.org/english/thewto_e/coher_e/tr_finance_e.htm

WTO [accessed 15 January 2018b] Why Do Trade Finance Gaps Persist: And Does It Matter for Trade and Development? *World Trade Organization* [Online] www.wto.org/english/res_e/reser_e/ersd201701_e.pdf

The disruptive power of e-retailing

16

THIS CHAPTER WILL FAMILIARIZE THE READER WITH:

- the transformation of the retail sector since the late 1990s and, with it, logistics and last mile delivery operations;
- the 'Amazonization' of customer expectations and the resulting compression of supply chains;
- the challenges facing retailers, logistics and express parcels companies in adopting this new business model including returns, city deliveries, payments and customs procedures;
- the development of the 'gig economy' and the flexibility that this has brought in matching peak and troughs of demand as well as impending government regulations;
- the growth of cross-border e-retail and the challenges and opportunities that this will create.

The disruption of retail supply chains

Retailing, and the logistics and supply chain industry that supports it, has been transformed since the late 1990s by the emergence of the e-commerce phenomenon. Well-known retailers such as Woolworths, Toys-R-Us, Sears and K-Mart, to mention just a few, have faced restructuring or even bankruptcy, unable to compete in a market that has come to be dominated by the likes of Amazon.com, Alibaba and eBay. These companies have brought a new business model to the retailing industry – stores open 24/7 via a consumer's laptop or mobile device, the ability to compare products and prices, and prompt, low-cost delivery to the consumer's door – or in some cases, even to the consumer's fridge.

The changing retail environment has led to a root-and-branch restructuring of the associated logistics and transport sector. Those companies that have been agile enough to embrace the new distribution channels with a host of new services have prospered. Not least among these have been the parcels companies responsible for last mile B2C deliveries. This trend has also created a welcome new revenue stream for the post offices previously struggling to come to terms with the inexorable decline of mail volumes.

The express parcels industry has undergone a major transformation over this period. At the outset, it was far from certain that many of the major express players, such as UPS, FedEx or DHL, would embrace home delivery due to the high costs involved in the number of undelivered parcels caused by 'not-at-home' end-recipients. Today B2C is an important part of the major players' thinking and revenues.

Looking to the future, delivery times are getting ever faster, with the number of same-day and one- or two-hour delivery services rising. This is having a knock-on effect on customer expectations. End-recipients are also demanding greater flexibility as well as more delivery options, fitting in around their lifestyles rather than around the operational demands of parcel delivery companies. Technology is helping to bridge this gap, leading to higher levels of customer service combined with fewer failed deliveries.

Alternative delivery solutions are also being developed. Lockers, in-car, or pick-up/drop-off networks are growing in popularity, and omni-channel retailers have placed emphasis on click and collect offerings that are not only convenient for customers but prove a useful source of revenue for retailers. Many logistics providers have tailored value-added solutions for transport, fulfilment and returns. They are also playing a role in many retailers' strategies as they support the expansion of services into new international markets.

One of the greatest areas of opportunity is expected to be in the cross-border segment of the market that is growing much faster than domestic volumes, albeit from a smaller starting point. Consultancy Forrester forecasts cross-border e-commerce growth of 17 per cent between 2017 and 2022, compared with 12 per cent for overall e-commerce (cross-border and domestic) (Forrester, 2017). Cross-border purchases have been forecast at 20 per cent of worldwide e-commerce by 2022, comprising some US $627bn (Rodriguez, 2018). Another report by DHL says that cross-border e-commerce accounts for 15 per cent of global e-commerce sales. By 2020, that share is expected to rise to approximately 22 per cent (DHL, 2016).

Of all markets, the Asia Pacific region is believed to be leading the way, in large part due to China, which is set to become the largest e-commerce cross-border market for both imports and exports. Rising incomes, an expanding middle class and dissatisfaction with domestic products are driving China's e-commerce growth.

At the same time the scope of cross-border e-commerce is also expanding. Fashion and electronics have long been cross-border top sellers, but consumers are now branching out further. Presently underserved product categories include beauty and cosmetics, pet care, food and beverage, and sporting goods.

E-commerce has the potential to link SMEs throughout the world with global markets, facilitated by the major digital e-retailing platforms. This can bring major economic benefits for those who are able to embrace the opportunity. However, as this chapter will discuss, there are many logistical challenges that will have to be overcome if the opportunities are to be spread evenly throughout the world. Failure to address these could result in the global economy becoming further split into the digital haves and have nots.

Definitions and players

The e-commerce logistics system can be simplified by categorizing the players involved.

E-fulfilment providers

The fulfilment of orders placed online by a customer can either be undertaken by the retailer itself ('inhouse') or by a third-party logistics (3PL) company ('outsourced'). Many large e-retailers, such as Amazon, will undertake the order processing, picking, packing, labelling and dispatch themselves, as this provides them with a greater level of control over the process. Many smaller e-retailers opt to use 3PLs as they can benefit from their investment in technology systems and their operational know-how.

The market has become blurred in recent years as Amazon has also provided logistics services to other retailers. 'Fulfilled by Amazon', as its offering is known, allows SMEs to store their products in an Amazon distribution centre. Amazon will then take care of the whole order process and also manage the last mile delivery. This has brought this e-retail giant into direct

Figure 16.1   Key players in the e-commerce logistics space

Major online retailers (largest e-fulfilment providers in the world)	Largest LSPs (revenue €500m+)	Mid-size LSPs (revenue €100m+)
JD.COM	XPO Logistics	Kuehne+Nagel
Amazon	Deutsche Post DHL Group	Clipper
Alibaba Group		SEKO
		(plus several others, visibility poor)

Other major online/ multichannel retailers		Smaller LSP players *(includes some major global contract logistics providers just getting into e-commerce, those not focusing on it and many small LSPs)*
Walmart		
Zalando		
Sears	**Major last mile players who could scale up in e-fulfilment rapidly**	
Rakuten		

	Others	**Start-ups**
	Ocado	ShipBob
FedEx		RedStag Fulfillment
UPS		Delhivery

competition with many LSPs, although for the time being many are content to enter into what has been termed 'co-opetition' – Amazon is not only a competitor but also a major customer for them as well.

The e-fulfilment market is becoming further confused as traditional last mile delivery companies (UPS and FedEx, for example) have started to provide e-fulfilment services as well as new start-ups (Figure 16.1).

Last mile delivery companies

Fulfilment isn't the only online retail challenge that is changing the logistics market. In the last mile, the key drivers of change that LSPs must respond to throughout e-commerce – quick, low-cost, high-quality delivery – is reshaping the way goods are moved through the final element of their journey.

Online retail has transformed the last mile. Having seen low growth in developed markets leading up to the rapid expansion of online retail, the express sector is now riding a wave of strong growth supported by e-commerce volumes on a near global basis.

The capacity of players in the sector to successfully respond to the rapid rise in volumes – especially during peak times – has been mixed. UPS, for example, struggled with peak volumes during the holiday seasons of 2013, while City Link, a UK operator, could not find a viable business model that allowed it to cope with high volumes at low revenue per unit. Indeed, online retail is causing a fundamental change in last mile operations.

First, the express sector is shifting from a predominantly B2B operation, where parcels were delivered to a smaller number of business addresses (usually located within the boundaries of major commerce centres and with high levels of first time delivery success), to a predominantly B2C operation, where individual parcels are delivered to individual addresses (often in residential areas potentially located much further apart, with fewer guarantees of first time success). The differences between the two delivery options highlight starkly different cost profiles:

- Deliveries of individual parcels to individual customers limit the potential for the delivery of multi-parcel consignments, raising the number of potential stops and the distances driven by each operative.
- The potentially greater spread of delivery locations increases the mileage. Greater distance between deliveries means more time travelling than undertaking the revenue-generating delivery.
- A failure to successfully deliver goods at the first attempt means the last mile provider incurs the expense of any subsequent delivery attempt.

This shift has taken place as the express market globalized, primarily in response to the rapid growth and development of the Chinese economy and the emphasis placed on the development of global networks, especially in the air, by UPS, FedEx and DHL. It has also come at the same time as postal operators have looked to online retailing as an escape route from their own problems of falling mail volumes.

Cross-border delivery

The cross-border delivery market is even more concentrated than domestic last mile markets, particularly at the premium end of the market, which is dominated by three companies: DHL, FedEx and UPS. The less premium end of the market is more competitive, with post offices playing a more significant role.

In Europe, where cross-border delivery services by road are significant, in addition to the three aforementioned integrators (DHL, FedEx and UPS), DPD (a subsidiary of the French post office La Poste) and GLS (a subsidiary of the UK post office Royal Mail) also have pan-European networks and play a significant role.

Reverse logistics (returns)

Online retailers increasingly offer a number of product features that facilitate a smooth and efficient returns service, including:

- pre-printed returns labels and resealable packaging included in parcels;
- an automated refund process with simple instructions;
- simple, clear procedures;
- an option to return merchandise to a physical location – either a bricks-and-mortar outlet, a post office or a location in an alternative delivery network, such as a parcelstore or locker.

In many scenarios, though, the introduction of such services means that the retailer is depending on the last mile provider to facilitate the returns process. This has an impact throughout the last mile network, not least in terms of the volume it generates and the cost implications that exert downward pressure on already thin margins. Last mile providers must therefore invest in supporting returns operations. Perhaps the most notable example of this is FedEx's 2015 acquisition of reverse logistics specialist, Genco Distribution Systems, for US $1.4bn. National post offices have been among the main beneficiaries, as many e-retailers require the end-recipient to package the goods and return them through the postal networks, which are the lowest cost option.

Challenges of e-retail

E-retailers require distribution systems that are often more complex than traditional ones. Besides the need to manage an increasing number of suppliers and varying inventory, the management of multiple delivery options, such as home delivery, in-store pick-up, lockbox or elsewhere, also becomes more difficult. Convenience and prompt delivery are expected as well as flexibility. The increasing demand for such delivery services has put a strain on parcel delivery companies and has led, not least, to the greater use of self-employed drivers (the so-called 'gig-economy'). However, there are regulatory as well as operational and social challenges, and some of these are highlighted later.

City centre deliveries

Cities across the world, in both developed markets and also emerging economies, are experiencing rapid increases in their population, as well as suffering from unacceptably high vehicle emissions, and this trend is causing major issues for the movement of parcels into, and around, these large population conurbations. Many cities have now implemented strategies to combat both congestion and pollution. These include:

- the introduction of congestion charges (London);
- restrictions on access times and zones where delivery vehicle can make deliveries;
- limiting access of different vehicles to specific days, for example by number plate (Mexico City, Beijing);
- regular road closures (Bogota);
- imposing car free days/zones (Paris).

Many are going further and have threatened the outright banning of diesel and, in some instances, petrol vehicles from city centres within a very short timescale. Although this may achieve political objectives, the impact of regulations and bans of diesel engine vehicles on last mile deliveries is yet to be fully understood. Cities compete globally on the basis of their efficiency, and despite politicians stating that the harmful effects on pollution must be eliminated, none will want to do so at the expense of jobs. This could be the outcome if urban supply chains become burdened with regulation and delays, with logistics costs rising significantly. However, these threats are also spurring many parcels companies to invest heavily in vehicles powered by electricity as well as alternative fuels.

Returns challenges

How retailers deal with returns is one of the most pressing issues facing the industry. According to US statistics, online returns average around 25 to 30 per cent (US Census Bureau, 2018). In the United States alone one specialist tech company, Optoro, puts the value of 2017 holiday returns at US $90bn and a staggering US $260bn across the year as a whole. Up to 30 per cent of e-retail consumers will return a gift with the most frequently returned items being jewellery, electronics, fashion and household goods (Optoro, 2018). On 3 January 2018, dubbed 'national returns day' by UPS, the express provider expected 1.8 million items to be returned, an 8 per cent increase on the previous year.

There is a heavy financial cost related to each return, with UPS (2018) estimating that it ranges from 20 to 65 per cent of the total cost of goods sold depending on the commodity involved. US-based technology provider, Datex, estimates that returning a 'bricks-and-mortar' shop-bought good costs the retailer on average US $3 and is usually back on the shelf by the next day. However, a return can cost an online retailer US $6 and due to the complexity of the process, takes at least four days before it becomes available for resale (Datex, 2018). This is probably itself an underestimation as the majority of goods never make it back into the supply chain. A consultancy, Clear Returns, estimates that, in the UK, £600m of stock, which had been bought over the Black Friday weekend, was still tied up in the return loop in mid-December (Ram, 2018).

Typically, most e-retailers would like to keep the volume of returns to a minimum for obvious reasons. However, in June 2017 Amazon launched its Amazon Prime Wardrobe service. This actively encourages consumers to buy more than they need so they can try fashion items on at home and return the ones they don't like or that don't fit. The service features at launch were:

- pick up to 15 items;
- try on for up to seven days;
- free pick-up of returned clothes;
- keep five or more for 20 per cent discount;
- free service for Prime members.

With the online fashion market growing fast, Amazon's plan is to win market share through this unusual innovation. In many respects the service already matches consumer behaviour. It has become accepted practice for consumers to buy several items, select the one(s) they want and return the rest.

However, Amazon has already started to change the terms of the service – reducing the number of items its customers can order to 10 in November 2017. The cost of the returns may have influenced its decision. The level of discount for multiple orders has also been amended, and while the service is being tested, more changes are to be expected.

Given that Amazon has led the way in the sector, it is likely that other competitors will follow suit, if they can afford to.

The role of the 3PL

LSPs are important players in reverse logistics. As the returns process is often regarded as 'non-core' for many manufacturers or retailers, there is a risk that the process can be neglected or underfunded. By outsourcing to a specialist logistics company, a focus can be maintained on the main business of selling while ensuring that customer service and inventory velocity are achieved.

It is also beneficial in terms of the balance sheet. E-retailers do not need to invest in warehouses in every market in which they operate as they can use those of the logistics provider, which can leverage its own investment over a number of customers. LSPs can also undertake inspection and refurbishment in addition to the storage and distribution of goods back into the supply chain.

A further benefit is that shippers do not need to invest in expertise, as LSPs can leverage their experience in the sector equally for small, medium or large companies.

Logistics or express parcels providers can play a more strategic role in the returns process than just handling or moving the product. As they are closest to the end-recipient, they are better able to make decisions on what to do with the return. This has several advantages:

- Operational decisions can be taken more quickly in the reverse logistics process.
- Products can be returned to the supply chain more quickly, repaired or disposed of.
- The returns process can be made more convenient for the end-recipient.

The expertise that LSPs have developed has allowed them to offer consultancy services, mapping out returns process and suggesting ways in which cost savings can be made.

Existing return solutions

For many e-retailers, the most crucial goal of their returns policy is to minimize the cost of transportation and delivery, and this, rightly or wrongly, takes precedence over inventory velocity – that is, reintroducing the product back into the supply chain. As speed is not usually an essential factor for this operation, and neither is there a need for the online purchaser to have a status update, a low-cost solution is generally preferred. The main principle is for the goods to arrive at a point of aggregation, which means in principle the last mile (or first mile in this case) transportation is performed by the end-recipient for returns and hence the e-retailers avoid these operational costs. The returns may be paid for by the e-retailer, or the recipient may be reimbursed by the e-retailer according to their terms and conditions:

- Post office – a vast majority of the returned items use pick-up and drop-off points (PUDOs) of the postal network.

- In store – for bricks and mortar retailers who have online presence, the return of goods to any of their shops conveniently located for the customer is chosen as their low-cost solution.

- Parcel shops – some carriers and independent operators offer dedicated parcel shops where goods purchased online can be returned.

- Parcel lockers – another solution is for recipients to return their goods to parcel lockers, which are increasingly common at train stations, car parks and garage forecourts.

The returns process still involves an element of inconvenience for the online shopper as it often requires the printing of return labels (relying on the recipient owning a printer) or, in some cases, a wait at home for the collection. Post offices have the restrictions of set opening hours and other options may involve a journey to a nearby self-service terminal to deposit the parcel.

Future returns solutions

The use of technologies that are being developed for last mile deliveries could, in the future, be leveraged into reverse logistics solutions. It is envisaged that, with technological advances, drivers could be contacted on demand through apps, text, SMS, social media or crowd-sourcing, and customers would be able to provide pre-notification alerts of parcels available for collection. It would also be possible for the customer to let the courier know when they are at home for them to collect. In a similar manner, they would be able to collect from a neighbour or from the boot/trunk of cars. As such, collection would happen in a matter of minutes, swiftly and with little inconvenience.

Visibility is also becoming more important, despite the traditionally low priority retailers have placed upon returns. The UK's Royal Mail offers a tracked service, which, according to its management, gives its customers access to tracking along key stages of the parcel journey, including confirmed delivery to returns processing centres, enabling the acceleration of returns processing and the resale of its products.

The 'gig economy'

Volatility in the e-retail logistics market, characterized by frequent peaks and troughs of demand, has meant that the vast majority of last mile delivery companies have adopted an outsourced model. Sub-contractors bear not only the cost of investment in transport assets but also carry the risk of revenues by being paid 'by the drop' or by the mile.

The e-retail market is such that so-called 'free shipping' is a major selling point for many companies. Of course, the costs of this marketing device are pushed onto the carrier, resulting in ultra-low rates of remuneration.

This has raised ethical concerns. The low barriers to market entry and a plentiful supply of people willing to take on a low-skilled job have meant that the amount paid by some carriers is barely enough to cover the cost of running a vehicle. There have been allegations that for some carriers their sub-contractors are 'disposable', that is, the carrier will be able to replace the owner-driver from a plentiful pool of new market entrants.

Cross-border e-retail issues and risks

Another potential challenge has been caused by the fast growth of cross-border e-commerce. This has been a positive trend for international express providers such as DHL, FedEx and UPS, but the explosion of SMEs now trading goods internationally has created headaches for customs authorities and other regulators who have to deal with:

- increased volumes of single item shipments;
- traders who are not used to the rules and documentation required to move goods internationally;
- traders who have little or no understanding of tax and duties that could be payable on their consignments.

While gaining access to millions, if not billions, of new customers is an attractive proposition for e-commerce companies, targeting purchasers in foreign markets is not necessarily the easiest of strategies.

Apart from the obvious language and currency barriers, there are a raft of additional factors that can impact a retailer's ability to successfully operate on a cross-border basis. A recent UPS study of European cross-border purchases (UPS, 2017) found that the top considerations when purchasing from retailers in another country included:

- payment security (75 per cent of respondents);
- clearly stating the total cost of the order including duties and fees (72 per cent);
- a clear returns policy (63 per cent);
- stating all prices in the shopper's native currency (63 per cent);
- the speed of delivery (62 per cent).

However, within Europe – an economic grouping largely governed by a set of compatible customs, taxation and trading regulations, with the vast majority of markets adopting a single currency – cross-border e-commerce is a far simpler proposition.

Trading conditions become far more complicated in regions such as Asia, where developed markets trade with emerging economies; countries have independent regulatory environments; many have different languages and currencies; and most are separated by large bodies of water. This results in a significantly different set of issues that e-commerce companies and their logistics providers must navigate.

Payments

Fraud is a major challenge faced by e-retailers operating on a cross-border basis. E-commerce sites need to use a reputable and robust payment system that is cognizant of local customer behaviour to reduce possible fraudulent purchases.

Many emerging economies are 'cash societies', ie where bank credit or debit cards are not widely used. Consumers in these markets often rely heavily on 'cash on delivery' (COD) payments, which comes with its own set of unique issues. COD purchases, where the goods are paid for on receipt of delivery – handing cash over to the delivery driver – incurs a very high return rate, especially on cross-border transactions where the transit time is far longer. Often, during the time that it takes to deliver the goods, the consumer has found a similar product locally. As there is no penalty or need to request a refund, the purchaser simply refuses to accept the delivery. This places additional cost onto the e-commerce seller, especially as the return element often also comprises an international shipment.

For those purchases that are completed, the last mile operator will need to collect the cash payment and then transport this to a secure facility. To reduce the risk, some companies use the services of local retail outlets that offer cash collection services. The funds are then sent electronically back to the merchant.

Also, cross-border payments should be fully transparent to ensure that all transport costs, local taxes, duties and fees are included so that customers are not surprised by additional government levies when their online purchases arrive at their final destination. Understanding local taxation and ensuring that the customer pays accordingly is crucial, otherwise the purchase may be returned, incurring additional, expensive, costs.

Cross-border returns

The cross-border returns element is also just as important as the last mile delivery and can negatively impact the perception of a business by local customers:

- Handling international returns is expensive and difficult for retailers/logistics providers to manage.
- Logistics solutions involve the gathering of returned items, determining if the items can be resold or disposed, and then submitting the items into the proper channel of distribution.
- Due to varying individual country laws and regulations, much of this handling is done in the country in which the returns occur.

Compared with domestic e-commerce, cross-border returns are far more expensive, and some retailers have adopted different strategies to try to reduce this expense. When UK-based e-retailer ASOS, for example, started to service US customers, it did so from its UK stockholding. To reduce returns cost, which can be as high as 50 to 60 per cent in the fashion sector, ASOS subsequently directed all US returns to a US distribution centre, the intention being not just to reduce costs but to also build up some inventory in the country.

Regulations

Regulations surrounding local and overseas e-commerce sales will differ country by country, and cross-border e-commerce sellers must be aware of these in order to adapt their approach in each target market.

A number of countries in South East Asia, and also Australia, are implementing additional taxes on online goods purchased from non-domestic sellers, and these costs will have to be either passed onto the consumer or borne by the retailer. Also, changes in tax-free import tariffs can impact growth opportunities, turning what was previously a profitable cross-border market into an unattractive proposition for overseas sellers within a very short timeframe.

Trust

Trust is one of the biggest issues facing companies wanting to sell their products online internationally. As e-commerce sites need robust payments systems to reduce fraudulent purchases, customers must be convinced that the websites they buy from are reputable and honest – a task that is far harder to check and police internationally.

Summary

The retail industry continues to feel the impact of e-commerce on a daily basis. Traditional bricks and mortar retailers that have not embraced an 'omnichannel' approach to sales are struggling against the might of Amazon and a host of other e-retailers that offer a wide range of high quality products, fast service and cheap prices.

However, even the e-commerce sector faces many challenges that, if not addressed, will curtail the growth of the sector. Cross-border e-commerce has the potential to aid economic development in many emerging markets around the world, but only if trade processes are streamlined and regulations reformed.

Other innovative solutions need to be developed to address inefficiencies in last mile deliveries in an urban context as well as the vast number of returned goods.

Bibliography

Datex [accessed 15 March 2018] Dirty Little Secrets of Holiday Returns (Part Three): 3PL Reverse Logistics – How 3PLs Can Help Retailers Maximize the Value of Returned Goods [Online] www.datexcorp.com/dirty-little-secrets-holiday-returns-part-3-3pl-reverse-logistics/

DHL (2016) *The 21st Century Spice Trade: A guide to the cross-border e-commerce opportunity*, DHL, Bonn

Forrester (2017) *Forrester Data Report: Online Retail Forecast, 2016 to 2021*, Forrester, London

Optoro [accessed 15 March 2018] Holiday Shopping Insights [Online] www.optoro.com/2017/12/

Ram, A [accessed 15 March 2018] UK Retailers Count the Cost of Returns, *Financial Times* [Online] www.ft.com/content/52d26de8-c0e6-11e5-846f-79b0e3d20eaf

Rodriguez, L. (2018) *The Role of Transport and Logistics in Promoting E-Commerce in Developing Countries*, UNCTAD, Geneva

UPS (2017) *2017 UPS Europe Pulse of the Online Shopper*, UPS, Brussels

UPS [accessed 15 March 2018] Rethinking Online Returns: Comparing the Return Policies and Processes of Top Online Retailers to Shopper Preferences – A UPS Study July 2015 [Online] www.ups.com/assets/resources/pdf/15UP31139_ReturnsExecutiveSummary_pages%20Final.pdf

US Census Bureau [accessed 15 March 2018] Quarterly Retail E-Commerce Sales: 4th Quarter 2017 [Online] www.census.gov/retail/mrts/www/data/pdf/ec_current.pdf

The ultimate disruptors

17

Amazon and Alibaba

THIS CHAPTER WILL FAMILIARIZE THE READER WITH:

- the strategies employed by two of the world's largest e-retailers, Amazon and Alibaba;
- how robotics has been employed to drive down logistics costs;
- the proactive roles that these e-retailers are playing in transforming logistics expectations and operations;
- the international expansion strategies of Amazon and Alibaba and the role of logistics in supporting these;
- the relationships that these companies have with logistics and last mile delivery operators and how these are likely to develop.

Introduction

Of all the companies that have caused systemic disruption in the retail and supply chain industries, two stand out: Amazon and Alibaba. Although Amazon is better known for its impact on the retail sector in the developed world, Alibaba has grown into the world's largest e-retailer and dominates the Asian market. They have not only transformed the retail sector but also the logistics industry in their respective markets.

Amazon.com, Inc.

Amazon.com has become a giant in the e-commerce sector, developing from an online retailer of books in the 1990s to a multifaceted platform spanning software services (Amazon Web Services), e-book readers (Amazon's Kindle) and even restaurant delivery operations. It also has a significant logistics operation, offering fulfilment services to its customers across the world. The company is listed on the NASDAQ exchange in the United States.

Logistics strategy

Amazon first began its journey as a logistics provider when Fulfillment by Amazon (FBA) was launched in 2006. Aside from Amazon Web Services, logistics represents the most obvious example of its strategy of developing internal services for external consumption.

With expenditure on fulfilment and outbound shipping amounting to about a quarter of its net sales, the maintenance and expansion of the company's logistics activities is both vital to the success of the company's marketplace operations and a massive cost centre for the business. As such, the company has embarked on a deliberate course to market its various internal supply chain services, with the dual aims of maintaining a leading internal supply chain to support its own operations, and to diversify the business into a sector that offers substantial top-line growth prospects.

Amazon's logistics strategy

Step one: reduce costs

Amazon's strategy has been to achieve economies of scale through its ownership of a vast network of warehousing and fulfilment centres and is justified by the volumes of material it puts through them. This strategy can be applied to air, road and sea freight to leverage buying power.

Step two: drive revenue growth

Mirroring the strategy of Amazon's cloud computing arm, Amazon Web Services (now the company's fastest growing unit), FBA provides services for external customers. Its services are accessible by retailers from its fulfilment centres.

In the future, Amazon will provide third-party transportation services for other shippers, thereby maximizing asset utilization (and reducing costs). 'We know we're very good at logistics. Why shouldn't we turn that into an infrastructure offer that others can use?' says Roy Perticucci, Amazon's European Head of Logistics (Koenen *et al*, 2018).

Figure 17.1 Amazon and key competitors

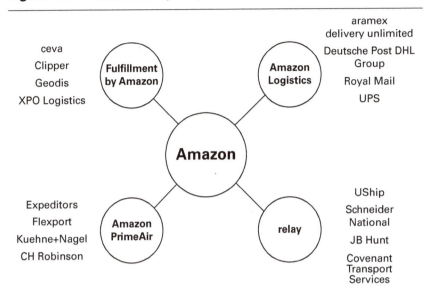

Amazon is at various stages of developing a compelling service offering within four core logistics markets: contract logistics/value added warehousing, express, freight forwarding and road freight. Figure 17.1 shows some of Amazon's key competitors.

Contract logistics/value-added warehousing

Amazon's logistics offering is underpinned by FBA, which targets small- to medium-sized businesses and individual sellers and provides such services as pick and pack, labelling, shipping, and inventory and returns management. In order to support these services, the company has had to develop a sophisticated inventory and order management capability.

In 2016, the service handled 2 billion items, with FBA adoption among Amazon sellers increasing by 70 per cent year on year. Significantly, FBA units shipped outside the United States increased by over 80 per cent during the year. The growth of FBA has led the company to develop a sophisticated system for warehouse fulfilment, based on robotics technology acquired from Kiva Systems in 2012. By deploying robots designed to bring picking shelves to human pickers for the fulfilment of customer orders, Amazon is able to increase the velocity of inventory fulfilment within the warehouse by as much as 75 per cent, while increasing inventory capacity by as much as 50 per cent due to the lack of picking aisles. All in all, installation of the system reportedly cuts operating costs by around 20 per cent (Kim, 2018). By the end of 2016 Amazon had installed 45,000 Kiva robots, across 20 of its fulfilment centres. By the end of 2017, the company had added an additional 55,000, bringing the total to 100,000.

Besides the development of these advanced systems to improve fulfilment operations, Amazon has also started to develop dedicated distribution services through its Seller Fulfilled Prime and Seller Flex programmes. Launched at the end of 2015, Seller Fulfilled Prime (SFP) allows Amazon marketplace sellers to ship to Amazon Prime customers from their own warehouse, rather than by routing products through Amazon fulfilment centres first. All distribution is coordinated through Amazon Logistics, a technology service layer that coordinates order and inventory management across a network of sub-contracted delivery companies.

Last mile delivery

Amazon initiated its last mile logistics programme in 2014 following a significant number of missed US deliveries by UPS and FedEx during the 2013 Christmas period. Besides the negative impacts of this specific instance, Amazon considers the reduction of logistics expenditure to represent a major strategic objective and continues to explore ways in which it can lower its overall shipping costs. Creative ways in which Amazon has sought to offset such expenditure include the continued expansion of alternative delivery options through the roll out of lockers and pick-up & drop-off (PUDO) points.

A more decisive change, however, has been Amazon's coordinated efforts to bring shipping management inhouse under the auspices of Amazon Logistics. A significant point of interest is that Amazon Logistics does not hire its own drivers or use its own trucks; rather, the operation consists of sub-contracting last mile delivery to a multitude of small companies and owner-operators. Amazon Logistics benefits from the relationship as it is able to exercise greater bargaining power over these contractors than it would in negotiations with the likes of UPS or FedEx and can therefore pay a lower rate for their services. Key to their express offering is service, reliability and speed. Amazon identified at an early stage that this was more important to their customers than the brand or livery of the delivery company.

Europe

While Amazon Logistics does not use its own transport assets, the company does provide the depots from which its contractors operate, leasing more than 20 such facilities in the UK alone. Though the network of such facilities used by the company is continuing to grow at a rapid rate, it is likely that the increased control and gains in bargaining power over contractors will result in enabling Amazon Transport & Logistics to shave costs from its outbound shipping bill.

Amazon has also opened a sorting centre in Munich, employing 130 workers. This could be seen as a step towards cutting out larger parcels companies (DHL and Hermes) but also acts as a benchmark to keep other carriers 'honest'. In the city, Amazon now has 240 delivery vans operated by six sub-contractors and, on launch, this operation reportedly took a third of DHL's volumes.

In other countries, the company has acted more directly to achieve the same aim. For example, in France, Amazon acquired a 25 per cent stake in parcel delivery provider Colis Privé during 2014. Total acquisition of the company was blocked on competition grounds.

India

In India, Amazon established its logistics service in 2012 and launched a third-party logistics service in 2013. Furthermore, in 2014, it introduced assisted shipping that allows sellers to ship products from their own warehouses using Amazon's logistics services. As part of its plan to ensure next-day delivery to customers across India, Amazon entered into an air cargo alliance with Patel Logistics in 2014, whereby the LSP moves goods from one airport to another. Once the products reach the respective airports, Amazon's other vendors such as Gati, Blue Dart and FedEx provide last mile delivery.

Middle East

In the Middle East, Amazon's acquisition of Souq at the start of 2017 was followed by the takeover of the subsidiary's primary express supplier, Wing, in September 2017. Wing has been developed with an IT infrastructure that supports mobile and web-based delivery solutions for businesses and individual consumers, and this fits with Amazon's emphasis on visibility and software integration.

United States

In the United States, the company has mainly focused on shifting its package delivery requirements towards the low-cost United States Postal Service and away from major parcels companies. The rise of Amazon Logistics, however, has presented another option for last mile delivery. Furthermore, while

Amazon Logistics aims to cut costs by employing independent contractors, the company is also working on an even more radical solution to the last mile problem: adopting the business model of Uber and crowd-sourcing last mile delivery. Named Amazon Flex, this operation was initially trialled in Seattle in 2015 and has since been rolled out to multiple cities in the United States and Europe. Amazon often deploys Flex drivers to service Prime orders, as the company is able to scale this resource up during peaks in demand.

Freight forwarding and air cargo

In January 2016, Amazon's Chinese subsidiary, Beijing Century Joyo Courier Service Co., was granted an NVOCC licence from the US Federal Maritime Commission, enabling the company to provide ocean forwarding services. This is consistent with the company's past supply chain actions, as it ostensibly represents an effort to improve its economies of scale. As China is one of Amazon's largest sources of goods it seems unsurprising that this is the first place where it would seek to in-source its ocean freight management requirements.

Large-scale sellers on Amazon's marketplace may be deterred from booking their freight forwarding with the company, as Amazon's NVOCC status allows the company visibility over both the supplier of the goods being shipped and the wholesale price paid by the importer. This threat of disintermediation is therefore a massive red flag to retailers, but for small sellers and producers, it offers major benefits: a streamlined cross-border e-commerce solution that purports to handle all marketing, order management, logistics and distribution right out of the factory gate.

Amazon has also explored opportunities for the deployment of air freight. Following a trial period in 2015, when Amazon tested the use of contracted aircraft flown by ATSG, it embarked upon chartered air freight operations in North America and Europe during 2016. In the former region, Amazon arranged to lease 20 aircraft on crew, maintenance and insurance (CMI) contracts with Atlas Air, as well as another 20 on a five-year CMI agreement with ATSG. Moreover, the deals allowed Amazon to acquire 19.9 per cent of ATSG's stock and 20 per cent of Atlas stock, with a possible expansion to 30 per cent for the latter, if the companies deepen their cooperation.

The logic behind Amazon's move into air freight is relatively simple: by acquiring its own fleet of aircraft it will have better visibility and control over its fulfilment operations. Due to the control and improved supply chain visibility brought about by such a move, Amazon will have a much more flexible and responsive capability to redirect inventory between parts of its network.

By insourcing part of its air freight requirements, Amazon is strengthening its ability to serve its customers during peak times, when its logistics partners have previously struggled to cope with a surge in package volumes. Having the extra capacity on hand will allow Amazon to relieve some of the pressure applied to its supply chain at such times and will supplement the services of its current partners. That being said, Amazon is a long way from being able to handle the entirety of its air freight requirements inhouse and it is debatable that it will ever do so.

Nonetheless, in the long term, there exists the possibility that Amazon will sell space on its freighters to companies looking to outsource their logistics and truly challenge the business of companies such as UPS and FedEx. It already offers fulfilment services to businesses selling through its website and with an integrated logistics network boasting supply chain visibility and computing power superior to that of many traditional express and parcel companies, Amazon could seriously disrupt the industry.

Road freight/trucking

Amazon's road freight operations are nascent by comparison to its position in the markets outlined earlier. Nonetheless, the company has taken a number of steps that will put the company in competition with external road freight companies in their own markets.

In 2015 Amazon purchased thousands of trailers in the United States to increase capacity for package delivery from fulfilment centres to sort centres. The significance of this move was that Amazon gained a uniform fleet of trailers optimized to interact with its existing logistics infrastructure, and therefore provided greater efficiency in the process of distributing inventory from hubs to spokes within its network. In addition, the company gained greater capability to reallocate inventory when demand shifts caused a shortage in certain parts of the network.

Importantly, there has been no indication that Amazon will be purchasing trucks, just trailers. As such, the company will still be contracting out the actual business of performing linehaul road transportation. Nonetheless, the move is designed to tighten the company's control over its logistics requirements, and in conjunction with manoeuvres to achieve a similar result for its air freight requirements, Amazon aims to achieve a more efficient, integrated inbound logistics system in support of its sortation and fulfilment centre network.

In November 2017, Amazon launched Relay, a dedicated app for truck drivers servicing its facilities. It allows truck drivers to enter information about their cargo in advance and then scan their phones to quickly check in and check out of facilities.

Amazon's logistics infrastructure

Having launched in the United States during 1995, Amazon was quick to expand into the UK and Germany shortly after, opening its first in-country fulfilment centres in these countries during 1998 and 1999, respectively. The company opened its first Japanese fulfilment centre in 2000, and subsequently opened up in Canada during 2002. This group of countries represents much of the core of Amazon's physical logistics network and, with the exception of Japan where the e-retailer comes second to Rakuten, it is the largest e-commerce player across each of these markets.

Amazon established a physical presence in the Chinese market through the acquisition of Joyo in 2004. However, it has been unable to gain traction in the country having been outcompeted by local players such as the dominant Alibaba. Thus far, China is the only country the company has seemingly failed to crack, possessing only a minor e-commerce market share of around 1.2 per cent.

While Amazon launched a French website in 2000, the company did not establish a physical presence within the country until 2007, instead shipping from its other European facilities. The company opened up its first logistics sites in Italy and Spain during 2011 and 2012, respectively, closely following its launch of dedicated websites for each country.

The company's other European facilities, in the Czech Republic (opened in 2013), Poland (2014) and Slovakia (2017), have all been established to serve other European markets, principally Germany, where Amazon has endured difficult industrial relations with its employees.

The company's most significant market entry since 2004 has been its establishment of in-country operations in India in 2013. Amazon's hierarchy views India as vital to its long-term growth, with expectations that it will eventually constitute the company's second-largest national market after the United States. Amazon has been keen to avoid the mistakes of its 'copy and paste' approach to entering China and has adapted to the idiosyncrasies of the Indian market, backing up its expansion in the country with a US $5bn investment commitment in 2014.

Shortly after its expansion into India, Amazon also invested in physical facilities in Latin America, with fulfilment centres opened in Brazil (2014) and Mexico (2015). Unlike India, however, the company has not committed as significantly to expansion in these territories; it has since added a handful of facilities in Mexico but has not built on its presence in Brazil. This is set to change though, with reports in 2017 indicating that Amazon is gearing up for an expansion in Brazil, broadening its product offering and physical presence.

The company's latest expansions have focused on the Middle East and Southeast Asia. Amazon opened up in Singapore and Australia towards the end of 2017, with its entry into the latter market expected for some time. Earlier in the year, the company established itself in the Middle East through the acquisition of Souq, the largest e-commerce player in

Table 17.1   Amazon: national markets served through dedicated sites

Country served	Year of entry	Market position	Main competitors
United States	1995	1	Walmart, eBay
UK	1998	1	Tesco, eBay
Germany	1998	1	Otto Group, Zalando
France	2000	1	Cdiscount, eBay
Japan	2000	2	Rakuten
Canada	2002	1	Walmart, Costco
China	2004	< 7	Alibaba, JD, Suning, Tencent, Yihaodian, Vipshop, Dangdang, Gome
Italy	2010	2	eBay
Spain	2011	1	El Corte Inglés
Brazil	2012	5	Americanas, MercadoLibre, Via Varejo, Magazine Luiza
India	2013	2	Flipkart, Snapdeal
Mexico	2013	3	MercadoLibre, Linio, Walmart
Australia	2013	Unclear	Myer, David Jones, JB Hi-Fi, Harvey Norman, Super Retail Group
Netherlands	2014	< 7	Wehkamp, Bol, Zalando, Coolblue, H&M, Hema, Thuisbezorgd
Singapore	2017	N/A	Lazada (Alibaba)

SOURCE Transport Intelligence

the region. The takeover of Souq has provided the company with a well-developed logistics infrastructure in the UAE, Saudi Arabia, Jordan and Egypt.

Table 17.1 lists the national markets that are served through dedicated sites.

Alibaba Group

Alibaba Group is the world's largest retailer. In China it operates online re-tail marketplaces including Taobao (China's largest mobile commerce desti-nation), Tmall (China's largest third-party platform for brands and retailers) and Juhuasuan (sales and marketing platform for flash sales), as well as the wholesale marketplace 1688.com and the Rural Taobao programme (ad-dresses consumption needs in China's rural areas).

Its international cross-border operations include AliExpress (global marketplace for buying Chinese goods), Alibaba.com (China's largest global online wholesale marketplace), Tmall Global (platform within Tmall for overseas brands to reach Chinese consumers) and Lazada (operates com-merce platforms in Indonesia, Malaysia, the Philippines, Singapore, Thailand and Vietnam – controlling stake acquired in April 2016).

Alibaba also offers cloud computing services, and media and entertain-ment services. Through a mixture of investment and cooperation Alibaba is involved with several non-consolidated companies including AliPay (online payments), as well as Cainiao (logistics) (Figure 17.2).

Figure 17.2   Alibaba e-commerce ecosystem

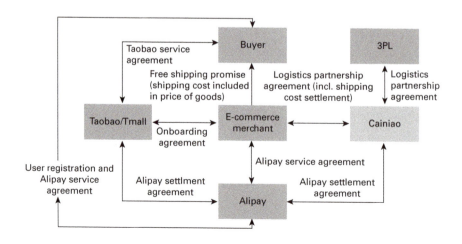

The Cainiao Network

Alibaba does not own its logistics operations, but rather partners with key providers. It takes a platform approach through a central logistics information system operated by Cainiao Smart Logistics Network Limited, which is a 51 per cent owned subsidiary.

Established in 2013, Cainiao Network is a collaborative logistics partnership that links together logistics providers involved in the delivery of packages from Alibaba's online platforms with the aim of sharing information to increase efficiency. It was initially formed from five express delivery companies, one retailer and two investment companies: YTO Express (Logistics) Co., S.F. Express (Group) Co., ZTO Express Co., Yunda Ltd. and Shentong Express Co.; Yintai Holdings; FOSUN Group and Forchn Holdings.

Each of the company's shareholders is tasked with a specific function in support of the business: FOSUN and Yintai develop and manage warehousing infrastructure; Forchn handles line-hauls; the parcels companies take care of last mile delivery; and Alibaba manages information and finance.

Cainiao Network does not deliver packages itself. Instead it operates a logistics data platform that provides real-time data to help the carriers improve the efficiency of inventory management and optimize delivery routes as well as enabling consumers to track their orders. According to Alibaba's annual results, 81 per cent of all items sold on its sites were delivered through the Cainiao Network.

During the 12 months ending March 2016, Cainiao Network and its logistics partners enabled the delivery of 12.2 billion packages from Alibaba's China retail marketplaces. Cainiao Network primarily derives its revenue from end-to-end logistics solutions and generates a significant portion of its revenue from providing these services to Tmall Supermarket.

The company was created with the overarching purpose of developing a logistics infrastructure capable of supporting Alibaba's explosive growth in China. It is unique in its scope, attempting to bring together several companies with partially divergent interests to provide the necessary logistics operations to underpin Alibaba's business. In doing so, Cainiao has created a technological ecosystem in which many of the largest Chinese express companies are embedded and, as such, reliant on its parent for shipment volumes.

As of 2017, Cainiao Network's 15 strategic express courier partners employed over 1.8 million delivery personnel in more than 600 cities and 31 provinces in China. Collectively they operated more than 180,000 hubs and sorting stations.

Six of the companies mentioned above are embedded in Alibaba's ecosystem and partner extensively with Cainiao. The exceptions to this rule, for different reasons, are EMS and SF Express. While the former is a state-owned entity, and therefore neutral, the latter has aggressively sought to carve out its own independent place within the Chinese Express industry and differs significantly from the other companies due to a focus on high-margin B2B business.

While SF was a founding member of Cainiao, the two had a major disagreement over data sharing during June 2017, damaging relations. Allegedly, Cainiao was demanding access to SF Express data that included information on the company's Hive Box locker service, which, in addition to supporting Cainiao deliveries, services deliveries for other e-commerce customers such as JD.com. SF is a preferred carrier of JD, which allows it to balance its volume exposure to Alibaba and diversify its customer structure (Zhang, 2018).

Although SF has been relatively successful in this approach, the other main parcels companies have found themselves effectively vassals to the company's empire. For example, in its 2016 IPO prospectus, ZTO disclosed that parcels related to Alibaba accounted for 75 per cent of its volumes during the half-year period to June 2016 (SEC, 2018). These firms have a much smaller exposure to Alibaba's main rival JD.com. When JD announced a shortlist of five preferred couriers (JD Express, SF Express, ZTO Express, Yunda Express and STO Express) in July 2017, YTO Express (in which Alibaba holds an 11 per cent equity position) noted that its exclusion from the list would not significantly harm its business, as JD accounted for only 2 per cent of its volumes.

Alibaba invested an additional US $807m into Cainiao in September 2017 in order to raise its ownership stake above the 50 per cent threshold (up from 47 per cent to 51 per cent) largely in response to a US regulatory probe into the company's transparency regarding the subsidiary.

Globalization strategy

Cainiao's role in international freight has remained limited. Nonetheless, the company has invested in the development of international gateways through collaborations with a variety of partners and takes custody of the data supply chain within China:

- The company's globalization efforts began in 2015, with a cross-border logistics partnership with the United States Postal Service, which was followed by similar arrangements with Spain's Correos and China Post, through Alibaba's Southeast Asian subsidiary Lazada.

- In March 2016 the company established a partnership with Borderguru, a subsidiary of Hermes. Working with Cainiao, Borderguru is now responsible for managing the whole logistics cross-border shipping process for European clients looking to sell their products in China, through Alibaba's Tmall Global marketplace.

- In October 2016 Alibaba completed an investment of 86.2m Singapore dollars for a 34 per cent stake in SingPost's logistics subsidiary Quantium Solutions International (QSI). It also obtained regulatory approval for a second investment of 187.1m Singapore dollars, which would raise its total stake in SingPost to 14.4 per cent. The collaboration will focus on strengthening QSI's end-to-end e-commerce logistics network in South East Asia and Oceania, including warehousing, fulfilment and last mile delivery.

- During November 2017 Cainiao launched an 'intelligent logistics park' in Dongguan, Guandong province, in partnership with supply chain services, technology and consulting business 4PX. With a total area of 21,000 square metres, the facility is designed to handle an annual throughput of 100,000 tonnes of parcels.

Despite these steps, the most intriguing international logistics development for Alibaba is not directly related to Cainiao. Acquired in 2010, and now the fastest growing unit within Alibaba's B2B division, One Touch is a business dedicated to supporting Chinese SMEs through export services, such as financing and customs brokerage. The chief incentive of One Touch for Chinese shippers is that it acts as a credit system, leveraging its access to customer data to negotiate directly with banks and provide individual exporters with cheaper financing than they would be able to gain independently.

In January 2017 One Touch established collaboration agreements with Maersk Line and WCA, the organization of independent freight forwarders. Both moves highlight Alibaba's growing interest in cross-border e-commerce, and likely foreshadow the company's plan for a broader global expansion.

Summary

Amazon and Alibaba have revolutionized the global retailing sector, as many bricks and mortar retailers have found to their cost. Not only have they delivered a new way of shopping but they have also changed customer expectations for good. In order to facilitate these changes, these companies have put in place logistics systems to fit their needs rather than adapt their business models to the existing industry structures. They have been able to do this due to their sheer scale, but at the same time this has become a necessity in order to suppress soaring logistics costs. As these companies compete for global dominance, they will surely be a major source for logistics and supply chain innovations for many years to come.

Bibliography

Kim, E [accessed 22 March 2018] Amazon's $775 Million Deal for Robotics Company Kiva Is Starting to Look Really Smart, *Business Insider* [Online] http://uk.businessinsider.com/kiva-robots-save-money-for-amazon-2016-6

Koenen, J, Hofmann, S and Schlautmann, C [accessed 22 July 2018] Signed, Sealed and Also Delivered, *Handelsblatt Global* [Online] https://global.handelsblatt.com/companies/signed-sealed-and-also-delivered-465329

SEC [accessed 22 September 2018] ZTO Express (Cayman) IPO Prospectus, *Securities and Exchange Commission* [Online] www.sec.gov/Archives/edgar/data/1677250/000104746916015850/a2229567zf-1.htm

Zhang, Y [accessed 22 March 2018] Cainiao-SF Data Standoff Ends; Problems Remain, *Global Times* [Online] www.globaltimes.cn/content/1049927.shtml

Conclusion
The future of the supply chain and logistics industry

THIS CHAPTER WILL FAMILIARIZE THE READER WITH:

- the profile of the supply chain and logistics industry in 15 plus years;
- which new innovations will be successful and their likelihood of industry-wide adoption;
- the impact that disruption will have on jobs in transport and warehousing;
- how supply chains may change in character, from global to regional or even local;
- futuristic solutions to logistics challenges presently in the early stages of development.

Introduction

Nowhere will the effects of 4IR be felt more than in the development of the transport, logistics and supply chain industry. However, it is far from clear whether the outcome for the industry will be positive or negative – much will depend on choices being made in the coming years.

It is also far from obvious which of the many innovations that are being researched and developed will go on to become mainstream. Figure 18.1 attempts to predict those that will be widely adopted and those that will remain niche.

Figure 18.1   Industry-wide adoption or niche application?

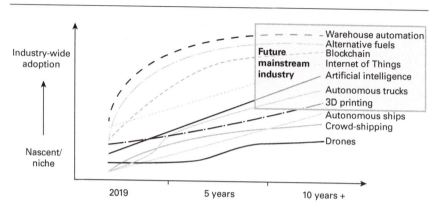

We consider that warehouse automation leads the way in industry-wide adoption over the next 10 years and beyond. Not only will automation become much cheaper over the coming years but trends such as labour shortages will make it much more attractive for warehouse operators to invest in capital goods rather than be squeezed by rising labour costs. We see that investment will ramp up significantly by the mid-2020s.

Second, investment in alternative fuels will rise significantly, driven by public policy decisions to impose diesel bans in urban areas.

The Internet of Things and AI will be steadily integrated within the supply chain and logistics sector, but there may be unexpected consequences and problems as the technology is adopted. Likewise, blockchain, after the hype has disappeared, will become just another form of technology, efficiently facilitating trade flows and increasing trust in commerce.

Other technologies will develop but, due to a number of challenges, will not be as widely adopted. Despite becoming technically feasible, autonomous trucks will still face regulatory hurdles as well as negative public perception. 3D printing will become an increasingly important part of the manufacturing process, but it will still be many years before costs fall to a level that will see it integrated into mass production. Crowd-shipping will be a niche part of the last mile delivery process although gradually gaining traction. Autonomous ships will gradually gain acceptance in the shipping industry, but the long investment horizons in the sector mean that industry change is by evolution, not revolution.

Drones, despite massive hype, will only ever fulfil a niche role in the industry, at least in terms of last mile delivery. However, in some geographies, particularly remote areas subject to existing extreme weather events or areas affected by global warming events where transport infrastructure fails, they will become vital tools. In developed economies, they will be more widely adopted in warehousing and other non-public spaces where they prove useful in terms of scanning items and stocktaking.

Speed of adoption

Although, as this book has pointed out, identifying innovations that will have a material impact on the industry is hard enough, it is even harder to determine the timing of the impact. For instance, it took a further decade after the dot-com boom (and bust) at the turn of the century before mainstream retailing was significantly affected. Likewise, it has been difficult to judge the speed of adoption of 3D printing, the Internet of Things or road freight marketplaces.

One of the reasons for this is that these innovations are not developed in a vacuum. The challenges they are designed to meet are ever shifting, and this can have a major impact on the levels of value they can generate. At a company level, the incumbent players in the market do not stand still, and they are often adept at assimilating new technologies or developing competing and more effective ones.

Take alternative fuels, for example. There is no doubt that if diesel engine technologies had not advanced to the extent that they have, the adoption of hydrogen cells, electric vehicles or biofuels would have been much faster. The fact of the matter is, however, that diesel engine vehicles have become more efficient, which has consolidated the technology's market leading position in terms of cost and all-round utility. Manufacturers believe that there are many enhancements to come, and if it hadn't been for the public policy imperative, there would be few commercial reasons for change.

In addition to this is the concept of an innovation 'ecosystem' (Adner and Kapoor, 2017). This essentially means that the required infrastructure needs to be in place before an innovative new business model can be adopted. Alternative fuels are, again, a good example. Before drivers or companies feel confident in investing in the new type of electric propulsion system, a comprehensive charging network must be built to address concerns over 'range anxiety'.

It is only when old technology has no more room for improvement, and when the infrastructure that supports the innovation is in place, that substitution can start to happen. It is rare that what Adner and Kapoor call 'creation destruction' occurs quickly. More often, technologies will exist side by side for a period until old technology or business models are abandoned. This description could apply to the continued use of paper documents in international trade. While everyone accepts that it can only be a matter of time before all processes are digitized, the ecosystems for this to take place are still not there. Likewise, hybrid engines are a very good example of this coexistence. The new technology works in parallel with the 'old', removing the problem of the lack of charging infrastructure.

Another example of this is printed barcodes and RFID sensors. It would seem logical that the amount of information that can be stored on a sensor and the uses to which this could be put would have led to fast adoption by the industry. However, the cost of the sensor versus low-cost printing, the ubiquitous nature of the barcode's ecosystems (from retailers to manufacturers and the logistics providers in between), and its reliability, have meant that the RFID 'revolution' has taken decades to occur.

The problem for market analysts or managers is that it is difficult to judge how quickly these infrastructure or ecosystem issues will be addressed, especially as the dynamic is continually shifting. Not only are there business investment and technological developments to take into account but also government intervention. Subsidies for green energy initiatives, which may kickstart a technology (or skew the market depending on your perspective), depend on public policy and vacillate depending on the administration of the time. The change in attitude towards diesel since the mid-2010s is a case in point. Once encouraged as a way of cutting greenhouse gas emissions, it is now vilified as a source of noxious pollutants despite no change in quantifiable evidence.

Future profile of logistics segments

It is possible to see any number of alternative pathways for each of the main logistics segments. However, in our opinion, the key attributes of each segment will be as follows (also see Table 18.1).

Road freight

In our view, by the mid- to late-2030s, diesel engines will be phased out as governments actively support alternative fuels. The demand for high frequency, small package, e-commerce deliveries will mean that electric vehicles become the main alternative for urban areas. Natural gas and hydrogen cells are the preferred technologies for longer distance and higher payloads.

Table 18.1 Logistics market attributes 2035

Logistics segment	Road freight transport	Warehousing	Freight forwarding/ international trade	Shipping	Express/parcel	Air cargo
Alternative fuels	Electric or hydrogen	Photovoltaic	n/a	Electric or natural gas 'clean' sulphur-free fuel	Electric or hydrogen	Electric
Digital technologies	Platforms/ exchanges Collaborative Shared	Shared Virtual Artificial intelligence	Digitized Control towers 4PL Blockchain/smart contracts Freight marketplaces	Digitized meta-documents Blockchain/ smart contracts	On-demand Artificial intelligence Crowd-shipping (niche) Route planning Dynamic delivery options	Digitized meta-documents
Automation	Autonomous (semi) platooning	Automated and robotic Augmented/virtual reality 'Tiny' fulfilment	n/a	Autonomous (semi)	Automated hubs Robotics Autonomous vans (semi)	Autonomous (semi)
Physical technologies	Predictive maintenance Asset tracking IoT tracking	Drones IoT inventory management	n/a	Larger ships IoT tracking	Drones (niche) 3D printing	IoT tracking
Notes	Higher utilization rates	'Smart' and green Smaller units	Broking becomes less important as segment increases value add through manager role	Lower unit costs Consolidated industry South-South volumes	Optimized for city deliveries	3D printing impacts intermediate high-tech volumes Faster clearance

Vehicles will have a high degree of automation, and platooning will become commonplace on main trunk roads. Investment in road infrastructure will mean that there is a continuous flow of data between vehicles and highways' control towers as well as between vehicles themselves. In most administrations, drivers will still be a requirement by law but have a negligible role in driving the trucks. However, drivers' hours regulations will have been loosened, which means that vehicle utilization will increase significantly, improving profitability.

Greater visibility of loads will mean an increase in vehicle utilization and more unitization of shipments will facilitate transhipment opportunities, speeding up deliveries. Networks will become more dynamic, with complex routing and delivery decisions being made by AI-driven transport management systems.

Warehousing

Warehousing will become largely automated. Robots will be responsible for most of the functions that would have been fulfilled by humans and will be controlled by AI. E-commerce will dominate the warehousing sector, so large numbers of single items will be picked on a frequent basis.

However, rather than large centralized distribution centres predominating, e-retailers make use of local warehouses to store most frequently ordered items, providing same day delivery services in urban areas. These warehouses will be based at retail parks, utilizing large retail premises that will increasingly become redundant in the 2020s as online sales grow in popularity.

Inditex S.A., the parent of Zara, has already announced that it is exploring the use of existing stores as mini fulfilment centres or distribution centres. This strategy allows them to fulfil customer orders from the closest store, in the event the item is not available in a central facility. This will become the norm.

Distribution centres will become greener, powered by solar energy. Heating and lighting will be of less consequence as human workers rarely enter the picking areas. Warehouse footprint will also decrease as autonomous trucks approach docks more efficiently and large car parks for workers are no longer required.

In addition, 'shared' warehousing platforms will mean that the market becomes much more flexible with many fewer long-term leases. Warehouse management systems will have visibility of inventory wherever it is located, and the distribution of stock across a wide geographical area will reduce transport costs and the risks of disruption to centralized operations.

Freight forwarding

Freight forwarding will still be an essential function in the facilitation of international trade. However, parts of the traditional role will have become automated such as quotation, documentation and freight booking. Instead, the forwarder will fulfil a 'control tower' role, acting as a neutral manager of shipment flows, assessing risks and rerouting as necessary. AI will play an important part of their offering.

Forwarders' unique visibility of multiple transport networks will mean, for many shippers at least, that disintermediation is pointless and the forwarder's ability to consolidate multiple shipments will remain a competitive advantage.

Shipping

The transportation element of the shipping industry will have experienced significant change by 2035. Propulsion will be by electric engines or liquid natural gas, and ships will be increasingly autonomous although still not entirely 'crewless'. Ships' spare parts will be 3D printed at facilities at ports and then flown to ships by drone. Sensors on board ships will provide for predictive maintenance.

Shipbuilding technology will increase the capacity of each ship, but this will limit the number of ports at which they will be able to call further. Networks of smaller feeder ships will become as important as the function of headhaul and backhaul. Transit time between 'hub' ports will decrease as fuel costs will fall, and there will be no need for slow steaming.

The requirement for alternative fuels may present problems for some of the larger vessels specifically designed for slow steaming as their engines may have to be replaced, which may not be cost effective. Instead, they may have a role as floating manufacturing or distribution centres that are able to be moved to where demand is required. 3D printing and other advanced manufacturing could very well take place on board, where the requirements are access to raw materials, power and decent communications.

Express and parcels

Electric vehicles will dominate the last mile segment of the express and parcels industry with dense networks of recharging stations. Increasingly vehicles will be autonomous, although a 'vehicle manager' will replace the driver. Their role will be primarily to move the package from vehicle to end-recipient.

The market will be characterized by a wide number of operating models. These will include drone delivery to remote locations, robot delivery in a specific urban context and crowd-shipping with increased use of public transport as well as personal vehicles. On-demand operations will become an important addition to the established hub and spoke networks of the express parcels carriers.

The huge volumes of e-commerce deliveries will require coordination by control towers using AI. Parcels hubs will be completely automated although faster moving items will be stored at local centres in urban areas for on-demand delivery.

Air cargo

The world's aircraft fleet will be powered by a mix of traditional jet fuel and hybrid electric. Reduction in jet engine noise will allow airports to operate 24/7, meaning that additional runways will be unnecessary. Eventually a step change in battery technology will allow the development of all-electric planes, reducing weight, increasing payload and eliminating emissions.

The reduction in the cost of air cargo will stimulate demand and make it economic for shorter distance movements of freight. The development of air taxis (as proposed by Uber) could result in high value, low weight cargo being moved on a localized basis by air.

All airway bills and other documentation will be digital, improving efficiencies and reducing clearance times. Use of sensors will enable air cargo to be tracked in real time as well as provide comprehensive data on the status and environment of the consignments.

A headwind for the industry will be the adoption of 3D printing, which will reduce the need for the movement of air cargo around the world.

The future for transport and warehousing jobs

According to Oliver Cann (2019) of the World Economic Forum, 'The Fourth Industrial Revolution, combined with other socio-economic and demographic changes, will transform labour markets in the next five years, leading to a net loss of over 5 million jobs in 15 major developed and emerging economies'. Although this figure applies to industry as a whole, the transport and logistics sector is not immune from the impact of the emerging technologies. It is not just manual positions that are at risk. AI will automate many of the positions presently filled by white-collar office workers.

However, there is an alternative view of this issue. Instead of looking at the new technologies as a threat, they could turn out to provide a boost to many companies. Labour shortages in the sector are endemic, and technologies that increase efficiencies, assist existing workers in their jobs or fill a labour gap will help to keep supply chain costs down.

Warehousing automation

As has been discussed earlier, robots are already starting to play an important role in warehouses. The logical conclusion of this trend is the development of so-called 'dark warehouses'. In fact unmanned and completely automated fulfilment centres are already beginning to come online. One such dark warehouse, built for Chinese e-retailer, JD.com, occupies 40,000 square metres in Shanghai's Jaiding District. The facility has the capacity to fulfil 200,000 orders per day and is operated by a combination of robotics and other automated technologies, which can self-calculate how to avoid collisions and optimize routes. The facility has just four human employees.

Such automation, though, comes with restraints – the facility can only handle certain types of goods, uniform in size, shape and weight, as the robotic picking arms cannot lift packages heavier than 3 kg. However, it must be assumed that advances in technology will extend the type and weight of products that are compatible with automation.

Truck drivers to truck managers?

The controlled nature of the warehouse environment (and for that matter cargo handling facilities and areas in ports and airports) means that the substitution of robots for labour could be viewed as an inevitability. Outside of highly regulated areas, however, it is far more difficult to replace human workers. Even if the role of the driver was completely eliminated, without considerable advances in robot technology, the delivery of the package from kerb to the end-user would still need a human, at least for the foreseeable future. Having said that, it is far easier to envisage a full load or even a part load being delivered by fully autonomous truck. The technology will be in place, but whether the public or politicians are ready to accept completely driverless vehicles is another matter. Therefore, it is likely that the role will change rather than be eliminated.

The transformation of global supply chains?

From the 1980s onwards, the world's economy has become ever more integrated, allowing manufacturers to unbundle and outsource production processes to remote suppliers. Globalization, it was assumed, would be unstoppable as manufacturers and retailers looked for ever cheaper sources of labour with which to produce goods for markets in the West, exploiting the comparative advantage that some countries have developed in certain sectors and processes. In some cases this advantage lay in the level of value-added that they could contribute; in others, to lower costs, especially those related to labour.

However, it is not necessarily the case that globalization will continue as the unrivalled supply chain dynamic in perpetuity. Although global movements of goods will continue for the foreseeable future, a rebalancing of supply chains will occur, first through the regionalization of downstream distribution and then to location-specific supply chains. Some of the drivers for this are highlighted below.

3D printing

3D printing will act as an accelerator of a trend towards localization of both upstream and downstream supply chains.

The technology has the potential to reduce the volume of intermediate goods – and consequently unravel the concept of 'Factory Asia'. Instead of components being produced in another location or country, there would be a rebundling of Tier 1+ activities. China is a major investor in 3D printing with the precise aim of recapturing value-added that is presently 'lost' to manufacturers in other Asian countries.

From a logistics perspective, the impact of this is that fewer transport and logistics services will be required as more goods are manufactured in a single factory prior to final distribution. Given that 3D printing is already being adopted widely by many industry sectors, this scenario really isn't too far off.

The impact of 3D printing on downstream supply chains is less imminent. 'Consumerization' of manufacturing, however, is definitely a possibility, in which case global and regional supply chains could be rendered redundant (in some sectors at least). Consumers may end up being able to print some objects in their home, or at least visit a local facility and have them printed there. This would eliminate the need for the movement of many products, although the types would be limited.

Growth of emerging markets

The transformation of emerging markets from being predominantly sources of low-cost labour for Western manufacturers to consumption markets in their own right has been occurring for some time. After the recession of the late 2000s, many countries in the developing world (such as China) were forced to focus their investment on domestic infrastructure to maintain their rate of economic growth as export markets slumped. This, combined with the increase in living standards, has meant that products manufactured in a developing region are more likely to stay there. Global economic growth has consequently not resulted in the high levels of trade that were seen pre-recession.

For many of the global consumer goods manufacturers, sales growth in emerging markets will not necessarily result in higher global flows of goods. That is because successful penetration of emerging markets relies on developing products for specific, local markets and delivering these quickly, cheaply and efficiently.

This, and the development of 'mega-cities', will mean that emerging markets will become the focus for supply chain investment. Asia, Latin America and Africa will develop their own logistics ecosystems rather than depend on connections to Europe and North America.

Focus of logistics on mega-cities

Another factor in the 'localization' of supply chains in emerging markets, will be the development of 'mega-cities' – usually defined as a city of over 10 million people. The top 10 fastest growing mega-cities in the world are all in emerging markets.

Mega-cities will create their own economies of scale, supplied by local/regional production facilities:

- Consumer goods will be customized to local tastes.
- Each city will develop its own unique ecosystem, which takes into account the movement of people, data, finance, energy, waste, goods and services.
- Transport demands will be specific to each city's needs and capabilities: poor planning and infrastructure will result in high logistics costs.
- Fulfilment, packaging, miniaturization and reverse logistics will require increased intensity of logistics provision.

An illustration of the challenges of this trend is that, in 2005, retailers and consumer goods manufacturers had to develop distribution channels in 60 cities in China to reach 80 per cent of the country's population. By 2020, these companies will need to be present in 212 cities to reach the same market (BCG, 2017). Logistics will increasingly be focused around cities rather than countries.

Science fiction or science fact?

Many of the technological innovations already outlined in this book would, just a few years ago, have been regarded as in the realms of fantasy. Therefore, although it would be easy to regard a number of the transport-related investments of wealthy individuals or companies as vanity projects, or at least unrealistic, they may well prove their detractors wrong. Three of these are highlighted below.

Elon Musk's Hyperloop

Hyperloop is an ambitious project that uses a sealed capsule inside a vacuum tube, propelled by magnetic levitation. The capsules could conceivably transport passengers or freight across long distances at speeds of 600 to 1,000 km/h.

Taking the top possible speed of 1,000 km/h, Hyperloop would allow a 4-day truck journey, or 23-hour flight, to be completed in 16 hours. It is also claimed the cost is just 1.5 times more than trucking, although this does not account for the vast sums needed to build the brand new infrastructure in the first place.

One of its uses could be for urban e-commerce deliveries. Hyperloop could give shippers the opportunity to build large distribution centres further outside population centres, thus making savings on more expensive city warehouse space. Hyperloop would be able to transport products into the city centre at rapid speeds, saving time, despite the longer distances between warehouses and population centres. The system would also allow larger distribution centres to serve multiple population centres at once. One touted proposal is for a Hyperloop connecting Barcelona and Madrid in just half an hour. A distribution centre built in the middle would have the ability to serve both centres.

However, with passenger transport being the most obvious application of the technology, there is no guarantee that freight movement would gain precedence.

Amazon's flying fulfilment centre

Amazon filed a patent for a flying fulfilment centre in December 2016. Resembling an airship with an underslung cargo compartment, this hub is designed to dispatch hundreds of delivery drones from above urban areas, with the idea that each drone would be able to glide towards its target drop zone, thus saving power and increasing range.

The patent filings assume that the drones would not have sufficient power to return to the airborne hub after conducting deliveries; instead, the vehicles would fly to the nearest ground-based facility, before being sent back up to the airborne hub in regular batches, transported by a smaller 'shuttle' airship.

Airships

There has been considerable interest in developing airships with the capability of delivering heavy cargo to regions with no airport infrastructure, especially in remote locations. Companies such as Lockheed Martin have invested considerable sums of money into these vehicles, which eventually will be able to carry more cargo than airplanes and be faster than ships. The latest designs for its Hybrid Airship deploy an air cushion landing system (ACLS), which allows the airship to land anywhere on 'hoverpads'.

A start-up company, 'Flying Whales' has attracted investment from the French government as well as a forestry agency and China's aviation industry corporation. The airship is being designed to extract timber from remote forests. Launch is due in 2022.

A UK rival, Airlander, is being developed to fulfil communication, cargo and surveying functions. The Airlander 50, presently in the design phase, will carry 50 tonnes of cargo in a loading bay consisting of 500 cubic metres. It is also aimed at the project/bulk cargo market.

Despite technical and economic challenges that have delayed commercial roll out, it is possible that by 2030 they will become common features in our skies.

Conclusion

Every aspect of society and business is being transformed by a new generation of innovative solutions – and the supply chain and logistics sector is no exception. Whether societal, economic or environmental, innovators are scrutinizing the industry's greatest challenges and developing new business models and concepts with which to address them.

Many of these innovators come from outside of the industry, and this has resulted in entirely new approaches to seemingly intractable problems. Using models from, among others, the financial services, IT and personal mobility sectors, and integrating these with advances in new technologies as well as ideas from the 'sharing' and 'circular' economies, no part of the business is immune from disruption.

Where does this leave the incumbents that have dominated the industry for so long? Or the relationships between shipper, carrier, forwarder and customer that are seemingly set in stone? Survival and success will rely on the ability of all parties in the supply chain to continually examine the value they generate and, where necessary, adapt to the new business environment.

There are many reasons for optimism. The improvements in logistics efficiency: reduced levels of environmental impact and a model that focuses on value generation rather than on labour costs, will create long-term sustainability for the industry. However, there are also many unanswered questions. If the logistics sector is transformed from one of high labour intensity to one characterized by high technology and automation, what are the societal implications for the many millions of workers no longer required? This will be a major conundrum for politicians.

Summary

By 2030 we will see the industry-wide adoption of many innovations that are presently in the early stages of development. Among the most successful will be warehouse automation, alternative fuels, autonomous vehicles, the Internet of Things, AI, 3D printing and blockchain.

The speed of adoption relies to a large extent on the improvements of existing technologies as well as the speed of adoption of the innovation 'ecosystem' on which these technologies rely. An example of this is the development of the charging network required to remove 'range anxiety', which will encourage companies or individuals to invest in electric trucks.

Every logistics sector will see major changes over the coming years. Digitized platforms will better match supply and demand, alternative fuels will reduce emissions, and automation will increase efficiencies and reduce costs. Disruption will affect many incumbent players unable to keep up with the speed of change.

Supply chains are also set to change. Globalized East–West flows of goods will be augmented by more complex regional and localized networks, especially those serving mega-cities in the developing world. At the same time completely new technologies may (or may not) change existing logistics systems, such as Elon Musk's Hyperloop.

Bibliography

Adner, R and Kapoor, R [accessed 22 May 2017] Right Tech, Wrong Time, *Harvard Business Review* [Online] https://hbr.org/2016/11/right-tech-wrong-time?referral=00060

BCG [accessed 5 April 2017] Winning in Emerging Market Cities, *Boston Consulting Group* [Online] www.bcg.com/documents/file60078.pdf

Cann, O [accessed 1 February 2019] Five Million Jobs by 2020: The Real Challenge of the Fourth Industrial Revolution, *World Economic Forum* [Online] www.weforum.org/press/2016/01/five-million-jobs-by-2020-the-real-challenge-of-the-fourth-industrial-revolution/

INDEX

Note: Numbers, acronyms and 'Mc' within main headings are filed as spelt out. Page locators in *italics* denote information contained within a figure or table.

CPSIA information can be obtained
at www.ICGtesting.com
Printed in the USA
LVHW071454290120
645191LV00020B/1774

9 780749 486334